D1452678

Christmas in nineteenth-century England

MANCHESTER
1824

Manchester University Press

STUDIES IN POPULAR CULTURE

General editor: Professor Jeffrey Richards

Already published

Christmas in nineteenth-century England

NEIL ARMSTRONG

Manchester University Press
Manchester and New York

distributed exclusively in the USA by Palgrave Macmillan

Copyright © Neil Armstrong 2010

The right of Neil Armstrong to be identified as the author of this work has been asserted by him in accordance with the Copyright, Designs and Patents Act 1988.

Published by Manchester University Press
Oxford Road, Manchester M13 9NR, UK
and Room 400, 175 Fifth Avenue, New York, NY 10010, USA
www.manchesteruniversitypress.co.uk

Distributed in the United States exclusively by
Palgrave Macmillan, 175 Fifth Avenue, New York,
NY 10010, USA

Distributed in Canada exclusively by
UBC Press, University of British Columbia, 2029 West Mall,
Vancouver, BC, Canada V6T 1Z2

British Library Cataloguing-in-Publication Data
A catalogue record for this book is available from the British Library

Library of Congress Cataloging-in-Publication Data applied for

ISBN   978 0 7190 7759 3 hardback

First published 2010

The publisher has no responsibility for the persistence or accuracy of URLs for any external or third-party internet websites referred to in this book, and does not guarantee that any content on such websites is, or will remain, accurate or appropriate.

Typeset in Adobe Garamond with Gill Sans display by
Special Edition Pre-press Services, www.special-edition.co.uk
Printed in Great Britain by
T J International Ltd, Padstow

STUDIES IN POPULAR CULTURE

There has in recent years been an explosion of interest in culture and cultural studies. The impetus has come from two directions and out of two different traditions. On the one hand, cultural history has grown out of social history to become a distinct and identifiable school of historical investigation. On the other hand, cultural studies has grown out of English literature and has concerned itself to a large extent with contemporary issues. Nevertheless, there is a shared project, its aim, to elucidate the meanings and values implicit and explicit in the art, literature, learning, institutions and everyday behaviour within a given society. Both the cultural historian and the cultural studies scholar seek to explore the ways in which a culture is imagined, represented and received, how it interacts with social processes, how it contributes to individual and collective identities and world views, to stability and change, to social, political and economic activities and programmes. This series aims to provide an arena for the cross-fertilisation of the discipline, so that the work of the cultural historian can take advantage of the most useful and illuminating of the theoretical developments and the cultural studies scholars can extend the purely historical underpinnings of their investigations. The ultimate objective of the series is to provide a range of books which will explain in a readable and accessible way where we are now socially and culturally and how we got to where we are. This should enable people to be better informed, promote an interdisciplinary approach to cultural issues and encourage deeper thought about the issues, attitudes and institutions of popular culture.

Jeffrey Richards

List of illustrations

All images courtesy of Manchester Metropolitan University Special Collections (the Laura Seddon collection of Victorian and Edwardian greetings cards).

Contents

General editor's foreword

There is still a popular belief that the nineteenth-century Christmas was invented by Charles Dickens and Prince Albert. But in this wide-ranging, carefully researched and subtly nuanced study, Neil Armstrong demonstrates that there was much more to it than that. The Victorian Christmas had its roots in previous centuries, but it was the product of many of the distinctive developments of the nineteenth century.

The now familiar iconography of Christmas emerged with the new printing technologies as Christmas cards, illustrated papers and seasonal advertising popularized the full range of Christmas trees, holly and mistletoe, Father Christmas and his reindeer, robins, yule logs, plum puddings and snowscapes. Christmas played a central role in the development of the Victorian domestic ideology, with the family promoted as the social ideal and the child romanticized. But Armstrong stresses the increasing importance of women in the planning and staging of Christmas and compares and contrasts the middle-class and working-class experiences of the festive season. He examines how the ever more elaborate nineteenth-century Christmas festivities led to new patterns of labour and leisure, with increasing demands placed on such groups as domestic servants, postmen and shop assistants. Christmas provided opportunities for employer paternalism but also employee exploitation.

Armstrong shows how Christmas provided a spur to the growth of secular philanthropy as the more enlightened elements of the middle class sought to use the season to mitigate the worst effects of modern industrial society. He examines the growth of the entertainment industry supporting Christmas, notably the pantomime, a national institution in Victorian Britain, but also a wide range of shows, spectacles, concerts and balls. He concludes by analysing the growth of the culture of Christmas shopping with ever more elaborate advertising, displays and stores. His research leads him to an intriguing paradox: that the traditional English Christmas whose erosion is so often lamented by the present-day press was actually the product of Victorian modernity.

Jeffrey Richards

Preface

My interest in Christmas arose from a recognition that the festive season might act as a prism through which the evolution of English society and its ideals, morals and values during the long nineteenth century could be illuminated. Thanks to the generosity of a studentship from the History Department at the University of York, I was able to develop these ideas into a PhD thesis between 2000 and 2004. During this period I benefited from the supervision of Edward Royle, who helpfully shared his expertise in Modern British social history and allowed me the freedom to experiment with various ideas and theories – not all of which have survived in this present volume. Whilst at York I also received helpful advice from the members of my thesis advisory panel: Elizabeth Buettner, Jim Walvin and Alan Warren. Both Jim Walvin and Hugh Cunningham provided extremely useful comments as examiners of my dissertation. Mark Ormrod also offered important support during the early phase of my academic career. Perhaps most importantly of all, the community of postgraduate students at York in the early years of the twenty-first century provided me with intellectual stimulation and friendship, particularly Mike Brown, Catriona Kennedy, Matthew Roberts, Emma Robertson and Helen Smith.

The survey of the historiography of Christmas which forms part of Chapter 1 appeared in an earlier version in the journal *Cultural and Social History*; I wish to thank Berg publications for their permission to reproduce this work, and Sean O'Connell for his help with drafting the article. Trev Lynn Broughton and Helen Rogers helped me develop my ideas on Christmas and the family during the completion of their collection on *Gender and Fatherhood in the Nineteenth Century*. I also wish to thank Jeremy Boulton for allowing me to teach a special subject class on the history of Christmas at the University of Newcastle, the students who allowed me to test out my ideas on them, and the staff at the School of Historical Studies for being so helpful and welcoming, with particular thanks to Joan Allen and Martin Farr. During a year at the University of Warwick advice, support and congenial company were provided by Maxine Berg, Catherine Cox, Margot Finn, William Murphy and Selina Todd. Subsequently, Patrick Major's invitation to submit an article to *German History* helped to further refine my ideas on the modern history of the festive season.

The book was completed at the University of Gloucestershire, and here Rebecca Bailey, Kate North, Martin Randall and Jonathan Spangler helped keep me sane. At the same time, I must thank the staff at Manchester University Press for their patience and expertise, my series editor Jeffrey Richards and the anonymous reader for their encouraging comments, and the staff at the Sir Kenneth Green Library, Manchester Metropolitan University, for allowing me to reproduce Victorian Christmas cards from the Laura Seddon collection. Helen Smith kindly proofread much of the book and helped polish my prose; the remaining faults are all my own. This book would also have not been possible without the love, support and intellectual stimulation over the past decade of my partner, Catriona Kennedy. Finally, I would not have been able to pursue an academic career without the financial assistance and encouragement of my parents, and the book is dedicated to the memory of my step-father, Rodney James Fry.

Introduction

In December 2006 the *Daily Mail* reported the launch of a campaign by the Christian Muslim Forum to 'save the traditions of Christmas from the interference of politically correct town halls'. In an attempt to establish the 'notorious local authority attempts to stamp out Christmas', the *Mail* twice cited the examples of Birmingham City Council's 'decision to name its season celebrations "Winterval" and Luton's attempt to change Christmas into a Harry Potter festival by renaming its festive lights "Luminos"'. At the same time the *Sun* newspaper declared as part of its 'kick 'em in the baubles' campaign that 'Scrooge bosses and council jobsworths are stripping away the joy of Christmas'. The litany of offences highlighted by the *Sun* included the outlawing of mince pies as a health risk, firms 'banning Christmas decorations in case they offend other faiths' and the removal of nativity scenes 'in case non-Christians find them offensive'.[1]

According to the British tabloid press Christmas was under attack. However, as Oliver Burkeman revealed in the *Guardian*, this 'phoney war' on Christmas 'relied on a grab-bag of stories that crumbled on closer analysis'. Luton Borough Council does not have a festival called 'Luminos' and does not use an alternative name for Christmas. When in 2001 it did hold an event called 'Luminos' in late November it did not replace the council's Christmas celebrations. Similarly, 'Winterval', which only ever occurred in 1997–98, was a campaign to promote Birmingham's newly regenerated city centre. Lasting from early November to January, it coincided with a range of traditional Christmas activities, including lights, a tree and carol singing. The Lord Mayor sent a card wishing everyone a merry Christmas, and a similar sentiment adorned a banner on the council's main building.[2] Despite the ease with which these reports can be dismissed, the perception that something is wrong with the way Christmas is being celebrated, that something is missing and the essential character of the festival is being suppressed, is an important one, and it is an idea which can be traced back as far as the seventeenth century. As an annual festival, Christmas inevitably makes us reflect on celebrations past and attribute difference, often interpreted negatively, as the product of the passage of time and the march of 'progress'. In 2006 the *Sun* commented: '[W]e are seeing centuries-old customs barred on daft safety grounds.'[3] The repetition of custom and tradition legitimates behaviour, investing rituals with a moral character which can only be undermined by the prevailing social and political trends of the day. In the early twenty-first century, these trends were, according to the tabloid press, a modern malaise of political correctness and the overbearing influence of state bureaucracy.

In each age, however, the people have a potential common cause for complaint, and in the seventeenth century it was the selfishness of the landed classes, which neglected the welfare and entertainment of their dependants in the country in favour of the pleasures of London during the festive season. This introductory chapter will trace the development of a nostalgic and sentimental Christmas discourse from its seventeenth-century origins through to the early Victorian period which is commonly associated with the emergence of the modern form of the festive season. This discourse is closely aligned with the rise of a literary print culture in England; it rests on the gradual expansion of the world of pamphlets, newspapers, periodicals and the growth of a book trade which by the nineteenth century was exploiting the Christmas season for commercial success. The expansion of the press and the book trade in England means that the following account is highly selective, and from the second half of the nineteenth century the number of books and countless articles on Christmas in newspapers makes recovering a coherent narrative of the festival a difficult task for the historian. Nonetheless, in the second half of the twentieth century a number of historians began to find a range of historical perspectives on the Christmas festival, and these will also be reviewed below.

The Christmas lament

Surviving household accounts for the Middle Ages and Tudor period reveal that all wealthy families purchased abnormal quantities of food for the Christmas season, and they were expected to use this to provide open-house hospitality, as the poet and farmer Thomas Tusser declared in the mid-sixteenth century:

> At Christmas we banquet, the rich with the poor
> Who then (but the miser) but openeth his door.[4]

Ronald Hutton, however, suggests that in reality hospitality in the form of food, drink and entertainment was largely restricted to 'social equals and immediate inferiors', and the extent to which Christmas hospitality was more widely diffused is open to question. As Hutton argues, the Elizabethan and Jacobean periods were marked by growing economic and social problems, and 'calls for a return to an ideal standard of old-fashioned seasonal hospitality may have been propelled by a growing need for the latter rather than an actual decrease in it'. In the early seventeenth century it was particularly significant that James I believed the quantity of hospitality to be decreasing at an alarming rate, as the elite increasingly chose to spend Christmas in London rather than dispense traditional hospitality and charity in their country seats. In 1616 James I made a speech denouncing this trend in Star Chamber, and called for the return of traditional country sports and pastimes in the context of the growing economic and social power of London. This speech can be seen as the beginning of a literary tradition of lamenting the loss of Christmas past. It not only helped to inspire at least one popular ballad, a poem by George Wither, Ben Jonson's *Christmas, his Masque* and in 1631, John Taylor's *The Complaint of Christmas and the Teares of Twelfthtyde*.[5] Like Jonson, Taylor personified Christmas, who on arriving in England on 25 December found that the 'many fine houses which [he] had often been well entertained at' no longer had open doors or smoking chimneys. Reaching the Lord of the Manor's house, Christmas found a 'serving-man leane against the wall, bewailing the miseries of the time present, and grieving at the alterations of the time past, despairing at the amendment of the time to come'. High woods which once protected the house had now fallen to the woodsman's axe, the deer in the park were very few, and the oxen in the meadows had all been driven to the cities. Worst of all was the follies of the young Master, who would rather smoke in the tobacco shops of London than make his chimney smoke in the country. Christmas railed against the landowners who would only feast the rich and ignore their charitable obligations to the poor (killed by 'prodigality, drunkennesse, and excesse') but found solace in the house of an honest country farmer who provided good cheer. Yet even the farming class were at risk from the perils of social and economic change, for 'when farmers began to make their sonnes gentlemen, and young gentlemen began to be devoured by usurers: then, then, charity lay on her death-bed'.[6]

In the seventeenth century perceptions of how Christmas should be celebrated were challenged not only by changing social and economic conditions but also by matters of religious belief and practice. As well as chiding the wealthy for neglecting their duties to the poor, James I complained of the 'Puritaines' in

London who did not keep Christmas at all.[7] In Taylor's *Complaint*, Christmas met a 'crafty' and self-obsessed cobbler who, too busy with work to observe a holiday, leapt from the visitor like a squirrel on learning the visitor's identity, declaring 'that the *Masse* was prophane ... and that some Papist had been [his] Godfather'.[8] The Godly perception of Christmas as a product of heathen superstition and Papist idolatry was a consequence of the Reformation. In the British Isles its most tangible impact was felt in Scotland when the reformed Kirk came to power in 1560. The following year it issued the First Book of Discipline, which claimed that the feasts of Christmas, the Circumcision, the Epiphany and those associated with the Virgin Mary, the Apostle and all other saints had been invented by the Roman Catholic Church; they were denounced as unscriptural and abolished. According to Hutton, until 1640 'only a tiny number of extraordinary radical English Protestants shared the hostility of the Kirk towards seasonal festivals'. This situation changed during the English Civil War. In 1643 the English Long Parliament signed the Solemn League and Covenant with the government of Scotland. The Long Parliament purchased military support, and one of the conditions the Scots imposed was reform of the Church of England, including its holy days. A literary debate on this issue began in England in 1643, and it was quickly established that no objective evidence for the birth of Christ existed, and the Christmas festival was supported by tradition and not Biblical authority. With Parliament in the ascendancy, a new national liturgy that excluded Christmas was issued in January 1645 and two years later its celebration was made an offence. Evidence suggests that the Puritan ban on Christmas was largely successful in terms of closing churches but achieved less when traditional and secular seasonal pastimes are considered. Furthermore, the loss of the Christmas festival exacerbated the hostility of the people towards a regime already made unpopular due to high taxation and the quartering of a large army near civilian populations. Consequently, Christmas 'could be made a rallying-point for condemnation of the government'.[9] As part of this process, pamphlets appeared which continued the tradition of the Christmas lament. *The Vindication of Christmas*, published in 1652, decried the 'lamentable Reformation' in which 'some over-curious hot zealous Brethren ... did do what they could to keep Christmas Day out of England ... by infusing an heretical opinion into the hearts of the people, to wit ... that plum-pottage was meer popery, and roast beef antichristian'. This attack was prefaced in the subtitle by 'twelve years observations upon the times, concerning the lamentable game called sweepstake; acted by General *Plunder*, and Major General *Tax*', with an 'exhortation to the people; a description of that oppressing ringworm called *excise*; and how high and mighty Christmas-ale that formerly would knock down *Hercules* ... strook into a deep consumption with a blow from *Westminster*'.[10] The complaints of the modern tabloid newspapers can be positioned in a long tradition.

The Restoration of the monarchy in 1660 brought with it restoration of Christmas in England. Customary hospitality, however, continued a pattern of slow and uneven decline in the proceeding centuries, and complaints continued to appear in pamphlets and newspapers. For example, in *Round about our Coal Fire*, published several times in the 1730s, the anonymous author commented on how 'the great festival was in former times kept with so much freedom and openness of heart, that everyone in the country where a gentleman resided, possessed at least a day of pleasure in the *Christmas* holydays; the tables were all spread from the first to the last, the sirloins of beef, the minc'd-pyes, the plumb-porridge, the capons, turkeys, geese, and plumb-puddings were all brought on board'. Now, however, the 'geese which us'd to be fatted for the honest neighbours, have been of late sent to *London*, and the quills made into pens to convey away the landlord's estate; the sheep are drove away to raise money to answer the loss at a game at dice and cards, and their skins made into parchment or deeds and indentures'. The author also mischievously warned that if the wealthy 'don't at least make their tenants or tradesmen drink when they come to see them in the *Christmas* holydays, they have liberty of pissing behind the door, which is a law of very ancient date'.[11]

The concern over the landed classes gambling during the festive season increased during the eighteenth century. In a series of editorials on Christmas in the 1780s and 1790s, *The Times* used the traditional festive lament to attack aristocratic vice, corruption and luxury, which was perceived as being linked with the fashion for refinement amongst the landed classes. Complaining of 'ostentation, dice and cards' in 1789, *The Times* regretfully stated: 'More refined in our manners, and more selfish in our conduct, every man studies his own gratifications, in preference to the happiness of his neighbour.' The consequences for the celebration of Christmas was that 'with the banishment of the sirloin, buttock and chine, hospitality took its farewell of great men's houses, and with the fripperies of French dinners came the parade of French nothingness, attended by cooks, hair dressers, and valets, sufficient to people a colony with epicures and fops, or ruin a kingdom of the hardiest people on the face of the earth'.[12] Such comments can be seen as part of the broader attempt in the period of the middle classes to stake a claim for full political citizenship by contrasting their superior attributes to the dissolute behaviour of the aristocracy.

In the context of Christmas, this meant representing the middle classes as the upholders of customs and traditions which guaranteed not only the English qualities of hospitality and conviviality but also social responsibility towards the poor. As *The Times* claimed in 1790, 'a system of refinement in luxury marks the tables of the rich – the middling rank of life are more enlightened and more select in their company'.[13]

The rejection of luxury and refinement had two further consequences for the Christmas lament of the late eighteenth century. Firstly, in an age of early industrialisation and significant population growth, more detail concerning the travails of the poor were provided in contrast with earlier accounts. As *The Times* commented in 1787: 'When we eat, we should recollect that thousands are without food – when we drink, that thousands are parched with thirst, and let the fire that renders us comfortable, at the same time inform us, that multitudes are perishing with cold. The prisons are full of debtors – their wives – their children, are perishing through want of nourishment.'[14] Secondly, women of the landed classes were censured in the Christmas lament for the first time. The growing middle-class ideology of gendered separate spheres, often linked with evangelical religion, placed a premium on women's moral worth in the private domain of the home as a counterbalance to the corrupting influence of the masculine public sphere. *The Times*, however, felt that fashionable ladies had neglected the domestic skills necessary for a successful Christmas:

> the education of the female part of the family being for some years committed to the mistresses of boarding schools or to private governesses, the art of domestic cookery is no longer practised by ladies, the study of the graces having kicked the drudgery of mixing pies, tarts, and puddings out of doors. It is much more fashionable now to possess the art of painting the face and whitening the hands, than to know the mystery of making raised crust or … calves feet jelly.[15]

An extension of domestic duty, particularly for ladies of leisure, was to perform good deeds in the community, and here again *The Times* found the female sex lacking: 'It would hurt the feelings of a modern lady to be employed in such *low occupations* as administering comfort and relief to those distressed objects.'[16]

In the early nineteenth century, these themes were further elucidated and expanded upon in Washington Irving's *Sketch-Book of Geoffrey Crayon, Gent*, first published in England in 1820. He was born in New York in 1783, the son of a Scottish Presbyterian immigrant who ran an importing business. Irving had already made a significant contribution to the development of Christmas in America with his 1809 *Knickerbocker's History of New York*: it referenced the figure of Saint Nicholas as a 'mythic patron saint of New Amsterdam', which played a part in the gradual emergence of the modern Santa Claus icon. In 1815 Irving embarked on a tour of Europe, but on reaching Liverpool he found that his brother Peter had fallen ill, and the English wing of the family was under threat of bankruptcy. In order to save his family from disgrace, Irving spent the next two and a half years working in Liverpool to restore the fortunes of the family. During this extended stay in England, Irving developed a keen interest in English romanticism and folklore, which eventually resulted in the *Sketch-Book*, a fictional account by a middle-aged American bachelor, Geoffrey Crayon, of his journeys around England.[17] In December, Crayon is on a tour of Yorkshire and is invited by an old friend to spend Christmas at Bracebridge Hall. In describing the celebration of Christmas at the Hall, Irving repackaged the traditional Christmas lament for the romantic age. As Crayon commented: 'I am apt to think the world was more homebred, social, and joyous, than at present. I regret to say that they are daily growing more and more faint, being gradually worn away by time, but still more obliterated by modern fashion.'[18] Crayon continued:

> One of the least pleasing effects of modern refinement is the havoc it has made among the hearty old holyday customs. It has completely taken off the sharp touchings and spirited reliefs of the embellishments of life, and has worn down society into a more smooth and polished, but certainly a less characteristic surface ... Pleasure has expanded into a broader, but a shallower stream, and has forsaken many of those deep and quiet channels where it flowed sweetly through the calm bosom of domestic life. Society has acquired a more enlightened and elegant tone, but it has lost many of its strong local peculiarities, its homebred feelings, and its honest fireside delights.[19]

The Squire of Bracebridge Hall was particularly keen that Christmas customs and hospitality be used to maintain hierarchical social relations as symbols of paternalism and deference. However, in the context of increasingly rapid social change following the long wars with Revolutionary and Napoleonic France, the squire recognised that social cohesion had become ever more problematic:

> The nation ... is altered; we have almost lost our simple, true hearted peasantry. They have broken asunder from the higher classes, and seem to think their interests are separate. They have become too knowing, and begin to read newspapers, listen to ale house politicians, and talk of reform. I think one mode to keep them in good humour in these hard times, would be for the nobility and gentry to pass more time on their estates, mingle more among the country people, and set the merry old English games going again.[20]

Yet the Squire's attempts did not suit the modern age, as Crayon revealed: 'The country people, however, did not understand how to play their parts in the scene of hospitality: many uncouth circumstances occurred; the manor was overrun by all the vagrants of the country, and more beggars drawn into the neighbourhood in one week than the parish officers could get rid of in a year.'[21] Even the Squire's attempt to mingle with his estate employees was doomed to ridicule:

> The Squire himself mingled among the rustics, and was received with awkward demonstrations of deference and regard. It is true, I perceived two or three of the younger peasants, as they turned their tankards to their mouths, when the Squire's back was turned, making something of a grimace, and giving each other a wink, but the moment they caught my eye they pulled gave faces, and were exceedingly demure.[22]

Though Irving's portrayal of the English Christmas was sentimental and nostalgic, he was clearly aware of its limitations as a model for modern social relations, but the enduring charm of text meant that subsequent generations found much to recommend in it. In 1890, for example, even the Liberal-orientated *Leeds Mercury* was willing to overlook the paternalistic dimensions of the *Sketch-Book:*

> Can anyone read such a sketch as Washington Irving's 'Bracebridge Hall', and not feel a glow of love for the days when this same Christmas who visits us and to keep high court and revel in the old English country house? Some of use could even afford to send our newfangled social theories packing … could we but join the group which stood round the old Squire's board … We know some misanthropes will tell us that the old days were socially iniquitous; that under the display of noisy hospitality there lurked the tyranny of class ascendancy; that the poor man only loved the rich because he knew no better; and that the rich was only kind to the poor when he wanted to make a display of his wealth, or rob them a little further on; that Christmas meant gluttony and drunkenness with a little perfunctory patronage, of religion thrown in, and so on. And we are called upon to be thankful for that, instead of all that, we have our daily penny paper, that the landlord is becoming extinct, that capital is grovelling at the feet of labour, and that every man who wants a dinner can get it gratis in the work-house. We confess it is hard at a season like this to realise the compensation of the age in which we live.[23]

Irving's *Sketch-Book* also coincided with the efforts of a number of anti-quarian writers who were afraid that what were perceived as authentic Christ-mas customs were in danger of being lost in the process of urbanisation. In 1822 for example, Davis Gilbert published *Some Ancient Christmas Carols* col-lected in the West of England because he was 'desirous of preserving them in their actual forms, however distorted by false grammar or by obscurities, as specimens of times now passed away'.[24] A more substantial collection was published by William Sandys in 1833 in *Christmas Carols Ancient and Modern*. Sandys commented that from the time of the Restoration, 'carol-singing was probably continued with unabated zeal, till towards the end of the last century, since which the practice has declined, and many old customs have been gradually becoming obsolete'. The reason for this, Sandys observed, was that:

> In many parts of the kingdom … this festival is still kept up with spirit among the middling and lower classes, though its influence is on the wane even with them; the genius of the present age requires work and not play, and since the commencement of this century a great change may be trace. The modern instructors of mankind do not think it necessary to provide for popular amusements, considering mental improvement the one thing needful … Still a cheerful observance of the great festivals of the year may well combine with this popular rage for reading, and the "Schoolmaster" might allow his Christmas holidays to be more than a mere cessation from labour for a day or two.[25]

Sandys recognised that the celebration of Christmas was intimately connected with leisure time, which was not always commensurate with the principles of utility, rational education and the growth of factory-regulated working hours which often characterised the early decades of the nineteenth century.

Irving also influenced on Thomas K. Hervey's *Book of Christmas* (1836), which featured largely descriptive discussions of the days from Saint Thomas's on 21 December through to Twelfth Night on 6 January, but these are prefaced with overviews of the season, and significantly, the signs and feelings of Christmas as well. Hervey argued that Christmas had been in decline since the puritan intercession of the seventeenth century, and that by the 1830s the 'revels of merry England' were under threat from the modern utilitarian spirit as well as the 'affectations and frivolities of society'. Once again, the expansion of urban England was identified as a particular problem, not only in terms of drawing young gentlemen into the dissipations of the town, but also through the 'annihilation' of the yeomanry. For Hervey, the cure for these ills was a revival of the old Christmas customs which would promote 'a reciprocal kindness of feeling as a community of enjoyment; and the bond of good will was thus drawn tighter between those remote classes, whose differences of privilege, of education, are perpetually operating to loosen it, and threatening to dissolve it altogether'. However, Hervey felt that the proper locations for Christmas festivity were 'the old manor house or the baronial hall', and despite Hervey's emphasis on feeling and companionship, one of his main complaints was that 'Christmas-tide [had] tamed away into a period of domestic union and social festivity'.[26]

As discussed in Chapter 3, Irving also placed an increasing emphasis on the power of Christmas to stir the emotions and affect 'domestic felicity'. This not only led a number of discussions of the sentimental and familial nature of Christmas appearing in periodicals in the 1820s, it also secured for the *Sketch-Book* the role of being one of the nineteenth century's festive urtexts, and, along with it, the continued tradition of the seasonal lament in the literary and popular culture of Christmas. Irving was also an influence on the most important writer on the festive season of all time, Charles Dickens, particularly Dickens's early Christmas writing in *Sketches by Boz* (1835) and the Christmas scenes at Dingley Dell in the *Pickwick Papers* (1837). It is, of course, *A Christmas Carol* which has become the most recognised Christmas story, which inspired many imitations and theatrical productions in the nineteenth century and has since inspired many television and film adaptations leaving Christmas at Bracebridge Hall completely overshadowed. With *A Christmas Carol*, Dickens has been credited with transferring the Christmas of the literary imagination from the English countryside to the modern urban world. The *Carol* only partly draws upon the tradition of the Christmas lament, and the nostalgic rural scenes of Scrooge's past are matched by the vigour and sentiment with which *some* in the present are able to celebrate the season, whilst his own redemption offers hope for a merry Christmas future, though the name of Scrooge has forever provided an instant moniker for those looking to identify the enemies of the festive spirit, as the recent example from the *Sun* demonstrates.

What Dickens did achieve, however, was to expand the terms of reference for his complaint concerning the modern celebration of Christmas. As Paul Davis highlights, *A Christmas Carol* first appeared shortly after the publication of parliamentary reports concerning the working conditions and exploitation of women and children in factories and mines. Dickens himself dated the genesis of the *Carol* from an address he gave to a working-class audience at the Manchester Athenaeum in October 1843. Davis noted that Dickens had been looking for 'an appropriate response' to the parliamentary reports and speculated that the Manchester address may have 'rekindled this earlier resolve'.[27] Consequently, the *Carol* was a very specific response to the poverty, hunger and working conditions of early Victorian England, and the inability of the poor law system to humanely cope with the most unfortunate in an industrialising society. And yet the *Carol* does not directly represent either industrial England or the urban poor. Though the Cratchit family experienced poverty, familiar as they were with the inside of the pawnbroker's and with a daughter apprenticed to a milliner, Bob Cratchit was a clerk rather than a manual labourer, the former being a social group well known for their aspirations towards gentility, and his family were closer in spirit to the ideology of bourgeois domesticity (and hence quite different from the scenes described by Hervey) than to the lurid descriptions of urban depravity offered by the social investigations of the period.[28]

The historiography of Christmas

For the greater part of the nineteenth and twentieth centuries, the history of Christmas in England was relegated to the preserve of antiquarians and popular historians, who perpetuated the nostalgic and sentimental perspective on the festival discussed above. These histories often relied on folkloric sources, contributions to periodicals such as the *Gentleman's Magazine* and *Notes and Queries*, and almanacs and collections of calendar customs which first began to appear in the early modern period and are still published today.[29] One type of approach taken in these histories can be found in William Sandys's *Christmastide: its History, Festivity and Carols* (1852), which examines the early origins of the festival before describing the Christmas celebrations of the English monarchs down the ages, emphasising the vitality of the customs of the past. As William Dawson explained in the preface to his *Christmas: its Origins and Associations* (1902), 'I saw ... that the successive celebrations of Christmas during nineteen centuries were important links in the chain of historical Christian evidences. I became enamoured of the subject, for, in addition to historical interest, there is the charm of its legendary lore, its picturesque customs, and popular games ... Henceforth, I became a snapper-up of everything relating to Christmastide.'[30]

Though popular histories and coffee table books on Christmas continue to appear,[31] a new approach appeared in the late 1970s with the posthumous publication of J. A. R. Pimlott's *The Englishman's Christmas*. Pimlott described the history of Christmas from pagan origins through to the twentieth century, but devoted five of his thirteen chapters to the Victorian period, putting particular emphasis on the role of trees, cards and carols, the development of Father Christmas, and the emergence of 'the business of Christmas': the Victorian period was identified as being essential to the development of the Christmas recognisable today. For Pimlott, this 'new' Christmas was 'carried forward by an irresistible momentum', establishing the role of children and commerce in the modern festival. Pimlott strongly contrasted the celebration of Christmas in the early nineteenth century with the situation after 1840. He emphasised the reduction in public holidays and the small coverage Christmas received in Regency newspapers and periodicals. In explaining the sudden popularity of Christmas in Victoria's reign Pimlott played down the popularly held notion that Charles Dickens and Prince Albert were solely responsible for this trend. Instead Pimlott argued that the popularisation was derived from religious revival (particularly the Oxford Movement) and humanitarian and romantic movements that emphasised the traditional virtues of 'neighbourliness, charity and goodwill' with particular focus on family and children.[32]

Though many of Pimlott's arguments were underdeveloped, he did provide a nuanced perspective on the celebration of Christmas in England, and *The Englishman's Christmas* remains an essential introduction to the subject. However, despite containing useful appendices that detailed potential avenues for research, *The Englishman's Christmas* was an unreferenced work, an indication that it was aimed at the popular market. The same can be said for the next two histories of the English Christmas to appear: J. M. Golby and A. W. Purdue's *The Making of the Modern Christmas* and Gavin Weightman and Steve Humphries' *Christmas Past*. Both works reveal the influence of Hobsbawm and Ranger's *Invention of Tradition* collection of essays, and argue that the Victorian middle classes 'reinvented' Christmas in terms of a nostalgic view of 'Merrie Englande' in order to promote social harmony and alleviate guilt created by material prosperity. Though *Christmas Past* is a tie-in publication accompanying a London Weekend Television series, Weightman and Humphries make an important contribution to the study of Christmas, offering a thematic exploration of the social experience of the festival and providing valuable oral testimonies of the Edwardian period.[33]

Invented tradition was now an established paradigm in the historical study of the English Christmas, and it gained further popularity in the 1990s when Geoffrey Rowell published a short article entitled 'Dickens and the construction of Christmas', highlighting the role Dickens played in the construction of what Rowell considers to be a Christian–social feast.[34] A collection of social–anthropological essays edited by Daniel Miller, *Unwrapping Christmas*, is also underpinned by the idea that the modern Christmas has been invented.[35] This work showed the value of social–anthropological interpretations of Christmas for historians. James Carrier explores 'The rituals of Christmas giving', identifying the Christmas present as 'a vehicle of affection that expresses private sentiment within a relationship that is personal and probably familial', whilst Mary Searle-Chatterjee examines the role that Christmas cards played in the maintenance of social networks, both within close intimate circles and looser social connections, and its dependence upon the work of female members of families.[36] Adam Kuper discusses the relationship between family and time in 'The English Christmas and the family: time out and alternative realities', presenting a model of Christmas family time based upon a desire for the repetition of childhood rituals, existing outside of history, and downplaying conflict and social hierarchy. Kuper argues that families experience the modern Christmas festival as a form of 'communitas', in which individual identity is subsumed in a spiritual community.[37] In the following chapters I make use of the term *communitas* to describe occasions in which small social groups, particularly families, achieve or attempt to achieve a feeling of togetherness during the Christmas festival which distinguishes it from normal experience.

There has also been a reaction against the use of invented tradition within the study of Christmas. In his scholarly survey of calendar customs, *The Stations of the Sun*, Hutton devotes ten chapters to examining Christmas customs, combining a synthesis of previous histories of the festival under the heading 'The reinvention of Christmas' with chapters discussing the decline of well documented rural–agricultural customs including the mummers' play and sword dance. He employs an unsentimental tone and situates decline within the changing social and economic relationships of the English countryside. He is critical of the folklorist tradition of studying custom with its emphasis on pagan survival, and also of historians such as E. P. Thompson for treating the working classes as relatively homogenous in both identity and interest and for glossing over the hostility displayed towards traditional customs by religious nonconformists and political radicals. Despite his scepticism towards the treatment of custom by the disciplines of folklore and social history, Hutton emphasises historical continuity when he argues 'that the rhythms of the British year are timeless, and impose certain perpetual patterns on calendar customs'. More specifically, he notes how a modern nine-day Christmas festival emerged to replace the medieval twelve-day festival, commenting that 'a sense of overpowering familiarity strikes a historian interested in the long-term development of the festival'.[38] Mark Connelly is also suspicious about invented tradition in his *Christmas: a Social History*. Preferring the term 'inflation' to 'invention', Connelly's useful volume examines the representation of Christmas in relation to Englishness, pantomime, the Christmas carol revival, empire, BBC broadcasts, cinema and shopping, stressing continuities over the period 1780 to 1952, and highlighting the role of Christmas as a cultural expression of English national identity.[39]

In America Christmas has also emerged as a valid topic for historical enquiry. For many years the standard work was the sociologist James Barnett's *The American Christmas*, which emphasised the fusion of disparate customs and the decline of dissenting opposition in the creation of a national holiday.[40] More recently, Susan Davis's '"Making night hideous": Christmas revelry and public order in Philadelphia',[41] and Stephen Nissenbaum's *The Battle for Christmas* recast the nineteenth-century American Christmas as a contest between proletarian street culture and middle-class respectability. The starting point for Nissenbaum's 'battle' is the puritan 'war' on Christmas in the seventeenth and eighteenth centuries, a battle replayed and recast in Clement Clarke Moore's 'A visit from St. Nicholas', the contrast between the parlour and the street, the conflict between personal and impersonal giving embodied in the Christmas gift, the relationship between generations in the middle-class home, the renegotiation of charitable giving to the poor, and the relationship between master and slave in the Antebellum South. Nissenbaum's imaginative work is based on an understanding of the potential of Christmas to answer broader historical questions and the importance of the history of holidays not existing in isolation. He also argues that whilst the Christmas he describes represented 'something of an invented tradition', the implication that real traditions existed before invented traditions is questionable. Nissenbaum calls for the recognition of the authenticity of all traditions, viewing them 'as dynamic forces that are constantly being negotiated and renegotiated'. Invented tradition, then, is 'a very useful historical tool', but is 'subject to abuse'.[42]

A similar caution regarding invented tradition can be found in Penne Restad's *Christmas in America*, a general history of the festival charting the evolution of the American Christmas from the colonial period to the twentieth century, but placing particular emphasis on the nineteenth century. Restad views invented tradition as a 'useful starting point', but is 'too singular and static' to explain the full historical dimensions of the festival in America. In common with Nissenbaum, Restad seeks to emphasise the 'elastic and ever-changing nature' of the American Christmas, especially through the 'interaction of political, social, economic, and religious realms'. Like Davis and Nissenbaum, Restad also locates the growth of the American Christmas within the emergence of the middle class during the first phase of industrialisation and urbanisation, but is more successful in connecting this with the domestic ideology and liberal Protestantism that underpinned it, demonstrating how Santa Claus, Christmas trees, and above all, gift giving were compatible with the Protestant ethic.[43] This theme of negotiation between market and religion is paramount in Leigh Eric Schmidt's *Consumer Rites: the Buying and Selling of American Holidays*. Placing Christmas within a context of annual holidays including Easter, Mother's Day and Valentine's Day, Schmidt reveals the relationship between Christianity and consumer culture to be 'symbiotic and conflictual, complementary and contested'. He emphasises how the market helped to foster a new kind of festivity based upon consumption and spectacle, including the gift-giving rituals of the home, where the anticipatory atmosphere induced by the idea of Santa Claus had a sense of 'religious waiting' inspiring 'spiritual awe' and 'advent mysticism'. For Schmidt, the rituals of shopping and gift giving became 'secular liturgies' competing with Church celebrations and showing the ability of the new Christmas 'to absorb and supplant it'. For their part, the Churches willingly participated in the market by holding Christmas bazaars. At the same time, Schmidt identifies a growing Christianisation of Christmas, embodied in the recounting of bible stories of the incarnation, the singing of religious hymns, the viewing of nativity scenes, the decoration of church interiors and the holding of special services. Concurrently, it was churchmen who were the most prominent in publicly criticising various aspects of the developing festival, from the wastefulness and meaninglessness of excessive giving, to the obscuring of the religious message and the treatment of the poor.[44]

A different perspective on the consumer undercurrents of the American Christmas can be found in William Waits's *The Modern Christmas in America: a Cultural History of Gift Giving*. Waits insists that religion did not play an important role in the emergence of the modern Christmas, and instead he offers the themes of industrialisation and urbanisation in the late nineteenth century, and efforts to reform the festival in the early twentieth century. Waits is keen to avoid the term 'commercialisation' because it blurred similar but distinct trends such as the use of money in connection with Christmas, the increased volume of sales, the growth of promotional sales at Christmas, the importance of buying and selling within the holiday, and the relationship between Christmas and a wider culture of consumption. Waits provides a nuanced perspective on Christmas consumerism, charting the rise of manufactured gift items, the feminisation of Christmas; and most importantly gift-giving relationships: between friends, married couples, parents and children, from the prosperous to the poor, and from employers to employees.[45] The wider significance of *The Modern Christmas in America* lies in Waits's application of an anthropological tradition of gift theory dating back to Marcel Mauss's *The Gift*,[46] and his positioning of the origins of modern American Christmas in the period after 1880, which offers an alternative to the consensus formed by Davis, Nissenbaum and Restad. However, because Waits relies almost exclusively on representations, his study is too narrowly based to make such a claim.

Most recently, these histories of the American Christmas have been criticised by Karal Ann Marling. Marling argues that Nissenbaum, Restad, Schmidt and Waits ignore the visual and material culture of Christmas in America, and she is keen to highlight the role of not only the objects and images of Christmas but also the feelings they inspire. Also important to Marling is the context of domesticity and the role played by women in creating the Christmas of the home. Her approach brings some rewards. Marling offers a more complex interpretation of the 'decontamination' theory of present-wrapping, arguing that wrapping may add value to the gift, and warning against the assumption that conflict existed between the home and the expanding nineteenth-century marketplace. Marling also recognises that Christmas trees had a significant role beyond the domestic interior, as they played an important part in civic ceremony as an embodiment of public virtue. In addition, she considers the effect of shop window displays at Christmas, which 'subordinated merchandise to visual drama' but also represented an impenetrable barrier between affluent and poor. Despite these rewards, much of Marling's work represents a familiar replaying of the existing literature, and she is unable to resist the often cloying sentimentalism of much of the popular literature on Christmas, captured in her advice that 'this book would make a great Christmas present for your Mom!'[47]

Taken as a whole, the recent American scholarship on the history of Christmas has been more successful in unlocking the potential of the topic, and this is due to the cautious use that has been made of the theory of invented tradition. I agree with Nissenbaum and Restad that invented tradition is a useful starting point for studying the history of Christmas. It is clear that in the nineteenth century the Christmas festival did undergo a significant expansion, often in ways which linked it much more obviously with the family, childhood and domesticity. When examining this trend, it is right for historians to question why and the extent to which successive generations of Victorians took elements of past customary practice and refashioned them for their own purposes. Invented tradition does not, however, provide a full explanation of how the modern Christmas festival came into being, nor does it completely explain the wider significance of the festive season in the broader national culture of England. What needs to be done is for the history of the festive season to be reconciled with a number of historiographical trends, in order to contextualise a series of related but distinct developments.

As Christmas became more associated with family in the nineteenth century, it is important to recognise the role the festival played in domestic ideology. In the 1980s, Leonore Davidoff and Catherine Hall were the first historians to demonstrate the ideological formation of gendered separate spheres for men and women of the English middle classes in the eighteenth and nineteenth centuries.[48] Linked to the separation of home and work that is associated with the growth of industrialisation and the expansion of commerce and often inspired by evangelical religion, domestic ideology privileged the role of women in their capacity as wives and mothers to provide a haven for men to escape the morally corrupting public sphere of work and politics. Though Davidoff and Hall's work remains the essential reference point for scholars of domestic ideology, their chronology and ideas have subsequently been contested or nuanced by a number of historians.[49] John Tosh, for example, has highlighted the important role that fathers could play in the middle-class household, whilst at the same time demonstrating how contemporary codes of masculinity were potentially unsettled by a feminised home environment.[50] John Gillis, meanwhile, has enhanced our understanding of the way in which middle-class families engaged in new ritualised behaviour, including celebrations and holidays.[51] In addition, historians of childhood have identified the nineteenth century as the high point of a middle-class ideology of childhood, which not only emphasised the need for children to be protected but also privileged the childhood imagination as a noble virtue, its indulgence felt to be essential for the development of the successful adult. As I noted above, Restad has paid attention to this context in her study of the American Christmas, and more recently David Hamblin has made the link between Christmas and domestic ideology explicit in the context of nineteenth-century Germany. Hamblin argues that Christmas was used to reconcile the tensions between the ideology and reality of middle-class life, which was often characterised by distant familial relationships, the product of work, education and the spatial segregation of the middle-class home.[52] Leslie Bella also demonstrates the potential for a gendered reading of Christmas past. She draws mainly on Canadian sources to argue that the Victorian period witnessed the feminisation of Christmas, which subsequently instilled in women a 'Christmas imperative', a desire to recreate the rituals of childhood, reinforced by the media and consumer society, and is responsible for women's disproportionate burden in preparing for Christmas celebrations today.[53]

As Simon Gunn has recently demonstrated, despite divisions based on occupation, religious belief and political affiliation, the nineteenth-century middle classes developed a confident public culture in which social leadership was demonstrated through artistic taste, the reform of public space and the provision and dominance of civic culture.[54] One potential consequence of this was attempts to reform working-class manners and morals, and, of particular relevance here, attempts to regulate working-class leisure time and customary habits. This often involved philanthropic endeavour, including practices such as home visiting and the promotion of temperance, and several historians have investigated the provision of rational forms of recreation and attempts to foster social control of the unruly lower orders.[55] As a concurrent development, however, more commercialised forms of leisure emerged and developed throughout the nineteenth century, of which music hall has received particular attention.[56]

The growth of commercial leisure can be seen as part of a broader trend towards a consumer society. John Benson dates the rise of consumer society from 1880, though W. H. Fraser's analysis of the emergence of the mass market, based on new manufacturing, distributing, advertising, retailing and shopping practices, begins earlier in 1850.[57] Not only did the late nineteenth century see the beginning of multiple chain stores like Boots but also – of particular interest to historians – the department store became an acceptable and appropriate space for middle-class women, part of a broader transformation making the shopping districts of urban England more respectable, particularly in the West End of London.[58] The history of shopping in the late nineteenth century has been a fruitful avenue for the study of gender relations, as shown by C. P. Hosgood's study of Christmas shopping. Hosgood is concerned with women's position within the gift-acquiring process, arguing that through shopping women had the opportunity to extend their authority both within their families and the community at large, which involved reclaiming a 'public street presence' and countering popular images of female shoppers who acted in an irrational and narcissistic manner by emphasising personal sacrifice for family enjoyment. By examining the representation of Christmas shopping in the popular press, Hosgood found that men's position at the forefront of shopping gave way by the 1890s to discourses of female dominance, whilst men became represented as subordinate and 'emasculated at Christmas, stripped of their authority – publicly humiliated'. However, by employing older Christmas discourses of inversion and role reversal, Hosgood maintains that these depictions ultimately trivialised women's achievement of extended public authority, since they reinforced the reality of continued subordination after a 'temporary suspension of traditional relationships'. The balance of authority was corrected in the New Year sales, where popular representations of women re-established paternal authority by employing military metaphors to show the 'cunning' and 'duplicitous' nature of women as 'the sale season saw them scrambling for items to sate their own petty cravings'.[59]

Despite the association of the expansion of Christmas with the Victorian middle classes, the working classes are hardly absent from this book, though there is not enough space to highlight the many social, economic, political and cultural distinctions that historians have made when discussing class, and I have had to draw some fairly crude distinctions for ease of organisation.[60] Though a number of general histories of the working classes have appeared,[61] the relative lack of primary sources detailing the intimacies of daily life written from the perspective of working-class people has led to a reliance on middle-class observations of the lower orders, particularly the work of social investigators and philanthropists, often with considerable emphasis on the problem of urban poverty.[62] Consequently, much more is known about working-class politics, for example, than the history of the working-class family, though some studies have managed to integrate both categories.[63] However, some working-class autobiographies exist that detail quotidian experience from the early nineteenth century onwards, and thanks to the oral history projects of the 1970s and 1980s, we know a lot more about the social life and private routines of the generations born in the late-Victorian and Edwardian period.[64] Despite these limitations, I have tried to demonstrate the active role that the working classes played in the development of the modern English Christmas. However, though Nissenbaum's idea of their being a 'battle for Christmas' in the nineteenth century has some explanatory purchase, it is not always evident which set of class-based values and practices were the winner, and in any case such a model overlooks the deep cleavages *within* the classes which make such generalisations deeply problematic.

Several scholars have suggested that the late-Victorian and Edwardian period is one that can be characterised as an age of modernity. In this context, modernity is evocative of the broad processes of modernisation: the growth of the state, scientific and technological development, urbanisation, democratisation, secularisation and consumerism; and the way contemporaries react to this. Often modernity inspires feelings of ambivalence; rapid social change can be intensely exciting, but it can also provoke fear and anxiety about what is being lost. Associated with these feelings is a keen sense of living in an entirely new age that has made a dramatic break with the past, though as Bernhard Rieger and Martin Daunton argue, the British experience of modernity can have more emphasis on continuity with the past than European nations that experienced violent political evolutions in the modern era. Rieger and Daunton suggest that British modernity rests on creating a continuum of progress between past and present. Consequently, a society's relationship with its past is an important aspect of modernity.[65]

The application of modernity to Christmas both enhances and complicates the theory of the invention of tradition, which has so often being the starting point of scholarly studies of the festive season. As this introduction demonstrates, the tendency to look back at Christmas and lament what has been lost in the face of economic and social change can be found from the seventeenth century to the present day; the early Victorians were not unique in doing so. Yet primary sources reveal significantly more Christmas-related activity from the 1840s than before, particular in relation to one of the most significant innovations of the period, the Christmas tree. It is useful at this point to think about periodisation in this history of Christmas. Despite the rapid expansion of the Christmas tree ritual in the 1840s and 1850s in public and private, in many ways this period of Christmas celebration has more in common with the descriptions of festivity found in the first four decades of the nineteenth century, based on the simple pleasures of warmth and good fellowship. Whilst the mid-nineteenth century is of enormous significance to the emergence of the modern Christmas in England, it is perhaps the modernity of consumerism and commercialism which makes the late nineteenth century seem like a more consciously new age of festive celebration, signified by the appearance at the turn of the century of Santa Claus as a commercial icon. Our contemporary tabloid newspapers bemoan the loss of a traditional Christmas, but the festive spirit they crave was forged in the heart of English modernity.

However, as Hutton suggests, strong continuities in the history of Christmas customs are a weakness of the theory of invented tradition, and continuities are apparent in all aspects of the festival. Furthermore, too much emphasis on the search for origins and explanations of Christmas present risks obscuring the specific meanings of festivities past. This book is intended as the first scholarly treatment of the English Christmas to draw together both the representation of the festive season and the various ways in which Christmases past were experienced. In this sense, it is not primarily a history of Christmas customs but rather a history of the Christmas season, including the build up to Christmas Day and the traditional twelve days of Christmas concluding at Epiphany, and the feelings, meanings and contests that the season inspired. More broadly, it is a book about the growth of modern England, in terms of both civil society and consumer society, but it is also a history of how these concepts relate to the family and, by association, a study of the role of the child in making Christmas such a significant part of the national culture. I focus on the nineteenth century as this was clearly a period of significant change and expansion in the celebration of Christmas in England and elsewhere, but I have also adopted a 'long nineteenth century' approach. The expansion of Christmas in the Victorian period can only be fully understood by examining the regency period which preceded it; equally, the Edwardian period is also included in this study as having much in common with the late nineteenth century.

Following the discussion of the tradition of the festive lament at the beginning of this introduction, Chapter 2 examines the print iconography of Christmas, demonstrating how a set of recognisable images of Christmas emerged in the long nineteenth century, appearing in illustrated papers, Christmas cards and advertising. This analysis of the visual signifiers of the festive season not only demonstrates the role of the market in shaping the associations of the modern Christmas festival but also allows for a detailed discussion of the emergence of the modern Santa Claus, as well as contextualising the increased use of children in festive images within broader debates about the representation of the child in nineteenth-century England. Whilst the increasing importance of children to the Christmas festival is a prominent theme of the whole book, the central importance of the familial context of the childhood Christmas is explored in Chapter 3. My discussion of the family Christmas balances the ideals and realities of a celebration that came to have a highly symbolic and emotional resonance with many people. I contrast the extent of the domestic celebration of Christmas before 1840 with what came after, and the festivities of the wealthy classes with those of the working classes, recognising that the growth of Christmas festivity relied on a number of factors that include not only leisure and material resources but also changing cultural, religious and occupational practices. Indeed, the expansion of the Christmas festival put considerable pressure on a number of workers who plight is discussed in Chapter 4. The preparation for the elaborate celebrations of Christmas in the home were undertaken largely by domestic servants, whilst the expansion of gift-giving and Christmas cards meant more taxing working conditions for shop assistants and postmen. Christmas could be an occasion during which employers made paternalistic gestures to employees to reinforce bonds of loyalty, yet the extra Christmas workload of postmen, servants and shop assistants simultaneously brought working people closer to the rituals of bourgeois and aristocratic festive celebration, but also made their own familial gatherings difficult or impossible. In the case of shop assistants this led to persistent campaigns for a longer Christmas holiday which were only ever partially met at best.

For those without work or suffering considerable poverty, Christmas might only be experienced as a form of philanthropy. Chapter 5 examines the practices of Christmas charity in the nineteenth century, emphasising continuity and change as traditional benevolence was reconfigured to meet the needs of mass urban society. This discussion is contextualised within the debates and practices of the reformed poor law, with particular emphasis on the Christmas festivities of paupers in workhouses. One of the most contentious issues was the provision of Christmas beer for workhouse paupers and demonstrates the role of the temperance movement in attempting to reform the festive season. The festivity of the workhouse was also an increasingly important aspect of the civic expression of Christmas in the nineteenth century, a theme further explored in Chapter 6, which explores the urban sites and spectacles of the public culture of Christmas that developed alongside the domestic. Christmas parties and balls held by civic dignitaries became a prime site for the performance of the ideal of childhood, though at the same time they raised concerns about the appropriate behaviour and public presentation of children, concerns which were also played out in the increasingly commercial domains of the public Christmas, in theatres, in the music hall and in the street. The impact of commerce on the Christmas season is also examined in the Chapter 7, which focuses on the cultures of shopping and advertising. The expansion of the trade in Christmas gifts is analysed alongside the increasingly sophisticated selling techniques of manufacturers and retailers, though these coexisted with more traditional practices. By the early twentieth century, an elaborate range of goods were marketed as Christmas presents which in turn dominated the rituals of the domestic celebration. The extensive role the market had come to play in a national celebration of the family and childhood also caused concern, as well as revealing the still class-specific nature of Christmas in the Edwardian period.

Notes

1 *Daily Mail*, 8 December 2006; *Sun*, 6 December 2006.
2 *Guardian*, 8 December 2006.
3 *Sun*, 6 December 2006.
4 R. Hutton, *The Stations of the Sun: a History of the Ritual Year in Britain* (Oxford: Oxford University Press, 1996), p. 9.
5 Ibid., pp. 9–19.

6 J. Taylor, *The Complaint of Christmas and the Teares of Twelfetyde* (London: James Boler, 1631), pp. 8–10, 19–24.

7 L. S. Marcus, *The Politics of Mirth: Jonson, Herrick, Milton, Marvell and the Defense of Old Holiday Pastimes* (Chicago: University of Chicago Press, 1989), p. 77.

8 Taylor, *Complaint of Christmas*, p. 6.

9 Hutton, *Stations of the Sun*, pp. 25–30.

10 *The Vindication of Christmas* (London: G. Horton, 1653), pp. 1–5.

11 *Round about our Coal-Fire* (London: J. Roberts, 1730), pp. 3–6.

12 *The Times*, 25 December 1789.

13 *The Times*, 25 December 1790.

14 *The Times*, 25 December 1787.

15 *The Times*, 25 December 1790.

16 *The Times*, 11 January 1788.

17 W. Irving, *The Legend of Sleepy Hollow and Other Stories*, ed. W. L. Hedges (New York: Penguin, 1999), pp. ix–x; S. Nissenbaum, *The Battle for Christmas* (New York: Vintage, 1996), p. 71.

18 Irving, *Sleepy Hollow*, p. 148.

19 Ibid., pp. 150–1.

20 Ibid., p. 178.

21 See the discussion on the reform of Christmas charitable customs in Chapter 5.

22 Irving, *Sleepy Hollow*, p. 179.

23 *Leeds Mercury*, 24 December 1890.

24 D. Gilbert (ed.), *Some Ancient Christmas Carols*, 2nd edn (London: John Nichols and Son, 1823), p. iii.

25 W. Sandys, *Christmas Carols Ancient and Modern* (London: Richard Beckley, 1833), pp. i, cxxv.

26 T. K. Hervey, *The Book of Christmas*, ed. S. Roud (Ware: Wordsworth Editions, 2000), pp. 22–4, 43, 71.

27 P. Davis, *The Lives and Times of Ebenezer Scrooge* (New Haven and London: Yale University Press, 1990), pp. 22–4.

28 C. Dickens, *Christmas Books*, ed. R. Glancy (Oxford: Oxford University Press, 1988), p. 57; Nissenbaum, *Battle for Christmas*, pp. 222–3.

29 See, for example, H. Bourne, *Antiquitates Vulgares; or the Antiquities of the Common People* (Newcastle: J. White, 1725); J. Brand, *Observations on Popular Antiquities* (Newcastle: T. Saint, 1777); W. Hone, *Every-Day Book* (London: William Tegg, 1825–26); R. Chambers (ed.), *The Book of Days* (London and Edinburgh: W. and R. Chambers, 1832); and more recently, S. Roud, *The English Year* (London: Penguin, 2006).

30 W. Sandys, *Christmastide: its History, Festivities and Carols* (London: John Russell Smith, 1852); W. F. Dawson, *Christmas: its Origins and Associations* (London: Elliot Stock, 1902). See also J. Ashton, *A Righte Merrie Christmasse!!! The Story of Christtide* (London: Leadenhall Press, 1894); T. G. Crippen, *Christmas and Christmas Lore* (London: Blackie and Son, 1923); and M. Harrison, *The Story of Christmas: its Growth and Development from the Earliest Times* (London: Odhams Press, 1951).

31 For example, see S. Callow, *Dickens' Christmas: a Victorian Celebration* (London: Francis Lincoln, 2003).

32 J. A. R. Pimlott, *The Englishman's Christmas: a Social History* (Hassocks: Harvester, 1978), pp. 85, 89.

33 J. M. Golby and A. W. Purdue, *The Making of the Modern Christmas*, 2nd edn (Stroud: Sutton, 2000); G. Weightman and S. Humphries, *Christmas Past* (London: Sidgwick and Jackson, 1987); E. Hobsbawm and T. Ranger (eds), *The Invention of Tradition* (Cambridge: Cambridge University Press, 1983).

34 G. Rowell, 'Dickens and the construction of Christmas', *History Today*, 43 (Dec. 1993), 17–24.

35 D. Miller, 'A theory of Christmas', in D. Miller (ed.), *Unwrapping Christmas* (Oxford: Oxford University Press, 1993), p. 3.

36 J. G. Carrier, 'The rituals of Christmas giving', in Miller, *Unwrapping Christmas*, p. 55; M. Searle-Chatterjee, 'Christmas cards and the construction of social relations in Britain today', in Miller, *Unwrapping Christmas*, pp. 176–92.

37 A. Kuper, 'The English Christmas and the family: time out and alternative realities', in Miller, *Unwrapping Christmas*, pp. 157–75.

38 Hutton, *Stations of the Sun*, pp. vii–viii, 419–22; E. P. Thompson, *Customs in Common* (London: Merlin Press, 1991).

39 M. Connelly, *Christmas: a Social History* (London and New York: I. B. Tauris, 1999), pp. 2–3.

40 J. H. Barnett, *The American Christmas: a Study in National Culture* (New York: Macmillan, 1954).

41 S. Davis, '"Making night hideous": Christmas revelry and public order in Philadelphia', *American Quarterly*, 34 (1982), 185–99.

42 Nissenbaum, *Battle for Christmas*, pp. 315–19.

43 P. L. Restad, *Christmas in America: a History* (New York: Oxford University Press, 1995), pp. viii–ix.

44 L. E. Schmidt, *Consumer Rites: the Buying and Selling of American Holidays* (Princeton: Princeton University Press, 1995), chapter 3.

45 W. B. Waits, *The Modern Christmas in America: a Cultural History of Gift Giving* (New York and London: New York University Press, 1993), p. 3.

46 M. Mauss, *The Gift: Forms and Functions of Exchange in Archaic Societies* (New York, Norton, 1967). For an overview of this literature see D. Cheal, *The Gift Economy* (London and New York: Routledge, 1988).

47 K. A. Marling, *Merry Christmas! Celebrating America's Greatest Holiday* (Cambridge, Mass., and London: Harvard University Press, 2000), pp. xiii, 18–20, 84–7, 161–5, 178–81.

48 L. Davidoff and C. Hall, *Family Fortunes: Men and Women of the English Middle Class 1780–1850*, 2nd edn (London and New York: Routledge, 2002).

49 See, for example, A. Vickery, 'Golden age to separate spheres? A review of the categories and chronology of English women's history', *Historical Journal*, 36 (1993), 383–414.

50 J. Tosh, *A Man's Place: Masculinity and the Middle-Class Home in Victorian England*

(New Haven: Yale University Press, 1999).

51 J. R. Gillis, *A World of their Own Making: Myth, Ritual and the Quest for Family Values* (New York: Basic Books, 1996).

52 D. Hamlin, 'The structures of toy consumption: bourgeois domesticity and the demand for toys in nineteenth-century Germany', *Journal of Social History*, 36 (2003), 857–69.

53 L. Bella, *The Christmas Imperative: Leisure, Family and Women's Work* (Halifax: Fernwood Publishing, 1992).

54 S. Gunn, *The Public Culture of the Victorian Middle Class: Ritual and Authority in English Industrial City 1840–1914* (Manchester: Manchester University Press, 2000).

55 For examples of this literature, see P. Bailey, *Leisure and Class in Victorian England: Rational Recreation and the Contest for Control, 1830–1885* (London: Routledge, 1978); A. P. Donajgrodzki (ed.), *Social Control in Nineteenth-Century Britain* (London: Croom Helm, 1977); and L. L. Shiman, *Crusade against Drink in Victorian England* (New York: St. Martin's Press, 1988).

56 The literature on music hall is extensive. For a useful introduction see J. S. Bratton (ed.), *Music Hall: Performance and Style* (Milton Keynes: Open University Press, 1986).

57 J. Benson, *The Rise of Consumer Society in Britain, 1880–1980* (Harlow: Longman, 1994); Fraser, W. H., *The Coming of the Mass Market, 1850–1914* (London: Macmillan, 1981).

58 E. D. Rappaport, *Shopping for Pleasure: Women in the Making of London's West End* (Princeton: Princeton University Press, 2000).

59 C. P. Hosgood, '"Doing the shops" at Christmas: women, men and the department store in England, c. 1880–1914', in G. Crossick and S. Jaumain (eds), *Cathedrals of Consumption: the European Department Store, 1850–1939* (Aldershot: Ashgate, 1999), pp. 97–108.

60 For a useful overview of the different approaches to class taken by historians of nineteenth-century Britain, see the introduction to C. Hall. K. McClelland and J. Rendall, *Defining the Victorian Nation: Class, Race, Gender and British Reform Act of 1867* (Cambridge: Cambridge University Press, 2000).

61 For a recent overview see A. August, *The British Working Class 1832–1940* (Harlow: Longman, 2007).

62 One example of an extensive body of literature is D. Englander and R. O'Day (eds), *Retrieved Riches: Social Investigation in Britain, 1840–1914* (Aldershot: Scolar Press, 1995).

63 For example, the historiography of Chartism is exhaustive, though Anna Clark has managed to integrate the study of politics, gender and everyday life, see *The Struggle for the Breeches: Gender and the Making of the British Working Class* (Berkeley: University of California Press, 1995).

64 P. Thompson, *The Edwardians: the Remaking of British Society*, 2nd edn (London: Routledge, 1992).

65 B. Rieger and M. Daunton, 'Introduction', in M. Daunton and B. Rieger (eds),

Meanings of Modernity: Britain from the late-Victorian Era to World War II (Oxford and New York: Berg, 2001), pp. 1–21; see also J. Harris, *Private Lives, Public Spirit: Britain 1870–1914* (Harmondsworth: Penguin, 1994), pp. 32–6; and A. O'Shea, 'English subjects of modernity', in M. Nava and A. O'Shea (eds), *Modern Times: Reflections on a Century of English Modernity* (London: Routledge, 1996), pp. 1–37.

2

The print iconography of Christmas

Having established how the sentimental and nostalgic discourses on Christmas emerged and developed from the seventeenth century onwards, it is also important to chart the evolution of a visual iconography of the festive season, and what this meant for contemporaries in the Victorian and Edwardian periods. This chapter examines how some of the products of developments in print technology in the nineteenth century, notably illustrated papers, Christmas cards and advertising, influenced the iconography of Christmas. In addition to analysing some of the most recognisable images of the festive season, including Christmas trees and Santa Claus, the chapter also considers the visual representation of Christmas alongside its growing notoriety as a festival for and about children.

Before the 1840s, there was little in the way of a distinctive Christmas iconography available in the illustrations which appeared in books, newspapers, periodicals and other forms of printed ephemera. Probably the most prominent image was mistletoe, which in eighteenth-century cartoons was hung above interior scenes of 'Christmas gambols' that conveyed merrymaking, mischief and licence, particularly among servants.[1] By contrast, in contemporary Britain and much of the world, the festive season is readily identifiable in a number of standard visual representations that include Christmas trees, holly, mistletoe and other decorations, Santa Claus, reindeer, stockings and (where appropriate) snowbound winter landscapes, perhaps featuring a robin. As the Christmas festival expanded in the Victorian period and new customs were developed, symbolic representations of Christmas proliferated and were made available to larger numbers of people as printing technology became more sophisticated and most significantly, the reduction in price realigned production towards the mass market. Though printed Christmas images became more widely available in a variety of formats, three in particular were important and influential before the First World War: the illustrated newspaper press, Christmas cards and, at the end of the nineteenth century, advertising.

The illustrated press arrived in the 1840s with such titles as the *Illustrated London News*, *Punch* and the *Lady's Newspaper*. The *Illustrated London News*, established in 1842, quickly paid attention to the Christmas season and introduced a Christmas supplement in 1848. Such was the extent to which the *Illustrated London News* attempted to visualise Christmas for a middle-class reading public, in terms of representing both past and present, that its images dominate coffee table books on the Victorian Christmas, such as Antony and Peter Miall's *The Victorian Christmas Book*, first published in 1978. Whilst *Punch's* depictions of Christmas were almost entirely satirical, the festive representations in the *Illustrated London News*, the *Lady's Newspaper* and later Victorian publications such as the *Graphic* and the *Sphere* were often either sentimental or humorous. The visual conceptualisation of Christmas in the illustrated press led to the representation of a number of different festive contexts, not least the way in which Christmas was celebrated in an imagined past. Mark Connelly notes how Queen Victoria's marriage to Prince Albert encouraged an interest in Anglo-Saxonism, and how the press featured representations of Anglo-Saxon Christmases stressing the hearty revelry of 'a united and happy people with rights guaranteed by time and agreement, not coercion or revolution'. Connelly also highlights the extent to which Tudor and Stuart Christmases provided a model for the celebration of Christmas, and in doing so has contested the argument of James Golby and Bill Purdue that the Victorians randomly selected aspects of Christmas from the past in order to 'invent' a Christmas invested in the ethos of 'Merrie England'. For Connelly, the Victorian 'interpretation of Christmas was closely linked to the Victorian reading of history', a deliberate and systematic process of historical selection and interpretation which allowed them to make sense of the present. Drawing upon the work of Roy Strong, Connelly argues that the Victorians were drawn to the Elizabethan age because 'both eras were marked by the development of national mythologies, were wedded to ideas of freedoms and liberties and both were expansionist'.[2] Illustrations of 'olden time' Christmases reflected the way in which the history of the festival was reconstructed in antiquarian studies such as Thomas K. Hervey's *The Book of Christmas* (1836) and William Sandys's *Christmastide: its History, Festivities and Carols* (1852), which focused, though not exclusively, on the activities of the royal court and ancient institutions such as Oxford University. In 1846, for example, the *Illustrated London News* featured the sixteenth-century custom of bringing in the boar's head at Queen's College. Another important influence may have been Joseph Nash's *Mansions of England in the Olden Time* (1839–49), and which included a scene of Tudor Christmas revels at Haddon Hall in Derbyshire, and a depiction of bringing in the Yule log at Penshurst Place in Kent. Both Nash's historical representations and those which featured in the illustrated press have been interpreted as promoting a paternalistic social harmony based on the benevolence of the elite classes.[3]

Another feature of the visual conception of Christmas in the illustrated press was the promotion of scenes of abundance. In the 1840s and 1850s the *Illustrated London News* and the *Lady's Newspaper* featured scenes of the Christmas display of poultry at Leadenhall market. Other scenes in this period emphasised plum puddings, and illustrations were often garnished with a display of fruit.[4] Whilst this demonstrates the continuity of the association of Christmas with the notion of plenty during a season of scarcity, in his discussion of the Great Exhibition of 1851, Thomas Richards argues that the organisation of the display of goods helped project an image of surplus, sustaining the idea if not the reality of mass consumption as well as registering and celebrating the increased prosperity of the nation.[5] The image of abundance was also present in literary representations of Christmas, with tables represented as literally overflowing with good cheer. These scenes offered a poignant contrast with the social reality for many in the 'hungry forties', and Tara Moore demonstrates that this disparity was played out in Christmas fiction, arguing that food was used to construct 'a national identity through a supposedly revived heritage in English dishes and customs', as well as promoting *noblesse oblige*, emphasised by the juxtaposition of the Ghost of Christmas Present with the waif-like figures of Ignorance and Want.[6] An emphasis on plenty was also apparent in Duncan's representation of the arrival of the Christmas train on the Eastern Counties Railway which appeared in the *Illustrated London News* in 1850. The crowded platform adorned with parcels and luggage was contrasted with a nostalgic 'country road scene in winter' on the opposite page, which evoked the popular narrative of the schoolboy Christmas homecoming described by writers such as Washington Irving and Thomas Hervey, with a stage coach travelling through a snowbound rural idyll. Bernhard Rieger demonstrates that representations of the modernity of transport technologies in the early twentieth century depended upon the juxtaposition of past and present, and similarly the meaning of Christmas in the nineteenth century combined an urban modernity and associations with country traditions. Though the parcel train brought 'good things', a sense of loss is conveyed in the contrast between the graceful social relations of the winter scene, where both evergreen gatherers and the schoolboys raise their hats in a Christmas greeting, and the harried and anxious people retrieving their goods at the railway station, too busy to acknowledge the strangers that surround them.[7]

The illustrated press was also keen to feature images of the Christmas family reunion popular in sentimental Christmas literature ever since Irving's *Sketch-Book* first appeared. In 1846 for example, the *Illustrated London News* featured a scene entitled 'Christmas is come', which showed three generations of a family gathered round the fireside, with the middle generation of adults raising their glasses to propose a toast to their elderly grandparents. This demonstrates the centrality of the pledging cup to the Christmas culture of the early Victorians, and images of alcohol and raised glasses were common during this period. Later in the nineteenth century the emphasis on drinking and toasting gradually disappeared from the iconography of Christmas. This can only partly be attributed to the growth of the temperance movement in Victorian England, which, as demonstrated in Chapter 5, never commanded the majority of middle-class opinion. The disappearance of toasting from respectable representations of Christmas owes more to its reconfiguration as a children's festival. An important part in this process was the royal family's decision to allow the *Illustrated London News* to reproduce a lithograph of the Christmas tree at Windsor Castle in 1848. The image featured the Christmas tree as an enchanting spectacle, and in contrast to 'Christmas is come', can be interpreted as a symbol of domestic ideology, as it celebrated the nuclear family rather than the generations and emphasised to a much greater extent the enjoyment of children. Though the generational image of Christmas festivity did not immediately disappear, the transformation of the domestic image of Christmas which had taken place was neatly captured by the illustrations accompanying Sandys's *Christmastide* in 1852. A lithograph of 'old' Christmas festivities featured dancing couples underneath the mistletoe, tankard raised (and discarded on the floor), and a barrel of ale. Children are present but peripheral to the scene. The following lithograph presents a Christmas tree scene, with the tree at the centre of a drawing room surrounded by children. The adult members of the party have now been placed at the periphery.[8]

The Christmas tree has remained an instantly recognisable symbol of both private and public Christmases since the mid-nineteenth century. Throughout the Victorian and Edwardian periods the illustrated press continued to provide illustrated scenes of Christmas trees, particularly in domestic context, often emphasising the mother's role as the creator of the home festival. Though Hunt's 'hoisting the Union Jack' which featured in the *Illustrated London News* in 1876 has been interpreted as symptomatic of the extent to which popular imperialism became part of the national culture in the last quarter of the nineteenth century, equally important is the way in which the mother is the central figure in the image, lifting her youngest child above the Christmas tree, whilst the father is positioned at the furthest remove from the totem of domesticity. However, some images removed adults from the Christmas scene completely, highlighting the enchantment and wonder that the Christmas tree inspired in the child, as demonstrated by the *Illustrated London News's* 'the private view' of 1865.[9] This reflected a broader trend, further discussed in Chapters 3 and 6, of Christmas of being a time for the display and performance of childhood innocence and spontaneity, which was expected to awaken the inner child in adults and spark memories of Christmases past.

A wide range of Christmas images continued to appear in the illustrated press in the late-Victorian and Edwardian periods, though there was a particular concern to show Christmas in usual contexts, or the current affairs which happened to coincide with the festive season. Consequently, illustrated newspapers were rarely innovative in terms of shaping the iconography of Christmas during a period in which the commercial dimensions of the festival developed significantly. From the 1870s, Christmas cards played an important role in the evolution of the modern signifiers of Christmas for the English, though during the nineteenth century the thematic range of images displayed on the cards was indicative of an unstable and unsettled iconography in the process of negotiation in a new mass commercial age. It is generally considered that the first Christmas card was commissioned by Sir Henry Cole and designed by J. C. Horsley in 1843. The design of the card was similar to many of the Christmas images which appeared in the illustrated press in the 1840s, with three generations of a family toasting the recipient of the card, an absent friend, though this scene was juxtaposed with images of charitable endeavours (which were also by no means overlooked in the press). George Buday, acknowledged as the leading authority on the history of the Christmas card, suggested that the representation of the family group in early Christmas cards 'carefully observed the disparity in age, and thus dignity, of the various generations of the family, placing each figure in its right place and relationship between the foreground and background in the composition'.[10]

The Christmas card did not immediately become commercially successful, and it was only after the invention of chromolithographic printing and the reform of the postal service that the custom of giving cards became firmly entrenched in English culture. Some of the early Christmas cards featured scenes of hunting, fishing and shootings, which Michelle Higgs argues were popular because they represented the tastes of the upper and upper-middle classes, and there were also cards which followed the illustrated press in depicting medieval and early modern re-imaginings of the festival. Religious cards emerged by the 1870s, but whilst these tended to concentrate on a recognisable set of images – the Nativity, the Madonna and Child (an image which was also promoted to a small extent in the mid-nineteenth century by the *Illustrated London News*), and 'the angels, the wise men [and] the shepherds with their flocks' – they formed, as today, only a minority of the Christmas card market. Buday argued that the dominance of secular cards in an age of considerable religiosity can be attributed to the widespread diffusion of religious culture and spiritual significance within the cultural practices of (largely middle- and upper-class) society; despite the prevalence of churchgoing and the popularity of the major Christian festivals, religious observance was not restricted to a specific spatial or temporal 'domain', and it was not necessary to restrict the subject matter of the material culture of the Christmas festival to its spiritual dimensions at the expense of the social aspect of the festivities. As has been frequently noted, not only was the proportion of religious Christmas cards low, but many illustrations had no obvious Christmas theme to them at all. A variety of animal Christmas cards were produced, including cats, dogs and horses, and spring and summer flowers were also popular, which has been interpreted as signifying the coming spring and summer, and also reflects the extent to which Christmas cards and valentine cards shared a culture and iconography in the nineteenth century. There were also many comical cards, which, though not festive in content, reflected the longer tradition of Christmas as the season of mirth, and cards which were topical, including the representation of political issues.[11] The great variety of Christmas cards in the late nineteenth century can be linked to processes of expansion which had influenced and were still influencing the festive season in England. Whilst this expansion emphasised key aspects of Christmas such as the importance of family and children, the growing undercurrent of consumerism created opportunities for the creative exploitation of the seasonal sentiment of goodwill, a period of change which both contributed to and was manifested in an unsettled iconography.

Though the content of many Christmas cards was decidedly unseasonal, a significant number did produce a recognisable canon of festive images. As Pimlott noted, cards showed holly, mistletoe, plum pudding, Christmas trees, bells, and particularly robins. The association of robins with Christmas pre-dated the Victorian age, as seen, for example, in the traditional carol 'the robin's appeal', but the connection was strengthened in the second half of the nine-teenth century. Whilst it has been suggested that the robin became symbolic of the postman exposed to the elements in winter, an idea reinforced by the character Robin postman in Anthony Trollope's *Framley Parsonage* (1860) and supported by Christmas cards showing a robin carrying a letter in its mouth, the robin also came to symbolise the vulnerable child at Christmas time in need of charity (see Chapter 5). Christmas cards also represented the shift towards Christmas being a festival for children and for watching what was perceived to be the innocent, spontaneous and playful essence of their nature. Buday traced the development of the representation of children in Christmas cards of the nineteenth century, arguing that they 'disclose the attitude of the grown-up towards the child', noting a gradual shift in the later nineteenth century away from the moralising tone in the mid-Victorian period where 'a certain naughtiness was considered charming and chic, a privilege of childhood and a sign of robust health'. If the earlier cards demonstrated an example of good behaviour and conduct for children, mirroring the content of improv-ing seasonal gift books for children prior to the development of the Christ-mas annual, then the shift was manifested in the sentimental representation of the ideal child, focusing on 'charm and prettiness', with a 'faint and precious' childishness performed in 'affection for flowers, their dolls, bricks, rattles and other toys'. Another way of emphasising the innocence of childhood was to portray children as little adults (which may also have emphasised the posi-tive attributes of children's play), cast in scenes such as courting couples, or undertaking activities requiring maturity. For example, a card produced by the Davidson Brothers in the early 1880s featured a young boy who had single-handedly cut down and carried home a Christmas tree from snow-covered woodlands (figure 1).[12]

However, the images of children made commercially available in the nine-teenth century through Christmas cards and other printed media is impossible to separate from developments in genre painting, the most obvious example of the connection between high art and commerce being the adaptation of John Everett Millais's images of childhood for commercial purposes, including the use of *Bubbles* on a Pears' Soap advertisement and the reproduction of *Cherry Ripe* as a chromolithograph in the Christmas edition of the *Graphic* in 1880. Scholars including James Kincaid and Anne Higonnet stress that the romantic notion of the innocence of childhood prevalent in the early nineteenth century gave way to a Victorian idea of innocence under attack, whilst Caroline Arscott argues that Victorian paintings of the child subject should not be seen so much

May peace and love and hope and glee,
Hang radiant on thy Christmas-tree.

I   Davidson Brothers Christmas card featuring a boy carrying mistletoe
and a Christmas tree.

in terms of fragile innocence but rather as 'blameless malefaction' encompassing both 'comedy and poignancy'. Consequently, a greater range of images and interpretations of children in Victorian Christmas cards is available than Buday's analysis allowed. In his discussion of Millais's *Autumn Leaves*, Malcolm Warner highlights how the children seem lost in thought and 'detached from

MY LOVE I SEND THEE WITH MY CHRISTMAS GREETING.

De la Rue Christmas card designed by G. G. Kilburne featuring a little   **2**
girl dreaming of her parents decorating the Christmas tree.

another', as well as the absence of the 'merriment, mischievousness, and all the livelier traits we normally associate with childhood'; in their place are a seriousness, with expressions 'tending towards sadness'.[13] Many Victorian Christmas cards featuring children could be interpreted in this fashion, including one produced by Davidson Brothers in the 1880s featuring two little girls reading whilst seated on a bed. This was one of several Christmas cards that provided an intimate view of young girls. The Seddon collection of greetings cards contain several from the 1880s which feature little girls in bed, either playing with dolls or dreaming of Christmas and Christmas presents. Another Davidson Brothers card, which bore the inscription 'wishing you a bright and happy Christmas', featured a little girl sitting up in bed, brushing the sleep from her eyes and staring directly at her doll, perched on the other end of the bed, whilst a De La Rue card designed by G. C. Kilburne, offering 'my love I send thee with my Christmas greeting', showed a little girl dreaming of her family decorating the Christmas tree (figure 2). These images offered adults a privileged view of the child's experience of Christmas and may have caused children who saw them to self-identify with the message of the magic of the festival. Often, the gaze of the children is drawn away from the viewer, indicating that the child is withdrawn in the delights of their own Christmas-inspired interior world, only accessible to the adult through the memory of Christmases past.

Oh! may this Happy Christmas, be
A time replete with joy for thee.

3   Davidson Brothers Christmas card featuring a girl in a fir-trimmed
coat with a muff.

There were, however, Christmas cards where the gaze of the little girl held the viewer's eye directly, such as an image of a young girl standing in a doorway, wearing a red fur-trimmed coat with a muff (figure 3).

In her controversial interpretation of *Cherry Ripe*, Pamela Tamarkin Reiss comments on how the bold gaze of the subject engaging the viewer head on could be interpreted as a sign of sexual invitation. Further 'sexual clues' in Reiss's interpretation of *Cherry Ripe* are absent from the image of the girl in the red fur-trimmed dress; the gaze and half-smile are perhaps more vacant and less engaging, yet there is a certain precociousness in the subject of the Christmas card and the image was produced not long after Millais's.[14] If this seems a somewhat far-fetched interpretation, Buday argued that the late Victorian audience enjoyed the charm of adolescents 'in the shyness and clumsiness of awakening sex', manifested in a genre of Christmas card popular in the last two decades of the nineteenth century. According to Buday, this genre rested upon both 'extravagantly overdressed and startlingly undressed "youthful beauty"', the former typified by the costumed boys and girls portrayed by Kate Greenaway, and the latter by the naked or semi-naked images of little girls produced by W. S. Coleman. Coleman's representations of adolescent girls on Christmas cards are of interest because of the way Christmas became a site for the contestation and negotiation of the boundaries of childhood and acceptable processes of maturation. Typical examples include an image of girl with a lute covered only in a diaphanous robe, and 'the bathers' of 1882 which featured a naked pubescent girl waist-deep in water (for a similar image see figure 4). As the following chapters reveal, Christmas was perceived to be a potentially dangerous occasion for the mingling of the adolescent sexes in a variety of contexts, and the festival afforded considerable opportunity for the intense scrutiny of both the child's behaviour and physicality, the most extreme example being the juvenile acrobats who performed in Christmas pantomimes (see Chapter 6). Yet the Christmas cards designed by Coleman received little criticism in the press, the most notable comment being that '*Punch* must protest … against nudities at Christmas time. It is too cold for them, if there were no other reason'. The reason for the general lack of comment in a decade in which social purity movements and concern for child welfare were prevalent, can be found not only in what Buday termed 'their somewhat affected innocence and conveniently arranged postures' but also because the subjects consciously replicated a classical iconography which was instantly recognisable to educated Victorians. In her analysis of the representation of women in Victorian advertising, Lori Loeb notes how contemporary advertisers borrowed the 'painterly conventions established by Frederick Leighton and popularised by Alma-Tadema', portraying fully mature women as Greek goddesses, with 'breasts partially exposed, arms and feet bared … half-dressed in a costume that is often unashamedly diaphanous'. If, as Loeb claims, classical images of the female subject in advertising 'engages in a sort of vaguely scholarly striptease, which the viewer may

MAY CHRISTMAS GLADDEN THEE AND ALL THOU LOVEST!

4   De la Rue Christmas card designed by W. S. Coleman featuring a girl in a lake,
picking waterlilies.

watch with impunity reassured that he or she is actually admiring high culture', then similar legitimating conclusions can be reached in regard to the representation of nude or semi-nude children in Christmas card illustrations. We can be certain, however, that all the images under discussion here commoditised the female body, whatever the age of the individual subject.[15]

Though the association of Christmas with children has remained absolute, the images of childhood discussed here have not remained part of the iconography of Christmas. The most enduring image to emerge from the nineteenth century is that of Father Christmas and Santa Claus, who made frequent appearances in the illustrated press, Christmas cards and children's annuals, and, from the turn of twentieth century, in advertising. The emergence of the Santa Claus icon in nineteenth-century England was the result of a series of complex and uneven processes which owed much to both national tradition and cultural transfer. The modern point of origin was New York, where Washington Irving's circle of patrician antiquarians, the Knickerbockers, particularly Clement Clarke Moore, were instrumental in forging a new mythical figure of benevolence from a number of European traditions, including Saint Nicholas of Myra, the English Father Christmas, the French *Père Noël*, the Dutch *Sinterklaas*, and the German *Christkindlein*, who through mispronunciation became known as Kris Kringle in the United States. Moore's poem, 'A visit from St. Nicholas', first published in 1822, played an important role in disseminating Santa Claus rituals, and in America Santa Claus became visually distinctive through the illustrations of Thomas Nast which appeared in *Harper's Weekly* between 1863 and 1886, in which Santa is portrayed as a rather scruffy, rotund, pipe-smoking, present-laden old man replete with back-sack and a crown of holly.[16]

It is not clear, however, how well-known Nast's illustrations were in England, and by the 1880s British illustrators and cartoonists had been developing their own take on Santa Claus. Whilst 'A visit from St. Nicholas' was not published in England until 1891, Susan Warner's *Carl Krinken: or, the Christmas Stocking* was published three times in London in 1854 and 1855, and the latter year also saw one of the first mentions of Santa Claus in the English press when Howard Paul reported on 'Christmas in America' for the *Illustrated London News*. Paul noted: '[T]his festive elf is supposed to be a queer little creature, that descends the chimney, viewlessly, in the deep hours of night.' References to Santa Claus were made in the English newspapers, periodicals and particularly children's magazines with increasing frequency from the mid-1850s onwards, though even as late as 1879 people could be confused as the origins of the icon, and have no clear idea as to his appearance. Both John Pimlott and John Tosh have emphasised Edwin Lee's contribution to *Notes and Queries* that year, in which he highlighted a 'Santiclaus' custom in the West country without reference to American cultural practices.[17]

The development of the iconography of Santa Claus was further complicated by the revival of interest in the Victorian period of the old English Father Christmas, who first emerged in the seventeenth century as a personification of feasting and games, but with no connection with presents and children.[18] He made an appearance as 'Jolly old Christmas' in the *Illustrated London News* in 1844, bearded, with a crown of holly festooned with bottles and glasses, offering a large Christmas pudding in one hand and taking a gulp from a Christmas glass, whilst in 1852 Father Christmas was the centre of a collage of festive images raising a toast in the *Lady's Newspaper* (figure 1). Similar images also appeared on Christmas cards in the 1860s and 1870s. For example, one card from the 1870s portrayed 'Father Christmas as the King of Misrule courtiered by a turkey, rabbit, goose, piglet and a couple of wine-bottles in full dress, knighting with his sword a huge "Sir Loin" of beef seen kneeling before his throne'. However, as early as 1856 images of Father Christmas began to appear which made him seem to have a softer and more sympathetic personality – a suitable companion and friend to children. That year the *Lady's Newspaper* featured Father Christmas fondly smiling at two young charges he held in his arms.[19] As children gradually became more central to the English Christmas, and with the slow dissemination of knowledge about Santa Claus, Father Christmas gradually took on more of the characteristics of the icon that had been imported from America, and the two figures became effectively indistinguishable.

It is widely believed that the image of Santa Claus with which we are familiar today was the product of Haddon Sundblom's illustrations for Coca-Cola made between the 1930s and the 1950s, in which Santa appears in a red and white fir-trimmed outfit, replete with white beard, boots, and a large belt. His girth and jolliness were emphasised, and his traditional pipe removed (and replaced in Sundblom's illustrations by a bottle of Coca-Cola).[20] Whilst it is true that Coca-Cola made a significant contribution to the establishment of a fixed iconography of Santa Claus by the mid-twentieth century, the notion that Sundblom effectively 'invented' the modern Santa Claus is an exaggeration, and the Santa Claus of the post-war era is clearly echoed in the some representations which appeared before 1914. However, like other aspects of Christmas iconography, the Victorian and Edwardian periods were a formative era of transition, in which recognisably new images of Santa Claus and Father Christmas appeared alongside representations which no longer seem expressive of the season. One obvious aspect of this relates to the colour of Santa's garments. For example, in 1856 an article in the *British Mothers' Journal* referred to 'his yellow Christmas coat', and later colour illustrations of Father Christmas and Santa Claus often featured blue garments, but the most prominent colour was the familiar red (though the many images that appeared in the press were black and white illustrations). A crown of holly remained a familiar adornment, but from the 1870s it was often replaced by, or appeared in combination with, a pointed hat, whilst the coat would regularly appear as long, loose (unless stretched over Santa's girth) and shabby, sometimes revealing a rough pair of boots, as seen in *Punch's* 'Strangers' of 1883.[21]

Most illustrations of Father Christmas and Santa Claus featured a white beard of varying length. The images of Father Christmas and Santa Claus which appeared in the 1860s and 1870s coincided with popular advocacy of the beard, which Christopher Oldstone-Moore has recently argued was a means of reaffirming masculinity and patriarchal authority in an age of rapid social change. Santa Claus's beard confirmed a grandfatherly demeanour which may have signified authority as the head of the family but potentially avoided confusion with the generation of men whose young children were growing up with the expectation of Christmas largesse. The extent to which Father Christmas and Santa Claus could ever be taken as a representation of modern manhood was tempered by the icon's elderly appearance, and the decline of beards amongst the younger generation from the 1890s confirmed Santa as something of an old-fashioned throwback. This idea was confirmed by a Williams' Shaving Soap advertisement of 1901 featuring Santa Claus removing his beard in an effort to keep up with modern men.[22]

The elaborate advertising that appeared in the daily press in the Edwardian period played an important part in promoting some of the recognisably modern aspects of Santa Claus's appearance. In some advertisements, including that of E. S. Stanhope's of York which appeared in 1907, the fir-trimmed coat was emphasised, whilst the prominent belt appeared on the Father Christmas advertising Marston's Burton Ale the following year. The combination of fir-trimmed garments and shiny belt and boots made the Santa Claus advertising Graves Gramophones in 1911 one of the most smartly dressed prior to the First World War. These images, however, continued to coexist with older depictions, including the Santa Claus employed to advertise Beecham's pills in 1904, whose maniacal facial expression and rough coat and boots suggested something of the old Father Christmas taking wry pleasure in the pain caused to Christmas revellers by festive overindulgence. There was also no guarantee that the men who dressed up as Santa Claus before the First World War adopted smarter and more modern forms of dress. For example, a photograph entitled 'Shopping with Santa Claus', which adorned the front cover of the *Lady's Pictorial* in December 1913, featured a man whose loose-flowing robes and pointed hat were embellished with small balls of cotton wool.[23]

Another significant aspect of the iconography of Santa Claus, and one that firmly separated him from the old English Father Christmas, was that illustrators were often greatly interested in his method of transporting the children's Christmas presents. The earliest accounts of Santa Claus in England featured his reindeer-pulled sleigh, and by the 1880s this was reflected in Christmas card illustrations. In the Edwardian period Santa's sleigh was also featured in advertising. In 1913 for example, Selfridge's placed an advertisement for Christmas shopping in the *Daily Telegraph* featuring Santa Claus speeding through a snowbound landscape.[24] However, by this period many representations took advantage of new transport technologies to help Santa with his burden and in the process make Christmas up to date and exciting for a new generation of children. From the 1890s onwards, images of Santa in airships began to appear on Christmas cards, whilst by 1910 an illustration by C. T. Hill appeared in Cassell's *Trips to Storyland*, featuring Santa Claus flying an aeroplane. Illustrations of Santa Claus driving a motor car began to appear around 1902, including an advertisement for Hopkin's Toy Bazaar in Leeds in 1907. If this demonstrated the adaptability of the iconography of Christmas which had emerged in the nineteenth century, Santa Claus's comfort with modernity was not quite assured. Illustrators could not resist humorously sending up Santa Claus, revealing him once again to be something of an anachronistic throwback in the modern age. For example, an illustration by S. J. Cash in the 1904 edition of *Partridge's Children's Annual* featured Santa Claus attempting to fix a motor car that had broken down in the snow, whilst, in a 1907 edition of the *London Magazine*, Charles Crombie depicted Santa Claus crashing an airship whilst attempting to deliver Christmas presents.[25] Christmas could be adapted to the conditions of the modern world, but in the public imagination, it was perhaps more suited to the not too distant past, encouraging nostalgic yearnings for the Christmases past of childhood.

Conclusion

The representations of Christmas which accompanied the advancements made in printing technology in the nineteenth century provided Victorians and Edwardians with a set of recognisable visual images which complemented but also transformed the associations of the season that were imagined and conveyed both in verbal gestures and the written word. The development of the modern iconography of Christmas operated in the context of commercial practices, and consequently the effort to both develop and supply the market led to an iconography which can be characterised as transitional and unsettled. This iconography partly reflected and partly stimulated both the continuing and the changing meanings of Christmas in the long nineteenth century, including the importance of children, and the way the festival came to embody domestic ideology as well as its capacity to encapsulate a vision of nation residing partly in an imagined past. However, these developments have to be considered alongside the lived experience of Christmas, to which the following chapters will now turn.

Notes

1 J. M. Golby and A. W. Purdue, *The Making of the Modern Christmas*, 2dn edn (Stroud: Sutton, 2000), pp. 36–7.

2 M. Connelly, *Christmas: a Social History* (London and New York: I. B. Tauris, 1999), pp. 16–18, 33–4; Golby and Purdue, *Making of the Modern Christmas*, p. 53.

3 A. and P. Miall, *The Victorian Christmas Book* (London: Dent, 1978); T. K. Hervey, *The Book of Christmas*, ed. S. Roud (Ware: Wordsworth Editions, 2000); W. Sandys, *Christmastide: its History, Festivities and Carols* (London: John Russell Smith, 1852); *Illustrated London News*, 26 December 1846; T. G. Crippen, *Christmas and Christmas Lore* (London: Blackie and Son, 1923), pp. 112, 136; P. Mandler, '"In the olden time": romantic history and English national identity, 1820–1850', in L. W. B. Brockliss and D. Eastwood (eds), *A Union of Multiple Identities: the British Isles, 1750–1850* (Manchester: Manchester University Press, 1997), pp. 78–92; *The Fall and Rise of the Stately Home* (New Haven and London: Yale University Press, 1997).

4 *Illustrated London News*, 21 December 1844; 27 December 1845; *Lady's Newspaper*, 25 December 1852; 20 December 1856.

5 T. Richards, *The Commodity Culture of Victorian England: Advertising and Spectacle, 1851–1914* (Stanford: Stanford University Press, 1990), p. 28.

6 T. Moore, 'Starvation literature in Victorian Christmas fiction', *Victorian Literature and Culture*, 36:2 (2008), 489–505.

7 *Illustrated London News*, 21 December 1850; B. Rieger, *Technology and the Culture of Modernity in Britain and Germany 1890–1945* (Cambridge: Cambridge University Press, 2005).

8 *Illustrated London News*, 26 December 1846; Christmas supplement 1848; Sandys, *Christmastide*, pp. 142, 152.

9 *Illustrated London News*, 23 December 1865; Christmas supplement 1876; Golby and Purdue, *Making of the Modern Christmas*, pp. 50, 63.

10 G. Buday, *The History of the Christmas Card*, 2nd edn (London: Spring Books, 1964), pp. 139–40.

11 M. Higgs, *Christmas Cards from the 1840s to the 1940s* (Princes Risborough: Shire

Publications, 1999), pp. 6–8, 19; J. A. R. Pimlott, *The Englishman's Christmas: a Social History* (Hassocks: Harvester, 1978), pp. 104–6; Buday, *History of the Christmas Card*, pp. 187–8.

12 Pimlott, *Englishman's Christmas*, pp. 104–5; Buday, *History of the Christmas Card*, pp. 140–2; L. Seddon, *A Gallery of Greetings* (Manchester: Manchester Polytechnic Library, 1992), p. 157.

13 L. Bradley, 'From Eden to empire: John Everett Millais's *Cherry Ripe*', *Victorian Studies*, 34:2 (1991), 179–203; J. Kincaid, *Child-Loving: the Erotic Child and Victorian Culture* (London and New York: Routledge, 1992); A. Higonnet, *Pictures of Innocence: the History and Crisis of Ideal Childhood* (London: Thames and Hudson, 1998); C. Arscott, 'Childhood in Victorian art', *Journal of Victorian Culture*, 9:1 (2004), 99; P. Funnell and others, *Millais: Portraits* (London: National Portrait Gallery, 1999), p. 107.

14 P. Tamarkin Reiss, 'Victorian centrefold: another look at Millais's *Cherry Ripe*', *Victorian Studies*, 35:2 (1992), 201–4.

15 Buday, *History of the Christmas Card*, p. 142; Higgs, *Christmas Cards*, p. 17; *Punch*, 28 December 1878; L. A Loeb, *Consuming Angels: Advertising and Victorian Women* (Oxford: Oxford University Press, 1994), pp. 34–5, 63.

16 R. Belk, 'Materialism and the making of the modern American Christmas', in D. Miller (ed.), *Unwrapping Christmas* (Oxford: Oxford University Press, 1993), pp. 77–80.

17 Pimlott, *Englishman's Christmas*, pp. 115, 118–19; *Illustrated London News*, 22 December 1855; J. Tosh, *A Man's Place: Masculinity and the Middle-Class Home in Victorian England* (New Haven: Yale University Press, 1999), p. 148. Some English people may have also heard the name Santa Claus from the passenger ship of that name which sailed between Liverpool and New York in the 1850s, and a racehorse named after the festive icon and active in the early 1860s.

18 R. Hutton, *The Stations of the Sun: a History of the Ritual Year in Britain* (Oxford: Oxford University Press, 1996), p. 117.

19 *Illustrated London News*, 21 December 1844; *Lady's Newspaper*, 25 December 1854; 20 December 1856; Buday, *History of the Christmas Card*, plate 45.

20 Belk, 'Materialism and the American Christmas', p. 77.

21 *British Mothers' Journal*, 1 October 1856; *Punch*, 29 December 1883.

22 C. Oldstone-Moore, 'The beard movement in Victorian Britain', *Victorian Studies*, 48:1 (2005), 7–34; *Illustrated London News*, Christmas supplement, 1901.

23 *Yorkshire Herald*, 7 December 1907; *Daily Mail*, 24 December 1904; 4 December 1908; *Leeds Mercury*, 16 December 1911; *Lady's Pictorial*, 6 December 1913.

24 Seddon, *Gallery of Greetings*, p. 172; *Daily Telegraph*, 1 December 1913.

25 N. Armstrong, 'Father(ing) Christmas: fatherhood, gender and modernity in Victorian and Edwardian England', in T. L. Broughton and H. Rogers (eds), *Gender and Fatherhood in the Nineteenth Century* (Basingstoke: Palgrave, 2007), p. 102; *Leeds Mercury*, 17 December 2007.

3

Family and childhood

The primary meaning of our contemporary Christmas is the celebration of familial bonds, manifested in family reunion and gift exchange, the latter taking on heightened significance when children are present. The common aim of these activities is to engender a mutual feeling of *communitas* that reaffirms the bonds of family and friendship through a highly ritualised set of group interactions. The conditions for the emergence and development of the modern family Christmas are contingent upon broader social, economic and cultural developments that took place in England from the late eighteenth century onwards. Though historians are divided on the precise chronology of industrialisation and its impact on both the structure and daily life of the English family and household, there can be little doubt that a gendered ideology of separate spheres emphasising the primacy of the nuclear family unit emerged, however difficult it was to adhere to in practice.[1] Linked to a growing celebration of domesticity in the late eighteenth and nineteenth centuries was an increased emphasis on childhood as a special and distinct period of life, with the innocence and imagination of the child requiring protection as a prerequisite for a healthy adult life.[2]

That both these trends were most fully elaborated during the mid-nineteenth century, coinciding with a small number of highly visible and recognisable Christmas customs, has led historians of the festival to interpret the modern English Christmas as an invented tradition.[3] Yet the rise of domestic ideology and the romanticisation of childhood have played less of a role in the historiography of the English Christmas than the willingness of the Victorians to repackage the past and, more specifically, the guilt felt by middle-class Victorians during the turmoil of the 'hungry forties'. Inevitably, class is a major factor in understanding the development of the family Christmas during the nineteenth century, since an increasingly elaborate domestic celebration was dependent upon considerable financial and labour resources, and sufficient leisure time in which to exploit them. Consequently, the family celebrations of the Victorian working classes will be considered here separately from those of the middle and upper classes that largely pioneered the modern family Christmas. However, in order to fully understand the evolution of the Victorian family Christmas it is necessary to highlight certain trends in the celebration of Christmas which were developing before the 1840s. What emerges from this study of Christmas in the context of family life, both before and after the accession of Victoria to the throne, is an often highly gendered set of social processes, customs and rituals which attempted to promote the family as an ideal and, by and large, celebrated childhood as something to be indulged: to be seen *and* heard.

Because of its contingency upon specific historical contexts, the experience of the Victorian family Christmas indicates the possibility that feelings have a history. As an imagined ideal, Christmas attained the power to stimulate and intensify a range of emotions, including familial love, benevolence and anticipation, but also loneliness and disappointment. As a period of ritual time, Christmas contained certain intermediary processes which helped to structure the emotional rhythm of the festival, including domestic decoration, gift exchange rituals, and household theatricals and entertainments, and these are explored in this chapter. At the same time there was a great deal of diversity in individual family practice, based not only on class but also on occupation, religion, region and personal temperament, amongst a wide range of factors which make generalisation difficult. Nonetheless, certain patterns are evident, and these must be understood in the broader frameworks of the history of the family and childhood, and not solely the Victorian invention of tradition.

Christmas before the Victorian age

Using evidence from Canadian women's diaries, Leslie Bella argues that many families only began to celebrate a domestic Christmas in the period between 1840 and 1870.[4] Similarly, accounts of preparing for and enjoying a hearthside Christmas are relatively rare in Englishwomen's diaries before Victoria's reign. It would be easy to conclude from this evidence that the modern familial Christmas was a Victorian construction. Undoubtedly, the celebration of Christmas in the Victorian age underwent a significant expansion. New popular rituals were introduced and disseminated, and more people celebrated a homogenising version of Christmas than ever before. However, the expansion of Christmas in the Victorian period cannot be fully understood without exploring important antecedents in Hanoverian England, developments which proved significant in laying a foundation for the emergence of a mass cultural celebration, as well as dictating how this expansion would take place.

In the eighteenth and early nineteenth centuries, individuals gathered together to celebrate Christmas in a variety of forms. Social and religious commentators often criticised the aristocracy and gentry for spending the Christmas season in idle dissipation. In a sermon preached on Christmas Day 1757, William Romaine criticised the landed classes for 'frequenting balls, masquerades, assemblies, card-tables, operas, plays, dancing, singing, and many other fashionable diversions'. Romaine also criticised 'the lower class of people [who would] be spending their time by all kind of rioting and excess'.[5] Romaine's comments suggest that the polite and plebeian forms of Christmas celebration in Hanoverian England had few familial characteristics. Whilst there is some truth in this interpretation, there is also evidence for the importance of domestic festivities. Christmas celebrations did take place in the great houses of the aristocracy and gentry, and though they typically involved a broad spectrum of guests, including wider-kin relationships, friendships and alliances, they could take on a semi-familial character. In 1812, for example, a Twelfth Night party was held at Godmersham Park in Kent where family members dressed up as characters from folk tales and nursery rhymes.[6] Gatherings also took place within families of the lower orders. In his study of popular recreations in the period 1700–1850, R. W. Malcolmson found that private family time coexisted with communal rituals during seasons of festivity, though the latter were declining.[7] On Twelfth Day 1802, William Holland, parson of Overstowey in Somerset, noted that one of his servants 'went off before dinner to her father's, being old Christmas Day when all the family are to meet'. He further remarked: 'I like the plan very much and I find it very much practised amongst the lower orders in this country.'[8]

Before the Victorian period, social commentators agreed that the true spirit of Christmas was to be found amongst the middling sort of people. In 1790, *The Times* declared: '[A]mong the trading part of the people, beef and pudding, and turkey and chine,[9] are almost synonymous with the day. The young people are invited to dine with the old, and a kind of general joy spreads itself around: business is forgot and pleasure takes the chair.'[10] In their study of middle-class families in the period 1780–1850, Leonore Davidoff and Catherine Hall found that Christmas was increasingly becoming a time for 'family gathering and pledging of loyalties', highlighting the example of a Suffolk village family who ran a bakery-cum-haberdashery, and, in the 1790s, used the parlour for Christmas family gatherings; during the rest of the year the family spent their time in the kitchen.[11] What prevented Christmas from being a cultural mainstay of the middling sort in this period was religious belief. A disproportionate number of families involved in trade were Protestant Nonconformists. Particularly amongst 'old' dissenting groups such as Quakers and Baptists, Nonconformists often rejected Christmas outright as a relic of Roman Catholic idolatry and superstition, entirely without biblical sanction. The perceived idle luxury of the rich and the revelry of the poor during the festive season served only to further alienate dissenters. Despite the potential for dissenting objections towards the celebration of Christmas in both social and religious terms, in 1824 the *Gentleman's Magazine* reiterated the common belief that the 'middle ranks' were the real upholders of the Christmas season. This evidence led J. M. Golby to conclude that by the 1830s the number of people observing Christmas was numerically small, but it was 'celebrated enthusiastically by members of the professional, clerical and shopkeeping classes'.[12]

The nature of this middle-class Christmas needs further clarification; it was only very gradually acquiring the characteristics of a festival embodying the domestic ideology in which families experienced communitas. Developments in the literary sphere proved to be very significant in this context. Samuel Taylor Coleridge's account of Christmas in the north German town of Ratzeburg, first published in *The Friend* in 1809, was significant in making children central to a Christmas experienced in the parlour, where a Christmas tree and gift giving provided a spectacle provoking emotional displays from parents and children alike.[13] Coleridge's account was only slowly disseminated in English society, eventually being republished in William Hone's *Every-Day Book* (1825 and subsequent editions), John Platt's *The Manner and Customs of all Nations* (1827) and the *Gentlemen's Magazine* (1828), as well as featuring in complete editions of the works of Coleridge from 1840 onwards.[14] Before 1840, its influence can be detected in literary circles. For example, according to her sister, the poet Felicia Hemans 'had always taken great interest in the description of the Christmas domestic festivals in Germany…, and all the innocent mysteries and pretty surprises which travellers have described so often, but none with so much truth and nature as Coleridge in his letter from Ratzeburg'. She 'always' attempted a similar celebration, where 'nothing seemed so important as the invention of different devices for the painted bags of *bonbons* destined to adorn the boughs of the "Christmas Tree"'.[15] It is also very likely that Washington Irving read Coleridge's account of Christmas. Irving's *Sketch-Book* managed to combine the traditional hospitality of the country house with the romantic and sentimental approach of Coleridge, indicating that Christmas could be a source of 'domestic felicity', where individuals are more sympathetic to and more dependent on each other for comfort and enjoyment.[16]

Though Irving did not include a Christmas tree at Bracebridge Hall, Crayon comments that after Christmas dinner ,'the hall was given up to the younger members of the family, who, prompted to all kind of noisy mirth … made its old walls ring with their merriment, as they played at romping games'.[17] Though many pre-Victorian accounts of Christmas make little mention of children, the festival was not devoid of meaning for the young. For example, there was a strong link between Christmas and education. Though nominally a school holiday, a culture of giving gift books of an improving nature for Christmas or New Year reminded children of their educational duties. The practice of 'Christmas pieces' also allowed children to demonstrate their educational progress. Decorated sheets of paper were sold to schools, where children would complete them with examples of their handwriting, and then take them home at the Christmas holidays. One such sheet, entitled 'useful and polite accomplishments', was completed by the seven-year-old John Stainton in 1779.[18] By the early nineteenth century, 'Christmas pieces' had become more spontaneous and performative, linked to trends in the performance of private theatricals, as well as becoming part of the general enjoyment of the festive season. For example, in December 1822, Stafford Pryse wrote to his mother noting that his daughters had just informed him that they were ordered to write some verses for Christmas as a matter of amusement.[19] It is, however, difficult to make generalisations about children's experience of Christmas in the pre-Victorian period. Educational and improving gift books coexisted with those that existed purely for enjoyment and amusement, such as *The Christmas Frolick; Or, Mirth for the Holidays* (1775). Other sources suggest that rational enjoyment reached its peak in the 1830s. In an 1838 article on Christmas games, the *Magazine of Domestic Economy* claimed: '[The] much-boasted march of intellect has driven from the field the noisy and boisterous games in which our forefathers delighted; but it has left us a sufficient number of such amusements to vary our enjoyments.'[20]

Children had certain expectations of the Christmas season. In the 1820s Robert Sharp of South Cave, Yorkshire, noted in his diary that schoolchildren would call at houses in the village demanding Christmas boxes.[21] The significance of this observation is that the expectations of the children in South Cave lay outside the home. This can be compared with Samuel Bamford's (1788–1872) account of his childhood in the Lancashire village of Middleton. Bamford's experience of the Christmas season in Middleton was almost exclusively communal in nature. In Middleton the holidays commenced on the first Monday after New Year's Day when all the work was completed, and the holiday was memorable chiefly for the sharing of ale and currant loaf between weavers' and colliers' families, the watch-night perambulations of the local Methodists, and the freedom of the children (having been released from work) to play games outdoors.[22] Bamford's account can be compared with that of Robert Collyer of Keighley, born a generation later in 1823. Like Bamford, Collyer's Christmas was influenced by working practices, and one year he recalled not being spared from the forge to go home; but the overall impression was that the 'Christmas tides in my early life were all in the homes'.[23] For the labouring classes in early nineteenth-century England, work practices clearly influenced the nature of the festive season. Generalisations are hard to make, since distinctive customs could be embedded in local community traditions and be influenced by occupation, region and religion. Whilst by no means a universal experience, some labouring people did enjoy a Christmas which at least partially reflected an investment in domesticity.

At every level of the social order in late Hanoverian England, there were families who celebrated Christmas in a familial context (but also many who did not). There is, however, a disparity between the increasing number of romanticised accounts of the Christmas season's power to create domestic felicity and the amount of evidence available in letters, diaries and memoirs of the period. This may be partly because those elite or evangelical families most likely to have generated and preserved such sources were also the least likely to have celebrated Christmas at this time, whilst the lack of family documents for the working classes is a challenge which historians of the nineteenth century are continually negotiating. Existing evidence of familial Christmases says little about important dynamics such as parent–child relations, nor about the gendered nature of Christmas preparation and celebrations. Bella argues that Irving and Dickens represented Christmas 'festivities led by male celebrants who define, stimulate and enjoy Christmas'. In contrast, women played a passive role, creating the domestic Christmas behind the scenes in the role of wife, daughter or servant.[24] Evidence from early nineteenth-century periodicals supports this. In a highly politicised letter to Leigh Hunt's *Examiner*, in 1818, one female resident from South Lambeth described herself as 'a wife, a mother, and an Englishwoman', stating: 'I have … been for some days past busily employed in preparing for Christmas *worthily*. My beef and mince-meat are ready … and my holly and mistletoe gathered.'[25] This 'Englishwoman' was responding to Hunt's vision of the Christmas festival as a symbolic manifestation of ancient rights and duties predating aristocratic corruption. Whilst her sentiment may not have been representative of all women, three years later an article in the *New Monthly Magazine*, attributed to Cyrus Redding, reported that after 'breakfast the busy housewife prepares her plum-puddings, mince-pies, and confectionary', indicating that such practices were commonplace.[26] After the accession of Victoria, however, commentaries by women on the meaning and nature of their Christmas labours became more frequent, suggesting that a subtle shift in the character of the festival had taken place.

Middle- and upper-class Christmases after 1840

Charles Dickens's *A Christmas Carol* is indelibly associated with the Victorian Christmas, embodying in popular memory all that the festival had come to signify. Yet the *Carol* was not representative of a paradigm shift in the history of ritual family time, but rather a representation of the nature of the family Christmas in the early 1840s, a pleasurable occasion demonstrating a cosy domesticity, celebrating close family bonds, and replete with feasting and games. As Mark Connelly comments, 'a society with no reference to what [Dickens] was talking about could not have reacted with such enthusiasm.'[27] However, when the *Carol* first appeared in print in 1843, significant changes to the structure and meaning of Christmas were taking place which Dickens's novella failed to represent.

The literary dissemination of German Christmas tree rituals was given considerable impetus by Prince Albert's introduction of a tree at Windsor Castle in 1840. Royal example contributed to the custom spreading rapidly in elite circles and high society in the 1840s. A lithograph of the tree at Windsor Castle was published in the *Illustrated London News* in 1848, which promoted the custom amongst the paper's middle-class audience. The actress Fanny Kemble recorded providing a Christmas tree for children in January 1843, and Rose Allen's memoir of domestic service at Hale Hall in Lancashire in the 1840s noted: 'Here stood the Christmas tree in all its glory, attended by two little girls dressed as angels, with wings of silver gauze, to distribute the presents: there was an immense number, many of them the work of different members of the family, showing much thought and knowledge of each other's tastes and feelings.'[28] At the same time, many protagonists imitated the Christmas trees they had seen elsewhere. Having seen a tree at a local country house in 1851,

Margaret Gatty noted in her diary that she 'got up a nicish [*sic*] little Xmas tree' at home.[29]

As soon as it appeared at Windsor Castle, the Christmas tree had a public as well as a private life. Christmas trees were erected at semi-public gatherings such as juvenile Christmas parties, in the commercial domain at venues such as the Crystal Palace, and in a variety of educational, religious and philanthropic contexts. It was in the family home, however, that the Christmas tree was most influential. Overlapping with Prince Albert's intervention was the appearance of a number of translations of German children's books, which emphasised the tree as a domestic spectacle which prompted awe and delight in children. For example, an 1849 translation of Johann Christoph von Schmid's *Christmas Eve* described how, as they were about to see the Christmas tree for the first time, 'children rushed into the room – but suddenly stood still dazzled by the glittering splendour. They could not speak at first for joy and surprise at this unexpected sight. They remained gazing with open mouths and steadfast eyes'.[30] The Christmas tree represented an intersection of the parallel and over-lapping ideologies of domesticity and childhood which influenced, if they did not govern, middle- and upper-class relationships in the nineteenth century. Though Christmas trees can be placed in a long-standing tradition of decora-ting domestic spaces with evergreens during the festive season, they created a new spectacle in the home, transforming the interior and adding to the experi-ence of a special occasion through the creation of an environment which was familiar yet different.

Before the widespread availability of electric lighting, the Christmas tree was illuminated by candles. This made the tree a spectacle of light occurring on distinct occasions during the festival. The ritual of 'lighting up' the tree helped structure the Christmas season by providing peaks of excitement and delight for children. The potential remoteness of parent–child relationships within the middle and upper classes can be characterised by the development of the nursery as a separate space governing the lives of children. The tree helped to consolidate Christmas as the primary event in the year during which families could renew emotional bonds. Children's delight at the Christmas tree was an emotionally gratifying reward for parents and other adult relations. Another important aspect of this process was that the tree promoted gift-giving, par-ticularly the indulgence of children. The growing popularity of the nursery encouraged the expansion of the toy industry, and Christmas quickly became the most popular time to provide children with toys.[31] Toys and other gifts both surrounded and were placed on the tree, adding to the spectacle of the occasion. In 1850 Charles Dickens configured the Christmas tree as a vessel for gifts and a toy in itself when he referred to the tree as 'that pretty German toy' in *Household Words*. Furthermore, Dickens made the Christmas tree an emblem of his Christmas memories of childhood, creating a narrative linking together 'Little Red Riding Hood', 'Noah's Ark', the *Arabian Nights*, *Robinson Crusoe*, *Sandford and Merton*, the Pantomime and Christmas ghost stories, and in the process privileging childhood imagination and reinforcing the ideology prevalent in William Wordsworth's *Ode on Intimations of Immortality from Recollections of Early Childhood* that 'the child is the father of the man'.[32]

Despite the growing importance of toys as Christmas presents, books and annuals remained important gifts for children. Reading played an important role in the expanded Victorian family Christmas, encouraging children's imaginations and structuring the rhythms of the domestic festival around narrative forms. The importance of reading for children at Christmas time can be illustrated by the memoir of Sybil Lubbock (1881–1943). Recalling how she and the other children would be sent to the schoolroom to sleep off Christmas dinner, she commented: 'Sleep indeed! – when each of us had a new bound Annual, provided, it would seem, for just such an occasion … To those who … had always drained their books dry in the course of the year, such a feast was joy indeed, flanked as it also was by new volumes of Sir Walter Scott or Dickens.'[33] The boundaries between fiction and ritual time were sometimes blurred and children were encouraged to perceive their Christmases in story-like terms. At, Hickleton, South Yorkshire, the 2nd Viscount Halifax (1839–1934) used to read books to his children during the Christmas festival, and would find ways to bring the story vividly to life, as his son the 1st Earl of Halifax (1881–1959) recalled: '[S]ometimes there would be a sudden and terrifying diversion – my father coming in, hobbling with a stick and dressed up as a witch, and the word passing round that this was indeed Gagool from *King Solomon's Mines*, which was being read aloud to us at the time.'[34] The Victorians also continued an older association between Christmas and the spirit world in the form of ghost stories, stimulating in children feelings of adventure, excitement and fear. For example, the Earl of Halifax recalled that after his father had read ghost stories, he and his siblings experienced a feeling of 'fearful mystery' as they hurried back to their bedrooms.[35]

Reading and storytelling can be placed in a wider context of play and theatricality at Christmas time. Private theatricals had played an important role in the country houses of the aristocracy and landed gentry since the eighteenth century, and in the mid-nineteenth century they were increasingly embraced by the middle classes, whose moral objections to theatre were waning. In middle-class households theatricals were most typically performed by children, possibly inspired by the Christmas scenes in Louisa May Alcott's *Little Women*, first published in 1868. Christmas theatricals were often melodramatic in form, and this encouraged participants, particularly children, to learn certain types of emotional performance. In her memoir, *A London Child of the Seventies*, Molly Hughes (1866–1956) described how, along with her siblings, she would perform an annual play at Christmas time, recalling how her brother taught her 'how to act when [she] wasn't speaking, how to listen with agitation, how to do "by-play", how to swoon, and once even how to die'.[36] Private theatricals encouraged the performance of children throughout the festival, particularly at key emotional moments. Other forms of play were also facilitated. In larger establishments, this could involve the removal of furniture to allow younger children to 'romp'. Romps were a form of organised chaos, seemingly providing children with the licence to behave in ways not normally tolerated, under the supervision of parents or higher servants.

During the Christmas season formal games, including cards, were played which included the whole family. The ethnologist Orvar Löfgren argues that Christmas amplifies the expectations and obligations of everyday family life, making confrontation likely.[37] In this context games could be a way of regulating and confining family tensions. The Earl of Halifax recalled that, after dinner on Christmas Day, it was traditional practice at Hickleton to play the card game Pounce Commerce, during which some 'of the grown-ups used to get very cross with others of the grown-ups', particularly if 'unsporting' practices were perceived to have been employed.[38] Another strategy for avoiding family conflict was revealed by Arthur Munby (1828–1910), who noted in his diary during Christmas 1860 that 'household unity' had been preserved 'by a careful avoidance of religious topics'.[39] Family tensions were not restricted to adults. The most freely acknowledged tensions emerge from autobiographies of childhood describing sibling rivalries, particularly when some children were allowed to dine with their family at Christmas, whilst others were confined to the nursery. Sybil Lubbock recalled her 'torrent of tears when it was decreed that [her] sister might go down to dinner, because Charlie, now a schoolboy, enjoyed this privilege, whilst [she, Sybil], his senior by several months, was sent ignominiously to bed'.[40] Tensions also arose in the gift relationship, which could symbolise subtle contests for moral authority. Horatia Gatty recalled how her sister Juliana Ewing (1841–85), the second eldest child of Alfred (1813–1903) and the writer Margaret Gatty (1809–73), 'was always the presiding Genius over birthday and Christmas-tree gifts; and the true "St. Nicholas" who filled the stockings that the "little ones" tied, in happy confidence, to their bed-posts'. Such a role was potentially significant when considering that Alfred was frequently absent from home coping with the demands of the large industrialising parish of Ecclesfield near Sheffield, and Margaret kept busy with the demands of publishing, as well recurring illness. Gatty indicated that Juliana had a rival for the position of 'Genius' in the form of a liberal relation, commenting that 'When Greek met Greek over Christmas presents, then came the tug of war indeed!'[41]

This account of Christmas in the Gatty household indicates the extent to which the festival was managed by women. As scholars including Michaela di Leonardo demonstrate, women in western societies carry out the majority of emotional labour in maintaining kin and friendship networks.[42] Repeated attempts were made to involve Margaret Gatty's sister Horatia in the celebrations at Ecclesfield. In 1870 Margaret wrote to her sister, '[S]omehow or other we must get you over.' When Horatia confirmed that she would visit, Margaret commented: 'I thought it a great blessing and happiness to meet, all of us, as we did and we should have been incomplete without *you* so I am grateful as well as pleased that you came.' Margaret's daughter Juliana was also involved, cajoling Horatia with the promise of a free cab; and when Margaret passed away, the responsibility of keeping Horatia in the Christmas circle fell to Juliana.[43]

The customary replication of family Christmases came to depend on mothers actively involving daughters, particular the eldest, in the preparations. In 1856 for example, Emily Wood (1840–1904) received a letter from her mother instructing her to find out what Emily's siblings wanted for Christmas. Two years later Emily indicated to her brother Francis just how much her Christmas responsibilities had developed: 'You must forgive me if you do not get so long a letter as usual but I am up to the neck in work for Christmas and rather behind hand … there is a possible Christmas tree which has to be worked for and a greater number of Xmas boxes than usual as Grandmama and Aunt Georgiana must be done. All this to my natural occupations … So I think you will agree my time is pretty well occupied.'[44] In preparing for Christmas, women made a personal investment in their labour, taking on tasks that might normally be undertaken by servants. Recalling the late years of her childhood in the 1860s, Jane Panton (1847–1923) noted that her mother would take hands-on charge of the Christmas Eve preparations, the decoration of the house with holly and ivy, washing the cut-glass chandeliers piece by piece, removing the loose covers from scarlet silk damask furniture, arranging the fireplaces with flowers, holly and virgin cork, turning the library into a cloakroom and the schoolroom into a place for refreshments, laying the supper table and making creams and jellies and custards.[45] At the same time, however, women did on occasion openly acknowledge the stress that Christmas could cause. In 1881 for example, Juliana Ewing expressed her relief at missing the Christmas preparations, describing it as being 'out of the fierce Ecclesfield stress just now'.[46]

The generation of women who first experienced the expanded domestic Christmas of the 1840s and 1850s keenly internalised the festive values they inherited from their mothers. Marriage inevitably led young women to leave their parents' Christmas hearthside, and yet memories of childhood reinforced the desire to return to the parental home during the festive season. In 1865 Emily Meynell-Ingram (previously Wood) wrote to her mother exclaiming, 'I too longed more than I counted for to be with you on Monday ... my eyes quite full with tears in thinking of you all and the old happy Christmas's we used to have and picturing to myself how you were all together then.'[47] Similarly, when Juliana Ewing was resident in Nova Scotia in 1868, the emotional effect of her husband playing 'Christians Awake' was that, in words written to her mother, she felt that she was 'not entirely in Canada'.[48] Both Emily and Juliana remained childless, and, significantly, returned to celebrate Christmas in their parents' households in late life.

Whilst an increasing emphasis on the importance of celebrating Christmas within the nuclear family unit of parents and children is apparent as the nineteenth century progressed, it never precluded the presence of wider kin and friends. It was particularly the case in aristocratic households that several generations could be present at Christmas under one roof. In the Edwardian period one visitor to Hickleton commented that the 2nd Viscount Halifax 'surrounded by his children and grandchildren ... was the life and soul of the merry party'.[49] However, such scenarios created tensions for newly married couples concerning which family to visit for Christmas. On Christmas Eve 1903, Agnes Lane Fox (1877–1962), daughter of the Woods of Hickleton, wrote to her mother: '[Y]ou cannot think how I long to be at home again with you and papa and to be running down the back stairs to your room to wish you a really happy Christmas ... I almost feel as if my Christmas would begin on Saturday when George and I get down to you and papa again.' The following day, Agnes's husband, Charles Lane Fox, explained to his father-in-law: '[M]y family have never let me be away on Xmas day ... I tried to persuade Agnes to go to you alone, and let me join her tomorrow, but she was so good about it and utterly declined to hear of it.'[50] Agnes felt the separation from her family at Christmas keenly, but ultimately had to subordinate her own happiness to wifely duty.

Women's investment in producing the Victorian family Christmas can be located in a broader scheme of gender relations. John Gillis argues that the Victorian Christmas was constructed by women for the enjoyment of men. Wives' emotional and physical labour enabled husbands to enjoy the abundance of the domestic Christmas environment, perform a playful and indulgent form of fatherhood, and even regress to a child-like state themselves.[51] David Roberts comments on the way in which the absent father of the landed classes could appear at Christmas or Easter, performing the role of the delightful papa who provided the children with great fun.[52] The 2nd Viscount Halifax played a significant role in entertaining children at Christmas, reading ghost and adventure stories, staging elaborate ruses, leading trips to the pantomime, and rearranging furniture to facilitate children's 'great romps' around the hall. His enthusiasm for Christmas also led him to play a role in the necessary preparations. In the 1870s and 1880s his diaries contain references to being busy with decorations, practical aspects of theatricals, wrapping presents and the writing of Christmas cards and letters. He also shopped for Christmas presents in London, though significantly he was following instructions from his wife.[53] Not all aristocratic fathers embraced Christmas so enthusiastically, however. At Lyme Park in Cheshire, Thomas Wodehouse, the 2nd Baron Newton (1857–1942), often voiced his disdain for Christmas, which caused his elder children to be a 'little blasé' about the festival. Wodehouse disengaged from the Christmas ritual practices at Lyme Park and consequently ceded symbolic authority to other prominent members of the household. For example, his wife opened the ball and led the servants' beef distribution. His lack of enthusiasm also opened up performative space for other male relatives to dominate the proceedings. His daughter Phyllis recalled how her Uncle William entered 'most whole-heartedly into the Christmas revels. He loved them because he not only loved children but was a child himself at heart'.[54]

John Tosh argues that the Victorian Christmas licensed middle-class fathers to play, and stresses that even the prominent evangelical father figure was not incompatible with a playful interaction between father and child.[55] Evangelical fathers of the early to mid-nineteenth century could feel a keen sense of emotional satisfaction from the Christmas reunion with their children. For example, in the 1830s and 1840s the Befordshire Squire, John Thomas Brooks of Flitwick (1794–1858) recorded in his diary the happiness he derived from the Christmas family reunion that took place when his children returned home from school.[56] Whilst early Victorian fathers could enjoy the opportunity for interaction with their children afforded by the Christmas festival, Tosh points to the emergence of the modern Santa Claus in the 1870s as representing a shift in the 'spiritual underpinnings of paternal authority' from the 'judging, watchful father of evangelical tradition' to the 'source of material largesse' in the form of Christmas presents.[57] The first descriptions of the modern Santa Claus appeared in English books and newspapers in the 1850s, and the stocking ritual associated with Santa Claus is a frequently recurring theme in autobiographies and oral history testimonies of protagonists born after 1880. These sources, combined with evidence from the public sphere, complicate the significance of Santa Claus as a source of paternal authority in the household. For younger children, the source of material largesse may have been confusing. Santa Claus quickly became established as a public icon of commerce and philanthropy, a figure which was not easily mapped onto a child's father. In a period in which the male breadwinner was cast as the ideal, it could be argued that giving Christmas presents to children represented a display of paternal authority. Yet some children, like William Fryer Harvey (1885–1937), perceived Santa Claus as representing parental rather than fatherly generosity, indicating that mothers were equally deserving of the obedience and respect that form part of the child's reciprocation in the gift relationship.[58]

The visit of Santa Claus placed children's excitement and anticipation at the heart of the narrative form that increasingly governed the ritual structure of Christmas. Regardless of the extent to which children internalised the myth of Santa Claus, his presence at least guaranteed a stocking full of presents. Memoirs reveal a variety of reactions. Some people, like Harvey and Joan Poynder (1887–1987), the daughter of the 1st Baron Islington, remembered their inability to sleep on Christmas Eve.[59] Other children managed their expectations by purposefully attempting to sleep and avoid contact with Santa Claus. Sybil Lubbock commented: '[W]e did believe that if we lay awake to *see* who filled the stocking the spell would be broken, and so we shut our eyes conscientiously as soon as we were tucked up.'[60] A common feature of these recollections is the performative nature of the gratitude expressed. William Fryer Harvey recalled the desire to enter his parents' bedroom and show them the contents of his Christmas stocking, whilst Sybil Lubbock commented on how she and her siblings would 'proceed ... to pour the varied contents of [their] stockings on their [parents'] beds'.[61] However, there were also potentially negative consequences of constructing the gift as the emotional climax of the festival. Richard Church (1893–1972) recalled: '[T]hroughout the morning these

gifts and the larger one given us at breakfast would keep us in a state of deliri-
ous ecstasy, an exultation that could only result in a corresponding fall. It came
always after tea, and it usually lasted right through Boxing Day, by which time
the more fragile of the treasures would be broken, and those left whole would
have lost their savour.'[62] The corresponding subsidence of high emotion, manifested in feelings of disappointment and anticlimax, may have signalled the
fracturing of Christmas ritual time, at least from the perspective of the child.

The increasing emphasis on the importance of Christmas presents represented a consumerisation of Christmas emotions, particularly for children. As
David Hamlin argues, the introduction of the Christmas tree and the rituals
surrounding Santa Claus in the nineteenth century encouraged the construction of the child as a 'desiring being'.[63] This process reached its logical conclu-
sion with the appearance in the late nineteenth century of Christmas lists. As
Maurice Baring (1874–1945) recalled, their presents were what they 'had put
down beforehand in a list of "Christmas Wants"'.[64] The consumerisation of
the family Christmas may have also marginalised the place of religiosity in the
nexus of Christmas emotions. Though there was no guarantee that families
and individuals would experience the sacred aspects of Christmas in emotional
terms, the happiness that Christmas engendered was frequently described in
terms of joy, a word which could be understood in explicitly religious terms.
This can be seen in the diary of the social reformer, Louisa Knightley of Fawsley
(1842–1914). On Christmas Eve, 1874, she recorded: 'It is really like Christmas in a story-book, with our happy family party, and the snow on the ground,
and the dear old hall hung with garlands, and carol-singing all round, and
underlying it all the deep, real joy of our Blessed Lord's birth.'[65]

However, the religiosity of the popular celebration of Christmas underwent
a subtle shift in meaning over the course of the nineteenth century. In the
early nineteenth century the spiritual meaning of Christmas was mediated by
the doctrine of the Atonement. This allowed the coming of Christ into the
world to be interpreted as a call for acts of redemption, and whilst this did
not preclude festivity, it stressed the need for the individual to be qualified
and entitled to a merry Christmas through appropriate conduct and actions.
This need lessened as the nineteenth century progressed, and the influence
of the Atonement gave way to the Incarnation. The increasing influence of
the Incarnation encouraged the Victorians to dwell on the mystery of Christ's
birth and to celebrate Jesus as a young child, providing a theological basis for
the construction of Christmas as a children's festival. Incarnational religion
also allowed the act of domestic feasting and celebration to be understood as

having spiritual significance in itself. For example, Paul Davis highlights how the mid-Victorian generation interpreted Dickens's *A Christmas Carol* as social gospel, with the Cratchits as the Holy Family.[66] The church historian Geoffrey Rowell argues that Incarnational religion is present in the family scenes of the *Carol,* where, 'the cornucopia of Christmas food and feasting reflects both the goodness of creation and the joy of heaven'.[67] If spiritual significance became firmly located in acts of consumption, then the motivation of religious feeling may have also become vulnerable as Christmas became more of a commercial festival and the emotions of Christmas became consumerised. Leigh Schmidt suggests that there is a dialectical relationship between Christianity and commerce which allows for emotional slippage between the consumer and the spiritual aspects of Christmas. Schmidt draws attention to the way in which children were encouraged to think of Santa Claus in deified terms.[68] The poet and critic Herbert Palmer (1880–1961), for example, recalled Santa Claus as being 'even stranger than God in being able to visit tens of thousands of homes at the same time'.[69]

In 1838 the *Magazine of Domestic Economy* contrasted the 'animal spirits' of children's exuberance with mature contemplation of the adult experience. Religiosity allowed adults not only to feel the happiness of Christmas joy but also to take stock and reflect upon the recent past, and perhaps mourn the absence of loved ones. By the Edwardian period the family Christmas was losing this capacity to contain multiple emotional meanings. Increasingly, religion was seen to be the opposite of merriment. Recalling that her family never had carols at Christmas time, Katherine Chorley, who grew up near Manchester, mused: 'Was it because mother's religion was so deep and personal and private that she could not bring herself to expose it to the gaiety of a Christmas party?'[70] Similarly, Phyllis Sandeman (born 1895), commenting on her family's reticence in showing enthusiasm for Christmas, stated: 'They might display anger but not joy – their joy, it seemed, was too intimate a thing to be shown to anyone – only, perhaps, to God.'[71]

Whilst religion had become less of a wellspring for the emotions of the Christmas festival as a whole, the secularisation of festivity was an uneven and incomplete process. The last quarter of the nineteenth century saw many dissenting families adopt the Christmas rituals of home and hearth. In some cases this adoption was entirely secular in nature. Quakers maintained a rigid objection to the Christmas festival past the mid-point of the nineteenth century, but the diaries of Elizabeth Cadbury (1858–1951) indicate a fully fledged family celebration in the 1890s and 1900s, without any spiritual underpinning.[72]

However, this was not the case in all Quaker households. Harvey, whose embrace of Santa Claus rituals has been noted above, recalled: '[O]f course we never went to church on Christmas Day and the meeting house on the twenty-fifth of twelve-month was closed'; however, breakfast was 'followed by Morning Reading. Mother reads a Christian hymn, or did we on this occasion sing? – and father an appropriate chapter from one of the Gospels.'[73] Gilbert Thomas (born 1891), the son of a Methodist shopkeeper in Gloucester, recalled that Christmas Day 'began with [his] father's chapter from *St. Luke* and ended with [his] mother's reading from *A Christmas Carol* [which] did justice to the Christian festival as well as the pagan feast'.[74] Whether or not the family Christmas was invested with religious meaning, the adoption of the rituals of the festive season by dissenters was a significant stage of the process of making the modern Christmas part of the English national culture.

Working-class Christmases after 1840

The positioning of the modern Christmas within the national culture also depended, at least partially, on the participation of the working classes. The multiplicity of experiences within the lower orders of the Victorian period makes generalisations difficult. Differences between skilled and unskilled workers, urban and rural labourers, and occupational and regional customs and practices all played a significant role in determining how or even if the Christmas season was observed. The family Christmas in the nineteenth century called upon significant resources in terms of money and leisure time, resources that were not always available. A significant number of labouring people experienced poverty at some point in their lives, and many experienced Christmas in an exclusively philanthropic context. Furthermore, the reliance of middle- and upper-class families on domestic service, and the growing consumerisation of the Christmas festival meant that large numbers of people were employed in the Christmas economy, placing particular restrictions on their own ability to celebrate Christmas in a familial context. The experiences of work and philanthropy will be explored in subsequent chapters, but here I will indicate some trends in the nature of working-class Christmases after 1840.

Before 1840, it was possible for familial and communal forms of Christmas celebration to coexist, and this continued to at least the mid-Victorian period. George Sturt (1863–1927), combined the memories of his own childhood with research into the life of his grandfather, William Smith (1790–1858), a potter and farmer based in Farnborough. His childhood Christmases were spent at the farm in the company of over twenty relatives, but the farmhouse kitchen was equally welcoming to the farmhands and other villagers, who told Sturt tales of spring-heeled Jack and of how on midnight on Christmas Eve 'the horses in the stable and the cows in the stalls went down on their knees in worship of the newborn Christ'. Through discussions with his Aunt, Sturt ascertained that the first Christmas tree at the farm had been introduced no earlier than 1857, in order to please two of Smith's young granddaughters. Christmas trees were also put to communal use, however, when a few years the later the nearby Longman family at Farnborough Park made a tree the centre of village festivity. At the same time, Sturt was very candid regarding the extent to which his own Christmas emotions had become consumerised: 'I have not forgotten how defrauded I felt to receive a present of clothes, instead of a really desirable toy.' Significantly, Sturt remembered how his desires cut across the 'good-tempered religiousness [which] was never far away': 'Rather a waste of time, I always felt it, yet it didn't matter much, more pagan delights, with presents, being sure to come on next day, and Christmas Day alone being frittered away with hymns.'[75]

The early and mid-Victorian Christmas of the urban working classes are the most difficult to reconstruct. Social commentators in the early nineteenth century assumed that traditional customs would be disrupted by the process of the urban migration. In his *Letters from England*, Robert Southey commented: 'In large towns the population is continually shifting; a new settler neither continues the customs of his own province in a place where they would be strange, nor adopts those which he finds, because they are strange to him.'[76] In December 1821, an article in the *New Monthly Magazine* attributed 'the drunkenness and gluttony among the lower orders', where the '*canaille* may be seen … in all the sty-grovelling stupidity of the most inexcusable sensuality, reeling from lamp-post to lamp-post', to urban migration.[77]

There is plenty of evidence to suggest the continuity of what can be considered, from the contemporary perspective of the respectable middle classes, as antisocial and immoral behaviour into the Victorian period. Provincial newspapers often printed summaries of police reports as evidence of the way in which the lower orders, and in particular the immigrant Irish, observed the Christmas festival. There were also concerns about working-class youths. In 1865 the *York Herald* reported that on Christmas Eve 'between eleven and twelve o'clock roistering parties of "fast" young men disturbed the ordinary quiet of the citizens'.[78] Such accounts implicitly contrasted the festive behaviour of the unrespectable working classes with those celebrating the Christmas of family, hearth and children. Yet police reports of Christmas disorder could reveal celebrations which replicated the recognisable coexistence of familial and communal festivity. As Martin Daunton argues, the 'bulk of working-class housing in England up to the mid-nineteenth century had been located in self-contained little worlds of enclosed courts and alleys; but within each cell, the residents shared space and facilities in a communal way'.[79] In one such environment in York in 1867, William Bell held a Christmas Eve party involving dancing, singing and ale-drinking. The party included an element of family reunion, as Bell's brother was visiting from Wortley. However, other members of the local community were also present, and since the party was held in Bell's kitchen, it was easily accessible from the street. Two policemen were able to interrupt the proceedings, leading to a violent confrontation which spilled back into the street, where the constables faced a group of angry young men threatening a 'milling'.[80]

This violent encounter was clearly provoked by the intrusion of alien and hostile agents. Festive disorder, fuelled by alcoholic consumption, could also take place within families. In 1868, John Wright held a Christmas party for family and friends in the East End of London. During the party, his son James, a 29-year-old labourer, started quarrelling with the wife of one of John's friends, and James subsequently struck his father in the face and damaged furniture and ornaments.[81] Evidence from the late-Victorian and Edwardian periods also suggests that the Christmas season could provoke acts of domestic violence. Though domestic violence was never restricted to the working classes, Jose Harris highlights how bank holidays became known as the 'saturnalia of beaten wives', whilst Robert Roberts described how 'Christmas or bank holidays could leave a stigma on a family already registered "decent" for a long time afterwards'.[82] Recalling her Edwardian childhood in the Potteries, Alice Towey noted that the Christmas period was characterised by fighting between her parents.[83] For dysfunctional and unstable families, Christmas could represent the exact opposite of the message of peace and goodwill, inverting the growing association of the festive season with familial happiness and a celebration of childhood innocence.

The meaning of working-class Christmas celebrations was often complex. Christmas ballads from the early to mid-Victorian period suggest the continuity of older attitudes towards the festival based on expectations of hospitality and the creation of an annual opportunity for cheer and mirth closely linked to the consumption of rich foodstuffs and alcohol. 'Christmas has arrived again' (1849) notes: 'the pudding fast is boiling, which will give to your stomachs great relief, and every pretty gaze is so smiling, as they gaze on the suckling pig and beef', and whilst the 'gin and beer is flowing, some drink can till they can drink no more'.[84] Christmas ballads often echoed the social commentaries of the early nineteenth century which condemned the drunken debauchery of the lower orders. For example, 'Christmas in 1859' commanded old women to run 'to the gin shop' and then 'go home like a fox, and thrash [their] drunken husband!'[85] The subtle difference was that the broadsides seem to be celebrating this culture, legitimating it as part of working-class social relations. However, some ballads introduced new meanings of Christmas. 'Christmas wih [*sic*] old friends at home' contrasted a soldier's experience of the Crimean war with the joys of a family Christmas:

> We will in happiness be mingling,
> Never more to roam,
> With my dear wife and loving children,
> This Christmas at home.[86]

'The Christmas log is burning', published in the 1860s, emphasised gathering round the hearth with emotional qualities redolent of Irving's Christmas at Bracebridge Hall:

> Who would not be,
> In the circle of glee,
> When heart to heart is yearning,
> When joy beats out,
> In the laughing shout,
> When the Christmas log is burning.[87]

By the late nineteenth century some working-class families were celebrating Christmas in ways which were comparable with bourgeois and aristocratic celebrations. Drawing upon the evidence of Charles Booth's investigations in London, Ellen Ross has concluded that 'by late Victorian times the holiday was certainly a moment of family celebration, with its special dinner, decorations, and often a Christmas tree'.[88] During a period in which mass-produced Christmas decorations were complementing or even supplanting natural evergreen materials, many working-class families adopted 'make do' strategies in order to participate in the national culture. For example, in Edwardian London, Claire Cameron recalled: 'I was hurried out to the kitchen, festive with colour-paper chains that Jack had strung across the ceiling, and my attention drawn to the "Merry Christmas" in frosted cotton-wool that adhered to the mirror.'[89] Other strategies included the creation of fairy lights by placing farthing candles in glass jars, and writing Christmas mottoes in chalk around the hearth.[90]

By the end of the nineteenth century, much more emphasis was being placed on children within working-class Christmases. Arthur Simpson of York (1893–1973) recalled: 'Christmas was always a terrible long time in coming, and we children looked forward to it as only children can.' The material culture of working-class Christmases was less sophisticated than their middle- and upper-class counterparts, but evidence suggests that lower-class children had a greater emotional investment in the rituals of festive food and gift giving. At the same time, the whole family understood the implications of such benevolence in the context of household economy. Simpson's longing for the Christmas season was signalled by his mother baking Christmas cakes some weeks before the festival. The children were allowed to scrape the sides of the mixing bowl and eat the 'raw residue for luck'. More practically, Simpson's mother saved the Christmas goose fat in a jar, to be rubbed on the children's chests 'at the first sign of a bronchial cough'. Every year Simpson received a Christmas stocking, filled with nuts, fruit, sweets and a 'sixpenny clock-work toy'. The desire to make the best use of such a boon made it the children's 'ambition … to see who could keep their clockwork toy serviceable the longest'. [91]

In providing Christmases for their children, working-class parents replicated to an extent the gendered performances of those higher up the social scale. Accounts of working-class childhood in the late Victorian and Edwardian periods recognised the mother as the figure who facilitated Christmas. Florence Atherton (born 1898) of Farnworth in Lancashire remembered that her 'mother always made a big Christmas pudding and nice dinner, turkey and everything else'.[92] Recalling that his mother used to prepare the Christmas stockings and hang paper chains, John Blake (born 1899) commented: 'Mum would then probably sit back and feel contented that she had carried out her duties to the family for Yuletide.'[93] Clare Cameron noted that her 'mother had to work harder than at any other time, so that everything should be spick and span for the relations who might drop in. There was much extra scurry, much extra cooking, and much greater care to be exercised with the weekly income'.[94]

If many working-class mothers had internalised the need to create Christmases for their families, only some fathers used the festival to perform a domesticated form of masculinity. There were some working-class families where domestic life was dominated by the mother, and the father was excluded from the 'emotional currents of the family'.[95] For example, none the of the working-class interviewees involved in both Paul Thompson's *The Edwardians* and Thea Thompson's *Edwardian Childhoods* revealed any distinct roles in the family Christmas for their fathers. Furthermore, most accounts do not make strong links between the Christmas stocking ritual and the father figure of Santa Claus. However, some working-class fathers were able to contribute to their family Christmases. Grace Foakes recalled that her father took her and her brother to Smithfield Market on Christmas Eve, where he purchased a turkey, oranges, nuts and sweets. Foakes remembered that her father was in regular employment during this period of her life, and always saved for Christmas. In the evening of Christmas Day the family would gather round the fire whilst Foakes's father roasted chestnuts.[96] Significantly however, the task of preparing the food lay with her mother, leaving her father to indulge in the more playful and seasonal activity of roasting chestnuts that symbolised a fatherly competence. In this case the gendered dimensions of the Christmas festival transcended the experience of class difference.

Conclusion

By the early twentieth century, most middle and upper class families in England were participating in a national culture of Christmas celebrations, though variations in practice inevitably endured. These included many Protestant dissenting families who reconciled themselves to a festival which celebrated domesticity and childhood. Though the Victorians felt keenly that their Christmas celebrations were linked to notions of national character, families were also celebrating their ideal selves. The affirmation and renewal of emotional bonds were a significant part of the attempt to attain *communitas*. As a set of social processes, *communitas* depended upon a combination of pre-existing customs and the rituals which emerged during the nineteenth century. These customs and rituals helped create the feeling that the Christmas festival existed outside of normal time. As a special occasion, Christmas time was shaped by its rituals which created emotional highs and lows, and entered into childhood memory in story-like form. And yet it is unlikely that many families were able to attain the purest feelings of domestic felicity that were propagated in the romanticised accounts of Christmas written by Coleridge, Irving and Dickens. The intense experience of a Victorian family Christmas was likely to amplify existing tensions, though most of the available evidence tends only to hint at disharmony; to admit that the family Christmas was less than perfect struck at the heart of its purpose.

A truly national culture depends on the participation of the working classes. By the late nineteenth century more working-class families were experiencing a Christmas that had some similarities with that of the middle and upper classes, though the working-class Christmas was always determined by the resources of time and money. There was likely to be a significant difference between those families on the cusp of lower middle-class status, and those of the so called 'residuum', whose only experience of Christmas was likely to have been in a philanthropic context. The expansion of the Christmas festival had important consequences for the working classes. Firstly, with the growth of a nuclear family-orientated celebration, came the decline of more communal forms of Christmas celebration, though overlap between the two forms persisted. Secondly, greater burdens were placed on key workers in the Christmas economy, making it harder for domestic servants, shop assistants and postal workers to celebrate a domestic Christmas of their own. In the following chapter, I explore the relationship between Christmas and work and how this contributed to the consolidation of a national culture of Christmas in England.

Notes

1 L. Davidoff and C. Hall, *Family Fortunes: Men and Women of the English Middle Class 1780–1850*, 2nd edn (London and New York: Routledge, 2002); A. Vickery, 'Golden age to separate spheres? A review of the categories and chronology of English women's history', *Historical Journal*, 36 (1993), 383–414.

2 H. Cunningham, *Children and Childhood in Western Society since 1500* (Harlow: Longman, 1995).

3 J. M. Golby and A. W. Purdue, *The Making of the Modern Christmas*, 2nd edn (Stroud: Sutton, 2000); G. Weightman and S. Humphries, *Christmas Past* (London: Sidgwick and Jackson, 1987).

4 L. Bella, *The Christmas Imperative: Leisure, Family and Women's Work* (Halifax: Fernwood Publishing, 1992), chapter 3.

5 W. Romaine, *The Necessity of Receiving Christ in our Hearts, set forth in a Sermon Preached at St. Dunstan's in the West, London, on Christmas-Day ... 1757* (London, 1758), pp. 12–13.

6 M. Hubert (ed.), *Jane Austen's Christmas: the Festive Season in Georgian England* (Stroud: Sutton, 1996), pp. 9–11.

7 R. W. Malcolmson, *Popular Recreations in English Society 1700–1850* (Cambridge: Cambridge University Press, 1973), p. 27.

8 J. Ayres (ed.), *Paupers and Pig Killers: the Diary of William Holland, a Somerset Parson, 1799–1818* (Stroud: Sutton, 2003), p. 64.

9 The bony part of a meat chop.

10 *The Times*, 25 December 1790.

11 Davidoff and Hall, *Family Fortunes*, pp. 359, 377.

12 J. M. Golby, 'A history of Christmas', in *Popular Culture: Themes and Issues* (Buckingham: Open University Press, 1981), block 1, units 1–2, pp. 15–16.

13 S. T. Coleridge, 'Christmas within doors, in the north of Germany', in *The Friend: a Series of Essays to and in the Formation of Fixed Principles in Politics, Morals, and Religion*, 3rd edn (London, 1837), vol. 2, p. 250.

14 W. Hone, *Every-Day Book* (London: William Tegg, 1825–26), pp. 1604–6; J. Platts, *The Manners and Customs of all Nations* (London, 1827), p. 263; *Gentleman's Magazine*, December 1828.

15 H. M. Browne Owen, 'Memoir of the life and writings of Mrs Hemans', in F. D. Browne Hemans, *The Works of Mrs Hemans, with a Memoir by Her Sister* (Philadelphia, 1840), vol. 1, p. 101.

16 W. Irving, *The Legend of Sleepy Hollow and Other Stories*, ed. W. L. Hedges (New York: Penguin, 1999), p. 149.

17 Ibid., p. 187.

18 J. A. R. Pimlott, *The Englishman's Christmas: a Social History* (Hassocks: Harvester, 1978), pp. 74–5; M. Harrison, *The Story of Christmas: its Growth and Development from the Earliest Times* (London: Odhams Press, 1951), unnumbered plate.

19 Shropshire Archives, Marrington Collection, 631/3/1276, letter from Stafford Pryse to Mrs Pryse, 19 December 1822.

20 *Magazine of Domestic Economy*, 1838, vol. 4, p. 137.

21 J. and P. Crowther (eds), *The Diary of Robert Sharp of South Cave: Life in a Yorkshire Village 1812–1837* (Oxford: Oxford University Press, 1997), p. 29.

22 S. Bamford, *The Autobiography of Samuel Bamford: Volume One, Early Days* (London: Frank Cass, 1967), pp. 132–6.

23 R. Collyer, *Some Memories* (Boston: Boston American Unitarian Association, 1908), pp. 8, 64.

24 Bella, *Christmas Imperative*, pp. 88–9.

25 *Examiner*, 27 December 1818.

26 *New Monthly Magazine*, December 1821, p. 613.

27 M. Connelly, *Christmas: a Social History* (London and New York: I. B. Tauris, 1999), p. 3.

28 F. A. Kemble, *Records of Late Life* (London: Richard Bentley and Sons, 1882), vol. 1, p. 369; R. Allen, *The Autobiography of Rose Allen: Edited by a Lady* (London: Longman, 1847), p. 139.

29 Sheffield Archives, Hunter Archaeological Society Records, HAS 40.7, diary of Margaret Gatty, 1851.

30 J. C. Von Schmid, *Christmas Eve, or Antony Kronor. The Orphan Wanderer. A German Tale. Translated by a Lady* (Oxford and London: Darton & Co., 1849), pp. 103–6.

31 K. D. Brown, *The British Toy Business: A History Since 1700* (London: Hambledon, 1996), pp. 21, 38; D. Hamlin, 'The structures of toy consumption: bourgeois domesticity and the demand for toys in nineteenth-century Germany', *Journal of*

Social History, 36 (2003), 858–64.

32 *Household Words*, 21 December 1850; Cunningham, *Children and Childhood*, pp. 72–4.

33 S. Lubbock, *The Child in the Crystal* (London: Jonathan Cape, 1939), p. 52.

34 Earl of Halifax, *Fullness of Days* (London: Collins, 1957), p. 32.

35 Ibid., p. 33.

36 M. Hughes, *A London Family 1870–1900* (Oxford: Oxford University Press, 1991), p. 27.

37 O. Löfgren, 'The great Christmas quarrel and other Swedish traditions', in D. Miller (ed.), *Unwrapping Christmas* (Oxford: Oxford University Press, 1993), p. 218.

38 Halifax, *Fullness of Days*, pp. 32–3.

39 D. Hudson, *Munby, Man of Two Worlds: the Life and Diaries of Arthur J. Munby 1828–1910* (London: Gambit, 1972), p. 87.

40 Lubbock, *Child in the Crystal*, p. 49.

41 H. K. F. Gatty, *Julian Ewing and Her Books* (London: SPCK, 1887), pp. 11, 15.

42 M. di Leonardo, 'The female world of cards and holidays: women, families and the work of kinship', *Signs*, 12 (1987), 440–53.

43 Sheffield Archives, Hunter Archaeological Society Records, HAS 43.256, letter from Margaret Gatty to Horatia Elder, 16 December 1870; HAS 43.257, letter from Margaret Gatty to Horatia Elder, 17 December 1870; HAS 43.259, letter from Margaret Gatty to Horatia Elder, 28 December 1870; HAS 62.3, letter from Juliana Horatia Ewing to Horatia Elder, Christmas 1870; HAS 62.146, letter from Juliana Horatia Ewing to Horatia Elder, Christmas 1880.

44 Borthwick Institute for Archives, University of York, Hickleton Papers, A2.267, letter from Mary Wood to Emily Wood, December 1856; A2.268, letter from Emily Wood to Francis Lindley Wood, 15 December 1858.

45 J. E. Panton, *Leaves from a Life* (London: Eveleigh Nash, 1908), pp. 214–15.

46 Sheffield Archives, Hunter Archaeological Society Records, HAS 61.529, letter from Juliana Horatia Ewing to Alexander Ewing, 8 December 1881.

47 Borthwick Institute for Archives, University of York, Hickleton papers, A2.88, letter from Emily Meynell-Ingram to Mary Wood, 27 December 1865.

48 Sheffield Archives, Hunter Archaeological Society Records, HAS 60.179, Juliana Horatia Ewing to Margaret Gatty, 27 December 1868.

49 J. G. Lockhart, *Charles Lindley, Viscount Halifax: Part Two 1885–1934* (London: Geoffrey Bles, 1936), p. 167.

50 Borthwick Institute for Archives, University of York, Hickleton papers, A2.125, letter from Mary Agnes Emily Lane Fox to Agnes Wood, 24 December 1903; letter from George Lane Fox to Charles Lindley Wood, 25 December 1903.

51 J. R. Gillis, *A World of their Own Making: Myth, Ritual and the Quest for Family Values* (New York: Basic Books, 1996), p. 104.

52 D. Roberts, 'The paterfamilias of the Victorian governing classes', in A. S. Wohl

(ed.), *The Victorian Family: Structures and Stresses* (London: Croom Helm, 1978), p. 65.

53 Borthwick Institute for Archives, University of York, Hickleton papers, A7.5, diaries of Charles Lindley Wood; A2.124, letters from Agnes Wood to Charles Lindley Wood, December 1875, 10 December 1878, 6 December 1879; A2.125, letter from Charles Lindley Wood to Agnes Wood, 11 December 1879.

54 P. E. Sandeman, *Treasure on Earth: a Country House Christmas* (London: National Trust, 1995), pp. 13–14, 35, 37, 76, 97.

55 J. Tosh, *A Man's Place: Masculinity and the Middle-Class Home in Victorian England* (New Haven: Yale University Press, 1999), p. 88.

56 R. Morgan (ed.), *The Diary of a Bedfordshire Squire* (Bedford: Bedfordshire Historical Record Society, 1987), pp. 6, 12, 55, 78.

57 Tosh, *A Man's Place*, pp. 147–9.

58 W. F. Harvey, *We Were Seven* (London: Constable, 1936), pp. 119–20.

59 Ibid.; T. Thompson, *Edwardian Childhoods* (London: Routledge, 1981), pp. 209, 222.

60 Lubbock, *Child in the Crystal*, p. 52.

61 Harvey, *We Were Seven*, pp.119–20; Lubbock, *Child in the Crystal*, p. 52.

62 R. Church, *Over the Bridge: an Essay in Autobiography* (London: William Heinemann, 1955), p. 109.

63 Hamlin, 'The structures of toy consumption', p. 863.

64 M. Baring, *The Puppet Show of Memory* (London: William Heinemann, 1922), p. 42.

65 L. M. Knightley, *The Journals of Lady Knightley of Fawsley 1856–1884*, ed. J. Cartwright (London: J. Murray, 1915), p. 272.

66 P. Davis, *The Lives and Times of Ebenezer Scrooge* (New Haven and London: Yale University Press, 1990), pp. 78, 81.

67 G. Rowell, 'Dickens and the construction of Christmas', *History Today*, 43 (Dec. 1993), p. 19.

68 L. E. Schmidt, *Consumer Rites: the Buying and Selling of American Holidays* (Princeton: Princeton University Press, 1995), pp. 139–41.

69 H. E. Palmer, *The Mistletoe Child: an Autobiography of Childhood* (London: J. M. Dent, 1935), p. 125.

70 K. Chorley, *Manchester Made Them* (London: Faber and Faber, 1970), p. 33.

71 Sandeman, *Treasure on Earth*, p. 33.

72 Birmingham City Archives, Papers of the Cadbury Family of Birmingham, MS 466/205/33, extracts from diaries of Elizabeth Cadbury re Christmas.

73 Harvey, *We Were Seven*, p. 120.

74 G. O. Thomas, *Autobiography, 1891–1941* (London: Chapman and Hall, 1946), p. 43.

75 G. Sturt, *William Smith, Potter and Farmer 1790–1858* (London: Chatto and

Windus, 1920), pp. 26–35, 227.

76 R. Southey, *Letters from England*, 3rd edn (London: Longman, 1814), p. 73

77 'Christmas Keeping', *New Monthly Magazine* (December 1821), p. 610.

78 *York Herald*, 30 December 1865.

79 M. J. Daunton, *House and Home in the Victorian City: Working-Class Housing 1850– 1914* (London: Edward Arnold, 1983), p. 12.

80 *York Herald*, 4 January 1868.

81 *East London Observer*, 2 January 1869.

82 J. Harris, *Private Lives, Public Spirit: Britain 1870–1914* (Harmondsworth: Penguin, 1994), p. 94; R. Roberts, *The Classic Slum: Salford Life in the First Quarter of the Century* (Manchester: Manchester University Press, 1971), p. 9.

83 P. Thompson, *The Edwardians: the Remaking of British Society*, 2nd edn (London: Routledge, 1992), pp. 306, 310.

84 Bodleian Library, University of Oxford, Harding Collection B.II (610), 'Christmas has arrived again'.

85 Bodleian Library, University of Oxford, Johnson Ballads 306B, 'Christmas in 1859'.

86 Bodleian Library, University of Oxford, Firth c.14 (352), 'Christmas wih [*sic*] old friends at home'.

87 Bodleian Library, University of Oxford, Firth 6.26 (361), 'The Christmas log is burning'.

88 E. Ross, *Love and Toil: Motherhood in Outcast London, 1870–1918* (New York: Oxford University Press, 1993), p. 88.

89 C. Cameron, *Rustle of Spring: an Edwardian Childhood in London's East End* (London: Skilton and Shaw, 1979), p. 63.

90 G. Weightman and S. Humphries, *Christmas Past* (London: Sidgwick and Jackson, 1987), p. 116.

91 A. Simpson, 'All in a worker's lifetime: the autobiography from the late Victorian times', unpublished typescript, York Reference Library (1972), pp. 6–7.

92 Thompson, *Edwardian Childhoods*, pp. 103, 111.

93 J. Blake, *Memories of Old Poplar* (London: Stepney Books, 1977), p. 12.

94 Cameron, *Rustle of Spring*, p. 51.

95 Ross, *Love and Toil*.

96 G. Foakes, *Between High Walls: a London Childhood* (London: Shepheard-Walwyn, 1972), pp. 57–8.

4

Work and leisure

This chapter examines the ways in which the ever more elaborate Christmas festival developed new patterns of labour and leisure in the nineteenth century. The opening section places leisure and holidays in a broader historical context, charting the expansions and contractions of the festive holiday period both before and during the Victorian age. One characteristic of the period is the attempt by employers to foster a culture of paternalism in which Christmas played a prominent role in masking the inequalities of the employer–employee relationship through symbolic gestures that attempted to affirm bonds of loyalty.

I go on to explore the experience of workers who played a key role in servicing the Christmases of the middle and upper classes. Distinctive rituals characterised the relationship between families and their servants, the latter being uniquely positioned to observe, but not often participate in, the family celebration of Christmas. If servants bore the burden of the labour which created the Victorian family Christmas, then shop assistants faced new pressures in dealing with the public demand for festive abundance and material goods. Often aspirational, and in necessary proximity to the commercial material culture of Christmas, shop assistants felt keenly that they were missing out on an important component of bourgeois culture and were vocal about their needs and desires for more leisure time to enable festive reunions with family and friends.

Though there was some public concern for the plight of shop assistants at Christmas, the public response to their campaigns for longer holidays was somewhat ambiguous, as consumers felt protective of their new rights. This ambiguity was absent, however, when the public discussed the postman's role in the Christmas festival. The popularity of the Christmas card from the 1860s and the expansion of gift-giving dramatically affected the working lives of postmen during Christmas, and the public strongly supported the practice of providing postmen with a Christmas box. Despite the custom being widely condemned in other contexts, the debates surrounding Christmas boxes demonstrate that despite the emergence of new consumer identities notions of personalised service persisted well into the twentieth century, were celebrated during the festive season and were configured by the sentiments that Christmas had come to embody.

Holidays and employer paternalism

The twelve-day Christmas holiday of medieval England, lasting from Christmas Day until Twelfth Night, began to decline by the sixteenth century, as the trend of rising real wages in the fourteenth and fifteenth centuries was reversed and workmen were forced to bear the economic burden of holidays. During the seventeenth century the number of holidays continued to decline due to puritan legislation, and whilst the main holidays, including Christmas, were revived after the Restoration, no major reversal in the decline of official holidays took place in the eighteenth century.[1] However, in many working environments, leisure time was maintained by customs that not only affected holidays but also led to irregular working patterns, set hours, and drinking and 'larking' at work.[2] These customs subsequently came under attack by employers looking to impose efficiency and 'clock time' upon their workforce.[3] Between 1790 and 1840, the pruning of the holidays surrounding Christmas was led by the government. The Custom and Excise Office, for example, closed between 21 December and 6 January on all seven dates specified by the Edwardian and Elizabethan Protestant calendars in 1797. By 1838 it was open on all these days except Christmas Day. Legislation in the nineteenth century both simplified and complicated the pursuit of holidays. In 1833, the Factory Act stipulated that Christmas Day and Good Friday were the only days (except Sundays) upon which workers had a statutory right to be absent from work.[4] In 1871 the Bank Holiday Act recognised the observance of Boxing Day, and the Holidays Extension Act of 1875 extended this to cover certain government offices. The Factory Act of 1901 guaranteed that women and young persons were entitled to have all bank holidays or equivalent in lieu.[5]

The Bank Holiday Act and the Holiday Extension Act set a general principle of holiday observation within commerce and industry, but the lack of a binding legal code led to great variations in practice throughout the nineteenth century. Sometimes the difference laid in the emphasis on a particular day.

New Year continued to be the most important day in Scotland but also had a strong resonance in the northern counties of England, whilst in the west of England Twelfth Tide was a significant day of celebration. In some industries older patterns of work prevailed: the cutlery factories of Sheffield granted between four and eight days of Christmas holiday; lace-making industries in Devon and Somerset enjoyed a week, which was also common in the brass trades; and some of the larger factories in Birmingham closed for a week or a fortnight for stock taking.[6] John Benson has found that nineteenth-century coal miners were notorious for insisting on celebrating a series of local feasts in addition to the major celebrations at Christmas, New Year, Easter and Whitsun.[7] However, in many areas of employment the payment of wages for holidays remained the preserve of the lucky few, and consequently workers did not always welcome an extended, or sometimes any, Christmas holiday. For those relying on outdoor employment, the bad weather often associated with the Christmas period could cause an unfortunate extended lay-off. In other instances, employers and employees took advantage of loopholes in the law. The 1833 Factory Act allowed dissenters to employ children and young people on Good Friday and Christmas Day with their own consent, but the Select Committee on Factories was told in 1840 that some manufacturers belonging to the Established Church were actually becoming dissenters in order to take advantage of this provision. On other occasions, workers simply rejected parliamentary regulations in favour of custom. At Henry Ashworth's mill at Turton, no one was compelled to work on Christmas Day, but many workers preferred to, because the local custom was to take a holiday on New Year's Day instead.[8]

The defence of custom became 'a key bargaining factor' for workers faced with threatening change. Hugh Cunningham highlights similarities in tone between workers' defence of custom and the writings of Tory paternalists such as Lord John Manners, as well as identifying a paternalistic undercurrent in the works of radicals such as William Hone. If there was a paternalistic element to the desire to regulate holidays by custom, it could also apply to the relationship between employer and employee at Christmas. Increasingly in the nineteenth century, employers saw the value of symbolic gestures towards their employees at Christmas and other key times of the year. As Cunningham has noted, when middle-class antiquarians commented on custom, they were separating out the 'more colourful leisure traditions of the past' as distinct from work habits; but for working people there was no clear distinction.[9] Studies of nineteenth-century leisure tend to stress the development of a regular and separate sphere of work, but it is possible that forms of Christmas sociability learnt in the home and in the community may have been replicated in the workplace. Whilst the expansion of the domestic celebration of Christmas in the nineteenth century contributed to a feminisation of festivity, this did not preclude the possibility of Christmas joviality in masculine worlds. The workplace could then, in turn, be the breeding ground for the continuance of more 'colourful' Christmas customs. For example, Cynthia Sughrue's study of festive sword-dancing teams in south Yorkshire shows that one team, operating in Woodhouse in the 1880s and subsequently transferring to Handsworth, were primarily recruited and maintained through friendships fostered in the collieries.[10]

In some instances Christmas paternalism took the form of philanthropy, as at Colman's mustard manufacturing plant in Norfolk, where the Colmans gave each workman a piece of pork at Christmas. The weight of the pork depended on the size of the family, a situation in which Caroline Colman displayed her 'useful knowledge', an expertise grounded in domesticity that allowed her to perform a public role.[11] She also distributed Christmas hampers and works' almanacs.[12] Philanthropic gestures could also be combined with employers preaching on their favourite subjects. Between the 1870s and the 1890s, the manager of York Gas Works, Mr Sellers, gave an annual Christmas address to the workmen. In 1879 he stressed to the workmen 'the wisdom of enjoy-ing Christmas in a sensible and manly way', urging industriousness and tem-perance, and the importance of taking 'your main enjoyment over your own firesides', and to 'put the education of your children in the highest place'. To complement this, children's books were provided for those men with children under the age of eleven. In 1882 he concerned himself with 'lying as a vice', and reiterated the message 'if you wish to be prosperous keep sober, if you wish to be respected keep sober, and if you wish to do your duty to your wives, to your children, or to your sweethearts, keep sober'. It is likely, however, that such addresses were not always taken to heart, and may even have caused resentment among the employees, as Sellers acknowledged in 1884: 'It is possible that some of you may think that sermonising in this fashion in a Christmas address is somewhat akin to a wet blanket.'[13]

Other evidence from York suggests that small employers were likely to provide a Christmas dinner for their employees. In 1848, Mr Varvill, a plumber, gave an 'excellent supper' to his servants and workmen, 'according to annual custom'. These gatherings often took place in public houses, as in 1859, when Mr Groves, a cabinet maker, entertained his workmen to a supper in the Waggon and Horses, Gillygate. Christmas could also inspire novelty.

For example, in 1881 the employees of Hunt's brewery dined together in a large mashing tub, which had been decorated with holly and evergreens.[14] These occasions provided employers with the opportunity to symbolically provide the Christmas feast in a fatherly fashion, but also fostered masculine social intimacies. Significantly, they became prevalent in the mid-nineteenth century, when the expanded domestic celebration of Christmas had become firmly established amongst middle- and upper-class families, and although these occasions offered a masculine alternative to the increasingly feminised Christmas of the home, they may also have contributed to the dissemination of the expanded Christmas festival, particularly to the 'respectable' working classes.

The expansion of Christmas in the mid-nineteenth century meant that for some firms or company divisions the festive season was an obvious time to hold their annual dinner. This was particularly true of the departments of the North-Eastern Railway Company (NER), whose annual dinners for the carriage and boiler-making departments were well established by 1863. From the 1860s the NER also developed a symbolic act of paternalism which drew upon an imagined past. Each employee was granted a piece of wood described as a 'yule log' to take home and burn on the family hearth.[15] This not only connected the company to the ideal vision of the family at Christmas time but also linked ideas concerning the ancient pagan origins of the Christmas festival to the modern industrial age. The earliest recorded occurrence of the yule log in Britain was by Robert Herrick in the 1620s or 1630s, though reference to its existence in Germany can be traced back to 1184. Sir James Frazer popularised the notion that the yule log was a pagan fire ritual from ancient Europe, though considerable doubt has been raised concerning this belief.[16] By 1913 this custom was operating as a potent local spectacle, and was captured in a photograph by the *Yorkshire Herald* as the workmen streamed out of the carriage and wagon works with their logs.[17] However, not all Christmas work activities were imposed from above by employers. In Leeds, for example, an annual tea and entertainment was established amongst rail employees in 1868, in order to raise funds for orphans of employees killed in the performance of their duties.[18]

For employers, Christmas could also play a part in the forging of a distinct company culture. Charles Dellheim argues that at Cadbury's a company ethos was embedded through 'ritual, myth and symbol', including social occasions at Christmas, New Year and summer. These rituals were intended to help create a unified spirit amongst the Cadbury family and their employees, part of a wider trend in the late nineteenth century of creating a 'culture of the employer family'.[19] The annual gathering of Cadbury Brothers' employees (held in December) was established by 1884, and consisted of a tea, hymns, organ solos, speeches and comic sketches, and the format remained essentially the same well into the twentieth century. Considering the persistence of Quaker objections to the Christmas festival, it is significant that the annual gathering was renamed the Bournville Christmas Gathering in 1904, and the Bournville Christmas Party in 1905.[20] Another Quaker chocolate producer, Rowntree's of York, had also instituted a Christmas party by 1905, though at Rowntree's the party was aimed at the children of the employees, complete with Christmas tree, gifts, and magic lantern scenes. From 1907 a children's treat was established in the factory's fire station, with Father Christmas distributing the gifts, strengthening the paternalistic ethos of the company. This reflected not only a desire to create a much more family-orientated culture of Christmas than the exclusively masculine celebrations of the mid-nineteenth century (though these continued in some sectors of employment), but also a form of employment that had become secure. In 1907 Joseph Rowntree reflected that in the early years of his business the company would have to 'reduce the size of the staff and to part with many workers' once the Christmas rush was over. In recent years, however, Rowntree's had been able 'to maintain full work throughout the year'.[21]

Domestic service

The workers who were most affected by the expansion of the Christmas festival were domestic servants. According to census figures, the number of domestic servants employed in England and Wales rose from 751,541 in 1851 to a peak of 1,386,167 in 1891, and did not decline below the one million mark until the late 1930s. Taking into account that around 60,000 servants in 1891 were men and boys, then residential domestic service can be seen as the largest single employer of women and girls, and it has been estimated that one in three young girls between the ages of 15 and 20 were in service. Whilst a number of historians have cast doubt on the methodology of compiling these statistics, it is clear that substantial numbers of young working-class women devoted most of the festive season to providing a Christmas celebration for their employers, a factor which reinforced the perception of domestic Christmas labour as feminine.[22]

The working lives of domestic servants were configured by expectations and values that were paternal and familial in nature, and there is evidence that many middle- and upper-class families sought to cement the social bonds between employer and employee through highly symbolic rituals performed during the festive season. Yet the very close proximity of domestic servants to the most private and intimate spaces of middle- and upper-class households made class relations more problematic than in other domains of work such as the factory or workshop. Indeed, the presence of servants in well-to-do households was something of a contradiction in an environment increasingly constructed as a haven from the competitive and morally corrupting public sphere, and middle-class suspicions of working-class propensities towards dirt and sexual transgression have been well documented by historians such as Leonore Davidoff.[23] As Christmas increasingly came to be seen as a celebration of the family, domestic servants occupied a strange and ambiguous position within it: performing essential labour, often privy to the elaborate performance of Christmas by the middle and upper classes, sometimes partially included in broader understandings of the family household, but also often separated from their own friends and relatives.

Servants were important to the domestic celebration of Christmas because they carried out much, though by no means all, of the physical work of Christmas in the home. This reliance on servants is demonstrated in a letter written by Geraldine Jewsbury (1812–80) describing Christmas in 1841, when she was acting as housekeeper to her father and younger brother:

> Listen! When, I got home from Leeds I found my servant ill, and I had to find a substitute in an instant! Well, this unlucky substitute left me a minute's notice on Christmas Day, and there was I, left with a servant ill in bed and eight people to provide dinner for, [and] nothing but myself to stand between them and starvation![24]

At the same time, the evidence highlighted in my previous chapter clearly indicates that women of the wealthier classes, in addition to managing the overall process of creating the perfect Christmas, also retained control of key tasks which most clearly symbolised their domestic authority and skill. However, in aristocratic households, where tasks were more fragmented, there was greater scope for the delegation of symbolic tasks. Davidoff highlights the ways in which upper-servants could often act as 'crucial agents in the performance of deference ceremonies'.[25] This was significant not only to the personal relationships of the household but also to how larger establishments operated as an institution in relation to the local community. For example, during Edwardian Christmases at Lyme Park in Cheshire, the butler acted as the master of ceremonies when estate employees came for tea and presents on Boxing Day.[26]

For the majority of servants, Christmas merely exacerbated their already considerable daily toil. One of the most detailed accounts of domestic service in nineteenth-century England can be found in the diaries of Hannah Cullwick (1833–1909). While the origins of these diaries lie in Cullwick's unconventional relationship with Arthur Munby, and his obsession with collecting and observing information on working women, she eventually began to write them for her own purposes and Liz Stanley argues that the diaries can be read as an accurate description of Cullwick's domestic labour and feelings. In 1863 Cullwick was in the service of Mr Foster, a beer merchant in Kilburn, and her diary provides a detailed account of the arduous tasks that she performed over the Christmas period. Cullwick's diary entries for the period from 23 December until Christmas Day describe how she woke early, on one occasion at four in the morning, and her days were filled by fire-lighting, cleaning and food preparation. On 23 December Cullwick noted that she 'was nearly sick wi' the heat & smell' of basting and roasting the turkey. By Christmas Eve Cullwick was very conscious of the contrast between the family's fun with a 'hot mince pie up wi' a ring & sixpence in it' and her own situation: 'We had no fun downstairs, all was very busy till 4 o'clock & then to bed.' On Boxing Day Cullwick recorded: 'I felt glad Christmas was over so far for if kept on long as it's bin the last 3 or 4 days I should be knock'd up I think.'[27]

In larger establishments, especially the country houses of the aristocracy, preparations for Christmas could be a large-scale operation. The 1st Earl of Halifax recalled from his late Victorian childhood that, for Christmas dinner, the gardeners would prepare the table with flowers, and around twenty people would be served six or seven courses on silver plates carried up two flights of stairs from the kitchen, though extra help was obtained from the village, stable and gardens to deal with the carrying and washing up. The additional guests who visited Hickleton during the festive season also generated extra work for the servants, as they were required to carry water to and from bedrooms, illuminate candlesticks and set fires in the guest bedrooms, though Halifax noted that 'on Christmas Eve members of the family used sometimes to practice self-denial for the benefit of the housemaids by not having a fire'.[28]

With servants being burdened with additional labours during key moments in the domestic celebration of Christmas, it is clear that they did not fully experience the potential joys of the festive season. Being resident in their place of employment during the Christmas season also meant that servants might be separated from their own families. However, some employers were willing to make allowances. In the 1860s and 1870s Hannah Cullwick was allowed by two different employers to have some personal time to visit relatives on Christmas Day, though the conditions attached to these leisure hours rarely made the occasions pleasurable. Whilst the Foster family went out on Christmas Day 1863, Cullwick was able to visit her sister Ellen, but had 'such a headache & felt so tired & sleepy [that she] sat in a chair & slept till five'. Whilst in the service of the Henderson family in 1871, Cullwick spent a very quiet but frustrating Christmas Day. The Henderson family went to church in the morning, and Cullwick was instructed by the mistress of the house to go out in the afternoon, and so was able to visit her sister for tea, but had to leave at half past seven, because the ladies of the Henderson household had gone out to dinner and were uncertain about their time of return. Cullwick commented: 'I felt dull & disappointed on the whole, spending the day neither here nor there.'[29]

Despite being afforded limited opportunities to visit relatives during the festive season, for Hannah Cullwick these were not the same as being able to *go home* for Christmas. Arthur Munby always returned to his family home in York for Christmas, and on Christmas Day 1872 Cullwick mused: 'I often think what a delightful pleasure that must be, going home for Christmas, but I've never once had it.'[30] There is reason to suppose that other servants did manage to have Christmas homecomings, as Davidoff's study of the 1851 Colchester census shows that three quarters of servants working in that vicinity had been born within a radius of ten miles, and other studies show that servants often worked within twenty-miles of their birthplace.[31] However, despite the relative proximity of many servants to their place of birth, some employers actively sought to minimise the contacts their servants had with the outside world, including blood relatives, for fear of morally corrupting influences. Yet the growing association of Christmas with the family in the Victorian age made such prohibitions more problematic during the festive season. These tensions were most clearly played out in institutions which aimed to reform and train so-called 'fallen women' for a career in domestic service. The administrators of these institutions believed that the families of those in their care had failed them, and yet from the 1860s inmates were encouraged to maintain links with their families through Christmas gift-giving. As the Matron of the York Penitentiary commented in 1865:

> The inmates, by willingly giving up the few luxuries allowed them, saved a little money, and were enabled to send presents to their friends at Christmas. A father

was much pleased to receive a silk handkerchief; one mother was surprised by the gift of a parcel of tea on Christmas Eve; the brothers and sisters of another inmate were made happy by a parcel of sweets as a token of love from the absent one.[32]

Despite encouraging gift relationships between inmates and their families, the York Penitentiary, in common with other institutions in the second half of the nineteenth century, operated on familial lines, with an emphasis on the need for 'family worship' and a matron cast as an 'authoritarian mother figure'. This ethos included the introduction of a Christmas tree in 1863.[33] One product of this was that some of former inmates continued to view the matron as a maternal figure after they had left the institution, and this relationship was celebrated at Christmas time. For example, one woman in the service of a clergyman's family sent a Christmas gift to the matron in 1874, whilst in 1897 a former inmate who emigrated to America wrote: 'I suppose by the time this reaches you it will be Christmas. I must say that I almost wish there was no Christmas: for when it comes round I want to be home so much it makes me miserable.' The idea of the institution as home also led some former inmates to return to the Penitentiary for Christmas, as four did in 1910.[34]

Whilst the evidence from the York Penitentiary suggests that some young women could not obtain a sense of home and belonging from employment in domestic service, it also highlights the potential for institutions to foster relationships of a familial character, and larger households – particularly the large country houses of the aristocracy – did operate as institutions representing dynastic power at community, county and national level. It is pertinent to examine the extent to which servants could become part of broader household definitions of family, as they often did in the early modern period, and by extension, form a part of the emotional community of Christmas celebration explored in the previous chapter. Servants were often able to watch communities of families and friends performing the domestic celebration of Christmas. In her memoir of service with a Lancashire gentry family in the 1840s, Rose Allen (born 1809) provided eyewitness accounts of festivities on Christmas Eve, which included the children's games of blindman's buff and snap dragon, and a boar's head supper and dancing. The following day, Allen witnessed the exchange of gifts by the Christmas tree, and a 'family concert of sacred music'.[35] In a similar fashion, in 1863 Hannah Cullwick was able to watch the Foster family and friends perform private theatricals.[36] Whilst these incidents were potentially important in disseminating domestic Christmas rituals of their own amongst the lower classes, the entitlement to watch but not participate emphasised class difference and the exclusion of servants from the emotional currents of the family and their friends.

There were, however, opportunities for servants to be drawn into the family Christmas, particularly in relation to the children of the household. As Davidoff and others highlight, servants played an important role in the formation of the child's world view, either through formal education or via the transmission of behavioural norms and gender and class expectations, because children spent much of their time in the company of servants. Significantly, accounts of playful interactions with servants occur often in autobiographical accounts of childhood. One of the Earl of Halifax's fondest Christmas memories was of being 'impelled round the [frozen] pond on a wooden chair' by the butler at Hickleton, and he also remembered how, along with his siblings, he was allowed to go down to the kitchen and watch the maids roast the joints of meat over a huge open fire.[37] Similarly, the painter and illustrator Ernest Shepard (1879–1976), who grew up in London in the 1880s, recalled how he and his brother Cyril would spend part of Christmas morning being a nuisance to the cook and the maids who were busy preparing Christmas dinner. Shepard also recalled happy memories of Christmas shopping with his nurse, Martha, who was the brothers' first point of contact on Christmas morning. One on occasion, Martha was greeted by a loud shout of 'Happy Christmas' as she entered Ernest and Cyril's bedroom, and she scolded the boys for lighting the gas without permission. An attempt to pacify Martha with chocolates was met with a stern order to put them away before the boys made themselves sick.[38] Clearly, in their relationships with the children of their employers, upper servants could take on aspects of parental affection and authority, but equally children learnt, especially at Christmas, that they had a licence to test that authority.

Christmas afforded upper servants the opportunity to symbolically assert their authority over the children by bestowing gifts, potentially a statement of the power relationship between giver and recipient. Recalling her childhood at Kingston Lacy in Dorset, Viola Banks (born 1900) noted how the cook would give the daughters of the house Christmas presents such as silver hair brushes and photograph frames.[39] However, the fondness the servants felt towards the children could be genuine, lasting long after they left the service of the household. Two former servants of the Wood family at Hickleton could not let the Christmas season pass without corresponding. In 1873, Mrs Moore, a former nurse to the children, sent a box of gifts for the family, whilst Mrs Pilgrim (died 1882), a former housekeeper, wrote to Charles Wood offering Christmas wishes to him and his wife and requesting that they kiss their young children. In the early 1870s the letters and gifts were reciprocated; for example, Mrs Pilgrim received a pen and holder set from the Wood family. However, the family gradually let their connection with Mrs Pilgrim weaken, despite the fact that she continued to send Christmas cards. Her continuing affection for her former employers, heightened by the emotions that Christmas engendered, was rather sadly captured in sentiments written on Christmas Eve 1880: '[I]t is such a long time since I heard from you that I think you must have almost forgotten me … however I cannot allow the season to pass without writing.'[40]

Despite these examples of Christmas gift exchange between families and servants, most of the Christmas gifts that servants received from their employers were impersonal and uniform. The poet and author Maurice Baring (1874–1945), who spent his childhood Christmases in Devon, recalled that the tree was 'lit up' after tea on Christmas Eve, and he and his brother would run back and forth with the servants' presents, beginning with the maids, who received materials for a gown, followed by the housekeeper and the upper servants.[41] These gift rituals could often reinforce the strict hierarchy of the household structure. At Lyme Park, for example, each servant received a piece of beef on Christmas Eve in order of precedence, and as Pamela Horn argues, such instances of largesse may have been one of the few occasions when lower servants had any contact with their employers. Whilst the symbolism of such rituals seems obviously to promote hierarchy and encourage deference, Davidoff argues that over time deference rituals could become an end in themselves, divorced of their original meaning. By the Edwardian period a certain amount of cynicism had developed in relation to the Christmas beef distribution, as Lord Newton's daughter recalled that her father's reaction to the servants' cheers was 'the most artificial part of the whole proceedings'.[42]

Ritual interactions between employers and servants developed significantly over the course of the nineteenth century. In the early 1800s, for example, the servants at Godmersham Park in Kent would receive a visit from the children of the house to sing carols, and the servants would also join the house party to toast the season.[43] At the beginning of Victoria's reign, William Tayler (1807–92), a footman in the service of a wealthy London widow, reported that there was 'a great deal of egg hot and toast and ale at these times and great sereymoney in puting [sic] up the mistletoe bow in the servants hall or the kitchen'.[44] By the mid-1860s there is some evidence of decline. Arthur Munby noted: '[M]y mother complains that servants do not so much care for Christmas matters: the mistletoe in the servants' hall [on Christmas Eve], which we used to have yearly, with its paper of verses written by the footman & addressed to the Master & Mistress, is now a poor & unregarded affair.' However, it was not Christmas that these servants objected to but the deferential nature of the ritual. The servants had a party amongst themselves on Christmas Day, during which Munby overheard pleasant 'female voices … singing hymns'.[45]

In the country houses of landed society, servants' balls became one of the major events of the Christmas season, but these were semi-public occasions representing the aristocratic household as a local and regional institution. At Hickleton, the Earl of Halifax noted the use of 'corporate' invitations, which included the principal local farmers and their wives, Doncaster tradesmen, and a selection of servants from other local houses. Proceedings would begin with the entrance of the lord and lady of the house. Servants clearly enjoyed these occasions; they were allowed to invite a friend, and generally the dancing continued until the early hours of the morning, long after the family had gone to bed. The servants would wear 'dance-clothes', but their status was always reinforced as they were expected to wear their caps, a practice Davidoff highlights as a source of much resentment.[46]

The characteristics of the servant Christmas experience described in this chapter persisted well into the twentieth century, but there were changes as well. In the late-Victorian and Edwardian periods there was much talk in the media of a 'servant problem', whereby middle-class families, particularly in urban areas, struggled to hire and retain good-quality servants, a consequence of widening educational and employment opportunities for young women.[47] Though undoubtedly exaggerated, the 'servant problem' did have an impact on the celebration of Christmas, particularly for families that employed only a few servants. Recalling the strain Christmas placed upon her mother in the Edwardian period, Katherine Chorley, who was resident in Alderley, near Manchester, noted that they 'never had many servants nor the kind of servant who could share the responsibility'. Also significant was that Katherine's mother was also sensible to the idea that servants should be given 'just time off'.[48] A concurrent development in the celebration of Christmas in the Edwardian period was a growing trend for families to spend either Christmas Day in particular or the festive season more generally in London hotels and restaurants, as well as in seaside resorts. This trend can be seen as a response to the difficulty of finding reliable servants to help create a festival celebrating the family ideal, particularly if members of the servant class were longing for their own family Christmases and resentful of rituals which celebrated an unequal power relationship and were designed to reinforce deferential behaviour.

Shop assistants and the campaign for a longer Christmas holiday

There are significant parallels between the experience of domestic servants and that of shop assistants in the nineteenth century. A series of parliamentary investigations demonstrated that shop life was based on long hours of monotonous work, low wages, and spartan and often unsanitary living and working conditions. Though it was less prevalent in the north of England, the 'living-in' system applied to many shop assistants, whereby they resided either above the shop or in dormitories adjacent to it. This allowed shopkeepers to maintain close control over their assistants through a series of petty rules and regulations, which, according to Chris Hosgood, kept shop assistants in a permanent state of adolescence. Though the experience of the shop assistant could vary significantly according to region, trade, owner and shop size, one general trend was that the workforce changed from being overwhelmingly male in the mid-nineteenth century to being fifty per cent female by 1914.[49]

Despite their poor working conditions, shop assistants were notoriously hard to unionise. It has been estimated that by 1910 only two per cent were members of the National Amalgamated Union of Shop Assistants, Warehousemen and Clerks (NAUSAWC). Furthermore, this modest growth was obtained only 'by moderating the combative tone of union rhetoric and activity'. If they could be motivated to seek reform at all, many shop assistants preferred to combine with employers in self-regulatory early-closing associations. Hosgood ascribes this situation partly to the genteel middle-class aspirations of many shop staff. Both the dress and the demeanour of the shop assistant at work acted as a mask shielding the public from the social reality of their existence; 'they had the bearing and look of gentlemen and gentlewomen', a situation that was especially reinforced in new commercial spaces like the department store. Another factor was that many assistants maintained the personal goal of one day owing their own shop.[50] Within this context, Christmas played an important role. As Christmas consumerism developed in the nineteenth century, linked to the expansion of gift exchange and material abundance in the home, shop keepers and assistants came under increasing pressure to meet public demand. At the same time, since the self-perception of shop assistants was grounded in aspirations to gentility, many entertained expectations of an ideal Christmas family reunion which the reality of shop life during the festive season could not match.

What made Christmas an issue for shop assistants and many other workers was the day that it fell upon. If Christmas Day fell on a Sunday shop assistants would lose a day's holiday, because they were already entitled to Sunday off. In practice, a moral holiday was often declared on the Monday to compensate for this, as happened in London in 1842.[51] The organisation of these holidays would operate in a local civic context, often by a combination of a declaration from the Lord Mayor and informal agreements amongst tradesmen. This system was not, however, legally binding, and shop assistants could still fall victim to uncharitable employers and local indifference.

By the 1850s, shop assistants had become vocal about their concerns about losing a holiday when Christmas Day fell on a Sunday. When this happened in 1853, two shop assistants in York wrote to the *York Herald*, anxious to secure a holiday on the Monday, and showing a keen awareness that action had been taken in other towns. A petition was also organised in York and presented to Lord Mayor, who subsequently issued hand bills declaring Monday to be a holiday.[52] In London, a group of five pawnbrokers' assistants appealed to the public for a general holiday observance on the Monday as the only way they could protect one of the two holidays they received each year.[53] These letters continued to feature, particularly in the provincial newspaper press, throughout the rest of the period in question. References to the need for rest and relaxation after long hours of work were often made, as were remarks about home, family and friends that reflected the growing importance of Christmas as a domestic festival. In 1859, a sympathetic tradesman called upon those who opposed the granting of a holiday to read *A Christmas Carol* (though ironically Dickens assumed that the food shops would be open for business on Christmas Day), and later in 1877 a former shop assistant recalled the happiness of 'spending old Christmas at the dearest place on earth, "home, sweet, home". Christmas brings with it many hallowed associations, who can forget a mother's kiss and tears of joy, and a father's loving smile and tender sympathy, on such happy reunions.'[54]

Early successes in campaigns for Christmas holidays lent added impetus to subsequent demands for a long Christmas vacation for shop assistants. New combinations of holiday, depending on which day of the week Christmas Day fell, were considered. When Christmas Day fell on a Tuesday in 1855, *The Times* reported that many provincial newspapers were carrying the news that a general holiday would be observed on Christmas Eve, thereby creating a three-day holiday.[55] In 1857, when Christmas Day fell on a Friday, tradesmen in the large towns of Essex closed on Saturday in addition to Christmas Day, whilst in 1858 a similar situation occurred in Derby and Lincoln when tradesmen closed on Monday 27 December.[56] In addition to the growing popularity of the family Christmas and the genteel aspirations of shop assistants, the demands for more holiday emerged in the 1850s because the availability of cheap rail travel made the possibility of reunion more of a reality. As early as 1846 a correspondent to *The Times* was calling upon the directors of railway companies to extend the validity of day tickets for several days over the Christmas period in order to allow clerks, warehousemen and shop assistants to travel home 'without trenching too much on their limited means'.[57]

For shop assistants, the momentum of the 1850s did not gain them any firm guarantees in the attempt to secure Christmas holidays. When Christmas Day again fell on a Sunday in 1859, more anxious letters appeared in provincial newspapers to secure a holiday on the Monday and a two-day holiday was the limit of expectations when the cycle repeated itself in 1864. However, campaigns for a longer holiday did become more ambitious as the nineteenth century progressed, and they were given a greater impetus by the expectations created by the Bank Holiday Act of 1871 and the Holiday Extension Act of 1875. Campaigns for four-day holidays were not uncommon. These holidays were never universally achieved, and demands were often met with compromise measures and even outright hostility from those with vested interests in shops remaining open. The civic decision on the declaration of holiday observance could effectively be left to market committees, since in many towns the pattern of shopping continued to be dominated by market day. In 1884, an attempt to alter York's market day in Christmas week from Saturday to Wednesday was rejected on the grounds that it would inconvenience the general public.[58] This was also one of the standard arguments used by tradesmen hostile to an increase in Christmas holidays. In the last quarter of the nineteenth century, this hostility could be manifested in public attacks on the character of shop assistants. In 1888, when Christmas Day fell upon a Tuesday, and a holiday on Christmas Eve and Boxing Day was campaigned for, one tradesman declared:

> The selfishness of employees is growing worse every year; they get their fortnight's holiday in summer, with wages paid; they have bank holidays, which ought never to have been adopted by traders; and are blest with about four hours a day less work than we old hands used to put in some years ago … I don't intend to give a third day's wage for a third day's no work to about a score of employees, half of whom will not turn up on Thursday.[59]

Employers could also imperil the agreements forged between trading rivals in relation to closing. In 1896 the secretary of the Early Closing Association (ECA), James Stacey, complained that the Christmas holidays of a 'large proportion of the assistants of East London [we]re threatened … by the attitude of a wealthy proprietor of a well known Commercial Road drapery house'; whilst in the West End, an agreement previously arranged between three large clothing firms was broken by two of them.[60] The intervention of the ECA reveals a difference of approach between London and the provinces. Shop assistants in London were, by and large, seemingly content to have their interests represented by the ECA, or its rival the Voluntary Early Closing Association, but many provincial towns and cities had no direct links with these organisations, and it is likely that the large numbers of letters from individual shop assistants campaigning for Christmas holidays was the result of the absence of representative organisations.[61]

Another strategy adopted by the ECA was to urge the public to modify its purchasing patterns, particularly its habit of late night shopping on Christmas Eve.[62] However, the combined strategies of the ECA could provoke a degree of hostility from the public. In 1901 one 'Working Man' described the ECA's efforts as the 'mischievous interference of a private and irresponsible society' and highlighted the contradiction of a Bank Holiday where shops were closed but 'theatres, picture galleries, and public conveyances [we]re crammed, "all the world and his wife" crowding the streets, and all places of public amusement [we]re thronged'. A 'housewife' complained that the ECA were making 'a very large proportion of the population of our large towns' exist for several days on stale food, and accused them of inflicting hardship on invalids and children.[63]

By the 1890s, medical authorities began to comment on the affects Christmas was having on shop assistants. In 1896 the *Lancet* reported:

> A week or fortnight before Christmas life in the shop becomes one continuous round of toil. Some of the employees who have homes in the country are forced by the exigencies of the occasion to leave town on Christmas Eve by midnight trains, which they are barely allowed time to catch, and thus with mental and bodily powers exhausted they reach their homes to take part in festivities which under the circumstances further exhaust vitality.[64]

Despite the concern for shop assistants, the *Lancet* overlooked the plight of the railway staff operating the trains late on Christmas Eve. The impact on the growing number of women in this workforce was also acknowledged when James Stacey commented upon the 'employees, many of them girls and women, who ordinarily work[ed] excessive hours, work[ed] unusually late in December, and continue[d] their exhaustive labour down to the last moments of Christmas Eve. Truly to them Christmas should have some compensation!'[65] George Gissing captured this situation in his 1893 novel, *The Odd Women*.

Discussing the deplorable conditions female shop workers faced, the character Monica Madden declares: 'Yes, it's bad enough now; but at Christmas! There was a week or more of Saturday nights – going on to one o'clock in the morning. A girl by me was twice carried out fainting, one night after another. They gave her brandy, and she came back again.'[66]

During the Christmas season of 1912, the Lord Mayor of York requested that retail establishments grant their assistants three days' holiday, a request that was ignored by a considerable number of shopkeepers.[67] The situation was further confused by the 1911 Shops Act, which attempted to enshrine a weekly half holiday for shop assistants in law but also stated that the holiday should not be enforced in the week before a bank holiday.[68] Different interpretations of the Act were put into practice, and the Home Secretary attempted to clarify it by stating that if tradesmen had remained open on the Wednesday before Christmas then they were obliged to shut an extra half day in Christmas week.[69] What remained most important, however, was the local civic context, and the Lord Mayor's involvement. The sentiment of a shop assistant who commented, 'Christmas time is a time for the reunion of the family, and the assistant who, as large numbers do, works a distance from home, has very few chances of joining the family circle, and … is kept at work until very late on Christmas Eve', suggest that there are strong continuities from the 1850s to the Edwardian period. By 1914, retailers, their assistants and the shopping public were still negotiating the acceptable boundaries between expectations of private family life and a rapidly developing consumer society. The Christmas festival, and all its sentiments and associations, had become central to both domains and was consequently an important site of contest for the complexities of modern life to be played out.

Christmas boxes and postmen

By the late Victorian period a mass consumer culture was a readily identifiable aspect of the English Christmas, and yet consumer society still coexisted with older service relationships, particularly personal service. The festive season served as annual occasion for rewarding personal service during the year in the form of Christmas boxes. A system of money being given to people in service had existed in England since at least the early seventeenth century. The practice of dropping money into an earthenware box kept by an apprentice, first recorded in 1621, had been widened to include domestic servants in general by the 1640s. By the 1660s the term 'Christmas box' had come to mean a cash gift paid to trades people. Complaints about this system began to emerge in the eighteenth century. In 1710 Jonathan Swift complained that he was being 'undone' by Christmas boxes,[70] whilst in 1756 the Bow Street magistrate Sir John Fielding commented that it was 'burdensome to private families':

> for, if in the course of the year, you should send for a carpenter to drive a nail or two, or an upholder to take down a bed, a blacksmith to mend your poker, or a bricklayer to repair a hole in a wall, you will certainly see all their apprentices at Christmas and add to these your baker, brewer, butcher, grocer, poulterer, fishmonger, tallow-chandler, glazier, corn-chandler, dustman, chimney-sweeper, watchman, beadles, lamplighters, not to forget the person who sells brick-dust to your footman to clean his knives, and you will have some idea of the Christmas boxes of a private family.[71]

While Fielding bemoaned the custom of providing Christmas boxes for services rendered, another Christmas box tradition involved the presentation by retail traders of Christmas boxes to their customers as a means of securing a regular clientele. The Christmas box was often given to the servants responsible for procuring the client's household provisions. Some shopkeepers found it to be an unprofitable system, complaining of servants who were perceived to be conniving with cheating trades people. It was typical for shopkeepers in a particular locality to co-operate in order to end the practice of giving Christmas boxes. In 1795 the butchers in the parish of Hackney announced this in a notice in *The Times*, whilst in 1825 the tradesmen of Trowbridge agreed to levy a fine of five pounds on anyone breaking a similar prohibition. In 1833 the York grocer Joseph Rowntree discontinued the custom of giving Christmas boxes to his customers, an action which caused a temporary downturn in trade.[72]

After 1850, notices detailing the abandonment of the practice of giving Christmas boxes appeared regularly, and the issue continued to cause considerable controversy. In 1898 a leading article in *The Times* repeated the familiar suspicions of the system: '[The] whole theory of this particular of Christmas boxes is that the tradesman and the domestic servant are to combine in a conspiracy to defraud their common employer … These so-called presents are given for no other motive than to induce the servant, either by omission or commission, to be unfaithful to his master's interests.'[73] However, whilst this situation might generate tensions within master–servant relationships, not all servant keepers agreed with *The Times*. One 'householder' from Hampstead argued that, there was nothing '"clandestine" in this matter as far as [they were] concerned': 'I know my cook has a Christmas box, and I know that my tradesmen – respectable men – give it … In this matter householders are greatly to blame; they should make a point of paying the tradesmen themselves.'[74] Legislation introduced in the Edwardian period, the Prevention of Corruption Act of 1907, only confused matters further. In December of that year a meeting of trades people was held in London in order to make 'the public … clearly understand that Christmas boxes given openly and without corrupt intentions were a legitimate form of interchange of human sentiment between any class of people and another'. In 1909, Sir Edward Fry, president of the Secret Commissions and Bribery Prevention League (SCBPL) reiterated his belief that there was 'no doubt that most Christmas boxes given by tradesmen to servants [we]re given as an inducement to show favour to the tradesman'. The SCBPL were particularly concerned with the measures some tradesmen were taking to avoid being prosecuted under the Prevention of Corruption Act. In 1907 'a mistress of five servants' complained that her grocer sent out a circular on Boxing Day, 'when so many head of households are out of town', stating that he would continue to provide a Christmas box unless he received contrary instructions. For the SCBPL this was applying the letter of the law, but not the spirit.[75] The issue was not resolved by the end of the period. In 1910 the *Grocers' Journal* lamented: '[The] question has been thrashed out year after year, and as each period of rejoicing comes round we find more and more adherents to up-to-date methods; but still the system survives.'[76]

Complaints about the Christmas box system were not, however, restricted to the role of domestic servants. In 1851 one tradesman complained that he had been visited in Christmas week by the rullymen and goods partners of the York and North Midland Railway Company, who, in collecting Christmas boxes, informed him that they had been and always would be especially careful with his goods. For this tradesman, such action did not only contradict the ruling by the railway company that porters in the passenger department should not be permitted to receive any fee; it also implied a threat of poor service in the future if a Christmas box was not paid.[77] For some people this amounted to begging. One commentator recalled his Boxing Day of 1877:

> Within a few minutes my door is assailed by three well-dressed young men asking to give them a Christmas box, on the plea that I have paid their master a good round sum for work executed by them – the beggars – during 1877. I have barely recovered from this shock when I am again interrupted in my work by a banditti of three very respectable looking 'apprentices' on a like errand. Then, we have also to expect a swarm of errand boys demanding black mail, and my dear knocker will have no rest for the day.[78]

In making these complaints, middle-class commentators inevitably resorted to prevailing stereotypes of class difference. One 'householder' was scandalised by the practice of allowing children to collect Christmas boxes:

> I am prepared to maintain that to permit children to go about at this season as mendicants is a step in the direction of pauperising their minds and destroying their self-respect. When I see some children begging from door to door for Christmas boxes, I feel inclined to ask – where is the independent British Workman now? Does he exist, and can it be possible that he will allow his sons and daughters to degrade themselves in this way? … No wonder, when adversity comes, that the British workman collapses, and becomes a cringing beggar, when these are the associations of his early boyhood.[79]

Further attempts were made to abolish, or at least regulate, the Christmas box system. In 1850 the custom of Christmas boxes being given to persons connected to the police courts was suppressed by the Home Office, and in that decade the Bank of England belatedly enforced a 1695 regulation preventing clerks from accepting Christmas boxes.[80] In the nineteenth century, workers also sought to protect what they perceived as their customary rights. On hearing of a new scheme being discussed to abolish Christmas boxes in 1848, a London special constable argued that the police should be exempt from any abolition, on the grounds of the great efforts they had made in combating Chartism that year. Working people were also vigilant in protecting their Christmas boxes from fraudsters. In 1827 the dustmen of St Martin in the Fields produced a distinctive medal by which real dustmen could be distinguished from impostors.[81]

Despite hostility to the Christmas box system, many people were still able to make distinctions concerning the types of service they were and were not prepared to reward. A 'householder' of York liked to give a present to his principal cab driver,

> who lifts many a heavy box without a grumble, and the lamp lighter, who gives my youngsters at the nursery window a cheerful nod every evening as he goes 'twinkle twinkle' down the street … but why should I be expected or asked to give to a parcel of boys and men to whom I owe no service at all? If I buy … a hat box, and have it sent up to my house, it is surely unreasonable that the errand boy should ask me to make him a present on the ensuing Christmas. I suppose his master paid him for bringing the article, and he did me no service in bringing it.[82]

The distinction centred upon personalised service and implied some form of intimacy, however artificial, between giver and receiver. According to the 'householder', the most deserving case for a Christmas box was the postman.[83] Performing a useful service throughout the year, postmen received a lot of public sympathy for their well-publicised low wages, and Christmas boxes were seen as a necessary way of supplementing these. Postmen were not helped by parliamentary enquiries investigating their pay and working conditions. Whilst Christmas boxes were exempted from a general ban on Post Office employees receiving gratuities in 1880, a committee that sat between 1895 and 1897 did nothing to address the postmen's demand for Christmas boxes to be converted into additional wages. Furthermore they were warned not to ask for Christmas boxes directly and not to let the non-receipt of a Christmas box affect the level of service they provided.[84] Postmen suffered further when the 1907 Prevention of Corruption Act created the widespread public misapprehension that Christmas Boxes were now illegal; and in the years leading up to the First World War regular notices were placed in the newspaper press by the postal authorities assuring the public that postmen were not covered by the Act.

The plight of postmen at Christmas was also exacerbated by the commercial success of the Christmas card from the 1860s onwards, and a corresponding increase in the parcel post, which might also be delivered on Christmas Day itself. The great strain this placed upon the Post Office workforce can perhaps be best measured in terms of the numbers of casual staff that were taken on in London in the late-Victorian and Edwardian periods: 3,000 extra workers were employed in 1889, rising to 10,500 in 1913.[85] The year-on-year increase in the amount of mail could be considerable, and such volumes of post led to intense working conditions. In 1903, workers on the 'South Mail', the travelling post office serving Bristol, Shrewsbury and York, were obliged to work for more than twenty-four hours with breaks only for meals and refreshments.[86] Public sympathy, however, remained highest for those Post Office employees with the greatest public presence, and this sympathy was reflected in the appearance of sentimental images of postmen delivering the Christmas mail in the illustrated press from the 1870s.[87] During the Christmas period of 1906, one correspondent of the *Yorkshire Herald* called upon York to copy London's example of cancelling a Sunday delivery in order to give the postmen a day's rest as a Christmas box, describing them as 'veritable beasts of burden, groaning under the heavy loads of good wishes, which they carry from door to door, cheerfully smiling (seemingly) under it all, because it is a season of "goodwill towards all men"'.[88] By the Edwardian age, the public had come to recognise postmen as the foot soldiers of Christmas sentiments, completing the task of sending Christmas wishes and material goods that maintained fragmented social and familial networks; as one commentator noted in 1902, the postman was 'the outward and visible sign of a link between ourselves and our friends in all parts of the world'.[89] The expanded English Christmas was based on a more elaborate and commercial culture of gift exchange than had hitherto existed, and it represented the shifting ways in which contemporaries maintained networks and associations in the modern world. At the same time, the postman could be a reminder of a more personalised and reassuring form of service, and the public was willing to recognise the postman as an essential intermediary in the process of creating and maintaining a merry Christmas.

Conclusion

The expansion of the domestic celebration of Christmas in the nineteenth century created additional burdens for those workers who played a pivotal role in supplying the labour and goods which supported the festivity enjoyed in the homes of the middle and upper classes. For the domestic servants who lived and worked in close proximity to their employers, and the shop assistants who had the greatest aspirations to gentility, Christmas inspired the need for family reunion and the desire for festive experience which corresponded to bourgeois norms. These needs and desires required financial resources which were sometimes beyond the means of the working classes, but, most importantly, all family festivity required leisure time, which was now at a greater premium. In their demands for longer Christmas holidays, nineteenth-century workers drew upon a combination of perceptions of traditional rights and accommodations to new social realities. In doing so, they were not generally helped by government intervention, and workers had to rely upon local civic authorities and the benevolence (or otherwise) of individual employers, who often used the Christmas season to pursue a paternalistic agenda in order to retain the loyalties of employees and maintain codes of acceptable behaviour. At the same time, there could be a great difference in the way Christmas was experienced both within and between different sectors of the economy. Though the development of the relationship between Christmas and the spheres of work and leisure partially rested on the emergence and expansion of a modern consumer society, the debates surrounding postmen and Christmas boxes reveals the persistence of a highly-prized notion of personal service celebrated annually during the festive season. Large numbers of the labouring classes experienced Christmas in a meaningful way through work, a process which contributed strongly to making the festival part of national culture, although for many the ideal form of celebration remained tantalisingly out of reach. Falling into poverty, however, meant that the experience of Christmas, if it existed at all, was mediated by philanthropy, and this is explored in the next chapter.

Notes

1 M. A. Bienefeld, *Working Hours in British Industry: An Economic History* (London: Weidenfeld and Nicolson, 1972), pp. 18–19, 38–9.

2 H. Cunningham, *Leisure in the Industrial Revolution c. 1780–c. 1880* (London: Macmillan, 1980), p. 58.

3 E. P. Thompson, 'Time, work-discipline, and industrial capitalism', *Past and Present*, 38 (1967), 56–97.

4 R. Hutton, *The Stations of the Sun: a History of the Ritual Year in Britain* (Oxford: Oxford University Press, 1996), p. 112.

5 J. A. R., Pimlott, *The Englishman's Christmas: a Social History* (Hassocks: Harvester Press, 1978), pp. 94–5.

6 Ibid., pp. 78, 94–5; Hutton, *Stations of the Sun*, p. 113.

7 J. Benson, *British Coalminers in the Nineteenth Century: A Social History* (Dublin: Holmes and Meier, 1980), p. 59.

8 Pimlott, *Englishman's Christmas*, p. 78; Cunningham, *Leisure in the Industrial Revolution*, pp. 61–2.

9 Cunningham, *Leisure in the Industrial Revolution*, pp. 62–73.

10 C. M. Sughrue, 'Continuity, conflict and change: a contextual study of three south Yorkshire longsword dance teams' (unpublished PhD thesis, University of Sheffield, 1992), pt 1, pp. 138–44.

11 L. Davidoff and C. Hall, *Family Fortunes. Men and Women of the English Middle Class 1780–1850*, 2nd edn (London and New York: Routledge, 2002), p. 432.

12 F. K. Prochaska, 'Philanthropy', in F. M. L. Thompson (ed.), *The Cambridge Social History of Britain 1750–1950. Vol. 3: Social Agencies and Institutions* (Cambridge: Cambridge University Press, 1990), p. 372.

13 *York Herald*, 22 December 1879; 26 December 1882; 22 December 1884.

14 *York Herald*, 8 January 1848; 31 December 1859; 24 December 1881.

15 *York Herald*, 3 January 1863; 2 January 1869.

16 Hutton, *Stations of the Sun*, pp. 38–40.

17 *Yorkshire Herald*, 26 December 1913.

18 *Leeds Mercury*, 27 December 1880.

19 C. Dellheim, 'The creation of a company culture: Cadbury's, 1861–1931', *American Historical Review*, 92 (1987), 29–30; P. Joyce, *Work, Society and Politics: The Culture of the Factory in Later Victorian England* (Brighton: Harvester Press, 1980), p. 181.

20 Birmingham City Archives; Papers of the Cadbury Family of Birmingham; MS 466/33, miscellaneous programmes 1884–1931.

21 *Cocoa Works Magazine*, January 1905; December 1907; January 1908.

22 L. Davidoff, *Worlds Between: Historical Perspectives on Gender & Class* (New York: Routledge, 1995), p. 22; L. Davidoff and others, *The Family Story: Blood, Contract and Intimacy, 1830–1960* (Harlow: Longman, 1999), pp. 158, 163–4.

23 See L. Davidoff, 'Class and gender in Victorian England: the diaries of Arthur J. Munby and Hannah Cullwick', *Feminist Studies*, 5:1 (1979), 87–141.

24 A. E. Ireland (ed.), *Selections from the Letters of Geraldine Endsor Jewsbury to Jane Welsh Carlyle* (London: Longmans, Green, and Co., 1892), p. 46.

25 Davidoff, *Worlds Between*, p. 24.

26 P. E. Sandeman, *Treasure on Earth: a Country House Christmas* (London: National Trust, 1995), p. 14.

27 L. Stanley (ed.), *The Diaries of Hannah Cullwick, Victorian Maidservant* (London, 1984), pp. 8–9, 112, 143–5.

28 Earl of Halifax, *Fullness of Days* (London: Collins, 1957), pp. 29–30.

29 Stanley, *Diaries of Hannah Cullwick*, pp. 143–5, 185.

30 Ibid., p. 261.

31 Davidoff, *Family Story*, p. 174.

32 *Annual Report of the York Penitentiary Society* (York, 1865), p. 9.

33 F. Finnegan, *Poverty and Prostitution: a Study of Victorian Prostitutes in York* (Cambridge: Cambridge University Press, 1979), pp. 166, 176, 191; *Annual Report of the York Penitentiary Society* (York, 1863), p. 9.

34 *Annual Report of the York Penitentiary Society* (York, 1874), p. 10; *Annual Report of the York Penitentiary Society* (York, 1897), p. 7; *Annual Report of the York Penitentiary Society* (York, 1910), pp. 4–6.

35 R. Allen, *The Autobiography of Rose Allen. Edited by a Lady* (London: Longman, 1847), p. 137.

36 Stanley, *Diaries of Hannah Cullwick*, pp. 143–5.

37 Halifax, *Fullness of Days*, p. 33.

38 E. H. Shepard, *Drawn from Memory* (London: Methuen, 1957), pp. 155–7.

39 V. Bankes and P. Watkin, *A Kingston Lacy Childhood* (Wimborne: Dovecote Press, 1986), pp. 55–6.

40 Borthwick Institute for Archives, University of York, Hickleton Papers, A2.126, letter from Mrs Moore to Charles Lindley Wood, 23 December 1873; letters from Mrs Pilgrim to Charles Lindley Wood, 24 December 1873; 26 December 1873; 31 December 1874; 24 December 1876; 24 December 1879; 24 December 1880; Mrs Pilgrim to Agnes Wood, 23 December 1875.

41 M. Baring, *The Puppet Show of Memory* (London: William Heinemann, 1922), p. 41.

42 Davidoff, *Worlds Between*, p. 24; P. Horn, *Life Below Stairs in the 20th Century*

(Stroud: Sutton, 2001), p. 13; Sandeman, *Treasure on Earth*, pp. 37–9, 50.

43 Letter from Fanny Knight to Dorothy Chapman, 25 December 1808, cited in M. Hubert (ed.), *Jane Austen's Christmas: the Festive Season in Georgian England* (Stroud: Sutton, 1996), p. 64.

44 Cited in J. Burnett, *Useful Toil: Autobiographies of Working People from the 1820s to the 1920s* (Harmondsworth: Penguin, 1977), p. 184.

45 D. Hudson, *Munby, Man of Two Worlds: the Life and Diaries of Arthur J. Munby 1828–1910* (London: J. Murray, 1972), pp. 234–5.

46 Halifax, *Fullness of Days*, pp. 34–5.

47 Horn, *Life Below Stairs*, pp. 8–12.

48 K. Chorley, *Manchester Made Them* (London: Faber and Faber, 1950), p. 30.

49 C. P. Hosgood, '"Mercantile monasteries": shops, shop assistants and shop life in late-Victorian and Edwardian Britain', *Journal of British Studies*, 38 (1999), 322–52.

50 Ibid.

51 *The Times*, 28 December 1842.

52 *York Herald*, 10 December 1853; 17 December 1853; 24 December 1853.

53 *The Times*, 16 December 1853.

54 *York Herald*, 10 December 1859; 18 December 1877.

55 *The Times*, 19 December 1855.

56 *The Times*, 12 December 1857; 4 December 1858.

57 *The Times*, 1 December 1846.

58 *York Herald*, 17 December 1864; 16 December 1884.

59 *York Herald*, 13 December 1888.

60 *The Times*, 15 December 1896.

61 W. B. Whitaker, *Victorian and Edwardian Shopworkers: the Struggle to Obtain Better Conditions and a Half-Holiday* (Newton Abbot: David and Charles, 1973), p. 58; *The Times*, 14 December 1899

62 *The Times*, 12 December 1881.

63 *The Times*, 29 November 1901; 20 December 1901.

64 Cited in *The Times*, 15 December 1896.

65 *The Times*, 23 December 1901.

66 G. Gissing, *The Odd Women* (Oxford: Oxford University Press, 2002), p. 41.

67 *Yorkshire Herald*, 19 December 1912; 28 December 1912.

68 L. Holcombe, *Victorian Ladies at Work: Middle-Class Working Women in England and Wales, 1850–1914* (Newton Abbot: David and Charles, 1973), pp. 123–31; Whitaker, *Victorian and Edwardian Shopworkers*, pp. 159–63.

69 *Yorkshire Herald*, 17 December 1912.

70 Hutton, *Stations of the Sun*, p. 23.

71 Cited in Pimlott, *Englishman's Christmas*, p. 73.

72 D. Davis, *A History of Shopping* (London: Routledge and Kegan Paul, 1966), p. 209; B. Bushaway, *By Rite. Custom, Ceremony and Community in England 1700–1880* (London: Junction, 1982), p. 258; A. Vernon, *A Quaker Business Man. The Life of Joseph Rowntree 1836–1925* (York: William Sessions, 1987), p. 81.

73 *The Times*, 10 December 1898.

74 *The Times*, 24 December 1898.

75 *The Times*, 6 December 1907; 27 December 1907; 1 December 1909; 24 December 1909.

76 *Grocers' Journal*, 17 December 1910.

77 *York Herald*, 3 January 1852.

78 *York Herald*, 27 December 1877.

79 *York Herald*, 28 December 1877.

80 *The Times*, 25 December 1850; Pimlott, *Englishman's Christmas*, p. 143.

81 *The Times*, 25 December 1827; 25 December 1848.

82 *York Herald*, 28 December 1877.

83 Ibid.

84 Pimlott, *Englishman's Christmas*, p. 143; H. Robinson, *Britain's Post Office. A History of Development from the Beginnings to the Present Day* (London: Oxford University Press, 1953), pp. 231–2.

85 *The Times*, 28 December 1889; 12 December 1913.

86 *Yorkshire Herald*, 26 December 1903.

87 See, for example, the *Graphic*, 28 December 1872.

88 *Yorkshire Herald*, 18 December 1906.

89 *Yorkshire Herald*, 24 December 1902.

5

Philanthropy

B y the early nineteenth century, England had a long tradition of providing for and treating the poor during the festive season. Though many commentators lamented the decline of these practices, the tradition endured throughout the century. This chapter examines the way in which Christmas was experienced by the poor. It emphasises the continuity of basic forms of Christmas charity throughout this period, and at the same time explores how seasonal good deeds were reconfigured to meet the needs of a mass urban society and the expanding celebration of family and childhood, drawing on both rationalism and sentimentality. The chapter contextualises Christmas charitable giving within the debates and practices of the reformed poor law, and highlights how the provision of Christmas fare to workhouse paupers became one of the most important examples of civic festivity. The workhouse also provided the site of one of the most contested Christmas practices in Victorian England: the provision of beer to paupers on Christmas Day. An analysis of the Christmas 'beer question' sheds light on the attempts of temperance advocates to reform the festive season and allows for a broader discussion of the motivations of the individuals who donated their time, effort and money to make philanthropy such a vital component of the public culture of Christmas.

Christmas charity

The first recorded evidence of Christmas charity in England dates from the medieval period. Christmas was a natural time to support the poor, a slack period in the farming cycle when earnings from harvest were exhausted and work was scarce.[1] In the thirteenth century, charitable giving at Christmas was based upon open-house hospitality through which manorial lords provided a feast for their villeins. However, as Felicity Heal and Ronald Hutton have shown, the traditions of the manorial feast declined in the late-medieval and Tudor periods. Most landowners reduced their activities to entertaining friends, relations and occasionally tenants. Examples of feeding the poor and keeping open house could be found, but these were exceptional cases. Heal suggests that levels of generosity declined even further by the early Stuart period. One consequence of this was the development of the literary complaint tradition discussed in Chapter 1, bemoaning the decline of Christmas hospitality at gentry seats and typified by John Taylor's *Complaint of Christmas*, which accused landowners of preferring to stay in London during the twelve days of Christmas in order to save money and avoid their manorial responsibilities in the country.[2]

Hutton argues that the pattern of declining hospitality continued throughout the Hanoverian period. As I highlighted in Chapter 1, in the late 1780s, *The Times* blamed the decline of Christmas hospitality on the cultures of politeness and sensibility, suggesting that genteel ladies had come to consider the practice of administering to the poor a vulgar experience. At the same time, aristocrats were charged with the accusation that they were too busy in the pursuit of vices such as gambling to help the poor at Christmas time. Despite this willingness to blame the landed classes, *The Times* also warned of the 'exquisite knavery' of robbers and pickpockets, 'whose outward dress and address denote the gentleman', recognising that the end of open-house hospitality could also be attributed to the changing nature of social relations, with dress and demeanour no longer a reliable indicator of rank.[3] Concerns about the safety of person and property were at the forefront of the gradual reconfiguration of the household and its environs as part of the private sphere, leading to a desire to protect the home from the incursions of the poor. Though Irving's 1820 account of the festive season was based upon a romanticised view of past English Christmases, he also hinted at contemporary concerns. This is epitomised by the story of the squire of Bracebridge Hall, who attempts to create an old-fashioned Christmas only for the manor to be 'overrun by all the vagrants of the county'; he subsequently restricts his invitations to 'the decent part of the neighbouring peasantry' on Christmas Day.[4]

Though open-house hospitality was rare by the early nineteenth century, in some locations the rural poor continued to claim hospitality as a customary right. From the 1820s, many hospitality customs were suppressed by the charity commission because they had no recognisable existence in law.[5] Bob Bushaway has uncovered evidence of suppressed 'folk charities' in early nineteenth-century Buckinghamshire. Until 1813 a custom existed at Princes Risborough in which a bull, a boar and sacks of wheat and malt were given away by the lord of the manor at six o'clock on Christmas morning. The process was reported to be accompanied by 'much intoxication and riot', involving the poor parading through the town the night before the distribution, and then marching in the morning to the lord's house, in a party that contained many strangers as well as parishioners. On arrival, they rushed into the house, 'inflicting wounds on one another with their knives'. This practice was subsequently discontinued and was replaced for five or six years with a distribution of beef and mutton to the poor. In the parish of Drayton Beauchamp there was a custom in which the inhabitants of the parish would go to the rectory on Boxing Day to eat bread and cheese and drink ale at the expense of the rector. The occasion was reported to cause so much rioting that the custom was abandoned and replaced by an annual distribution of money. By 1827 the increase in population had made this practice untenable, and the rector began to withhold payments. Parishioners continued to visit the rectory to demand money but were always refused.[6] Hutton argues that the retreat from hospitality led to the rise in 'begging customs', including doles for elderly and indigent females on St Thomas's Day, and mumming and wassailing groups who sought hospitality from wealthy houses and offered entertainment in return. Begging customs reached a peak in the early nineteenth century before gradually declining, due to the rationalisation of charity, rising living standards and, in the early twentieth century, the introduction of old age pensions.[7] Many dole customs were a way for communities to support individuals and families during times of hardship, and dolers did not regard themselves as 'beggars' because they were not permanently dependent on charity but merely claiming a customary entitlement.[8]

As Hutton argues, the expectation that landowners would offer some form of hospitality to tenants and guests remained in place until the late nineteenth century, when the 'decline of British agriculture and increasing rural depopulation put paid to the old social and economic relationships of the countryside'.[9] In the Victorian period new philanthropic events were introduced at Hickleton, though the Wood family were careful to preserve the privacy of the more intimate spaces of the household. From the 1840s, village children were invited to see the Christmas tree, and this event was held in various spaces, including the village schoolroom, the carpenter's shed, and the front hall of the house.[10] Though the legality of customary rights had been undermined by the work of the charity commissioners in the first half of the nineteenth century, many landed families continued to have a strong sense of obligation to their local communities. For example, at Nunwell House on the Isle of Wight, the custom of distributing beef and bread on Christmas Eve, established as a charitable trust in the lifetime of Sir William Oglander (1769–1852), was still being practised in the 1890s. The family solicitor John Wilson Fardell reported: 'So far as I can see there does not appear to be a legal obligation to do this, although as you will see there is some obligation in the matter. All Lady Oglander did with reference to this charity was to do what Sir Henry did in his lifetime and which his father, Sir William, also did.'[11]

Bushaway stresses that the distribution of institutionalised charities and bequests should be distinguished from folk charities, since the latter did not permit discrimination between the deserving and undeserving poor.[12] Many of the Christmas charities active in the nineteenth century fell into the former category; their legal basis meant they were able to survive much longer. In York, for example, one charity founded upon a legacy from Leonard Thompson in 1698 distributed money every December to the poor in the parishes of St Martin and St Helen; and the parish of St Martin also benefited from a December coal distribution by Dr Beckwith's coal charity, founded in 1770. Both were still operating in the Edwardian period.[13] Christmas charity bequests continued to be established throughout the nineteenth century. In 1883, the parish magazine of St Philip and St James, in the same city, advertised tickets for flour and coals relating to the will of Mr Roper, which stipulated that the bequest benefit 'persons of good moral character, whose position in life renders such a gift welcome, and who with some kind of regularity attend the church', though the editor lamented that the vicar and churchwardens 'might prefer not to be so restricted in their choice'.[14] However, like many small bequests, parochial Christmas doles were increasingly felt to be inefficient, and many were reformed in the second half of the nineteenth century. The result of this can be seen in Batley, where a Christmas dole was established in 1874 following the amalgamation of seven different charities.[15] Some benefactors remained stubbornly attached to their chosen form of bequest. A charity was founded in 1889 at Great Yarmouth by the will of Cornelius Harley Christmas, providing a distribution of bread, coals and money to the poor in the week before Christmas Day. The bequest contained an attached instruction to the trustees to convert the whole bequest into cash for immediate distribution should the public authorities try to interfere with the gift. David Owen speculated that Cornelius Harley Christmas's generosity was motivated by a sentimental attachment to the nature of his surname.[16]

Whilst the recent historiography of philanthropy has sought to resist whiggish narratives of the inadequacy of private philanthropy being rectified by the gradual development of state-provided welfare,[17] a patchwork of Christmas dole bequests was an inadequate means of keeping a rapidly rising population warm and well fed in midwinter, particularly as many new urban environments had no ancient bequests or endowments to rely upon.[18] However, much charitable activity, both at Christmas and throughout the year, was informal and difficult to quantify. It included donations made to church offertories, or the large number of donations of materials, food, clothes and decorations which various institutions relied on to provide Christmas treats. Much of Christmas informal giving was based on personal transactions between the donor and recipient, including the Christmas boxes discussed in Chapter 4. Although it is hard to substantiate, a large number of personal transactions probably took place within communities of poverty.[19]

The complaints about Christmas boxes discussed in Chapter 4 had been common since the eighteenth century, but they reached a new height in the 1860s when they combined with a powerful discourse challenging acts of giving that did not discriminate between the deserving and the undeserving poor. In his study of the East End of London in the 1860s, Gareth Stedman Jones reveals how contemporaries perceived the virtual breakdown of the machinery of poor relief in terms of the 'deformation of the gift'. He argues that the deserving poor became demoralised by the ease in which the undeserving poor could take advantage of the expansion of indiscriminate charity. Many of the gifts were channelled through organisations, but they were motivated by sentiment, lacked coherent methodology, and often overlapped with each other.[20] Weightman and Humphries argue that by the mid-Victorian period the big cities acted as magnets at Christmas for 'casual labourers, the unemployed, tramps, and travelling criminals', creating the perception that 'respectable working-class folk would be demoralised by the midwinter wealth and Christmas revelling of the casual poor'. Christmas was a likely time for migration by the indigent poor, but while Weightman and Humphries suggest that the rationalisation of charity that took place under the auspices of the Charity Organisation Society (COS) from 1869 greatly reduced seasonal migration, Peter Mandler has uncovered evidence from Manchester and London to suggest that it was still prevalent in the Edwardian period.[21] Ellen Ross draws attention to the suspicion of 'charity mongers' as 'both stock literary figures and the bête noire of the whole charity world'. Drawing upon the social investigations of Charles Booth, Ross highlights the case of Mrs Parks, wife of a drunken invalided soldier, who was able to get two or three dinners for her children during the Christmas season.[22] Such a systematic 'working' of the charity system suggests that by the late nineteenth century, Christmas could play an important role in the survival strategies of the poor and destitute. In some industries paid income remained temporary and seasonal, and the availability of Christmas charities must have played a considerable role in the poor 'getting by'.

Despite the existence of 'charity mongers', Weightman and Humphries argue that the reform of Christmas charity that arose under the influence of the COS strengthened the established categories of deserving and undeserving poor through the introduction of means testing.[23] There is evidence that the COS collaborated with and provided means testing for Christmas charities in the late Victorian period, as it did in York for Edith Milner's charity, which provided Christmas meals to the poor in their own homes.[24] The sentimental appeal of Christmas might seem to contradict the rational, scientific principles of the COS, but as Alan Kidd demonstrates, nationally the COS was a disparate organisation with a wide diversity of ideas and practices, as is demonstrated by the Christmas appeal made by the Bethnal Green branch in 1872. The practices of the COS also alienated 'many within the charitable community', and despite charity reform in the second half of the nineteenth century, many new Christmas-orientated charities came into existence during this period. [25]

The new Christmas charities that appeared in the late Victorian period were a product of the growing power of Christmas sentiment and its place in the national culture, but they also reflected the way in which poverty had reappeared on the national agenda, in part thanks to a new generation of social investigations, including Andrew Mearns's *The Bitter Cry of Outcast London*, published in 1883. The 131 organisations which made a Christmas appeal in *The Times* in 1872 included not just organisations wishing to provide either a Christmas experience for the poor or just the basics of survival, but organisations that exploited the sentiment of Christmas in order to raise general funds for everyday expenses. Hospitals were prominent in the exploitation of the Christmas sentiment, with thirty-two of the institutions making an appeal in 1872. Roy Porter highlighted how philanthropy had been an essential part of hospital finance since the eighteenth century, and the continuing importance of philanthropy to hospital finance can be seen in the way Edwardian hospitals used staged images of wards featuring Christmas decorations in their annual reports to present a positive image of the institution to its subscribers.[26] Keir Waddington demonstrates how hospitals also diversified their charitable activity with measures that 'mixed "seriousness" with "entertainment"', including annual dinners or balls that would be the 'social and financial highlight of the hospital's year'.[27] The 2nd Viscount Halifax attended balls at Doncaster Infirmary early in the New Year and reinforced philanthropic links with Doncaster tradesmen who supported the infirmary by inviting them to the servant's ball at Hickleton.[28]

The Christmas appeals of hospitals and other institutions in the second half of the nineteenth century gained the support of local religious, civic, political, military and commercial elites. Though the expansion of Christmas charity was part of the development of a national culture it also reinforced a local civic identity. One consequence of this was that it became common for the beneficiaries of Christmas charities to be addressed by lord mayors, MPs and, by the Edwardian period, their wives. Lady mayoresses came to perform a very public role in the civic Christmas, as demonstrated in York when in 1904 Lady Vernon-Wragge distributed packets of tea to the elderly poor of nineteen institutions and gave boxes of oranges to children at a further five institutions.[29] The link between the civic and the national could also be important for a charity society's appeal for funds. In London Sir William Treloar's crippled children's Christmas hamper fund of 1913 had published in *The Times* a full-page advertisement that featured the portrait of George V alongside those of the Lord and Lady Mayoress of London and the 21 mayors of metropolitan boroughs. This provided readers of *The Times* with an esteemed example to follow, and contrasted the spectacle of 'fairy Christmas London' with a sentimental description of the experiences of poor crippled children.[30]

The crippled children's Christmas hamper fund is an example of a specific type of charity that emerged in late Victorian England: the charity organisation specifically designed to provide a festive experience for the poor. Whilst there were no examples of this type of charity in *The Times* in 1872, by 1892 appeals appeared of behalf of organisations such as 'East-End Christmas Dinners' and 'Christmas Cheer for the Homeless and Destitute'. Especially prominent were charities for children, which drew upon the broader discourses sentimentalising childhood in the nineteenth century. In the context of Christmas, it became common to refer to destitute children as 'poor robins', presenting them as innocent and vulnerable. Robins were one of the more popular images to appear when the Christmas card became commercially successful in the 1860s. At first comic, the depictions became sentimental in the 1870s, and in the 1880s there was a fashion for cards showing dead robins accompanied by morbid and sentimental texts.[31] In 1880 the parish magazine of St Simon's, Leeds, noted the church's intention of 'providing a Christmas dinner for the little robins of the parish'. Kathleen Heasman attributed the term 'robins' dinners' to the Rev. Charles Bullock, editor of *Home Words*, who inserted an appeal in the paper at Christmas 'for all the hungry human "robins"'.[32]

One of the most prominent ways in which philanthropy illuminated the relationship between Christmas and childhood was through press campaigns to provide poor children with toys. In 1879 the readers of the *Truth* supported an exhibition of toys which were distributed amongst children in London hospitals, workhouses, workhouse schools and infirmaries.[33] By the Edwardian period local newspapers in provincial cities such as Birmingham, Leeds and Manchester were organising large-scale campaigns to provide toys as Christmas presents. In Leeds the *Yorkshire Evening Post* appeal began in 1908, when the paper assisted Albert Knight, Vicar of Christ Church, Leeds, in providing over 1,600 Christmas presents for the poor children of his parish. Knight was inspired by the question one young girl had asked the clergyman: 'Please, sir, are we havin' any toys at Christmas?' The response to this question revealed the extent to which children were now believed to have innate rights, and how *all* children had come to form expectations about Christmas. The following year the *Yorkshire Evening Post* extended the appeal to the whole of Leeds, estimating that there were 10,000 children who 'never receive[d] a visit from Santa Claus'. The paper asked for 10,000 toys, principally dolls, to be sent, appropriated from the 'corner of some well-stocked nursery', and further appealed to an 'army' of ladies to dress the dolls. After the dolls were exhibited, they were distributed to children in various schools throughout Leeds. These campaigns deployed new journalistic techniques which were part of the landscape of urban modernity. Almost every day the readers of the *Yorkshire Evening Post* were provided with a running total of the number of toys received, which by 17 December had reached 29,753. There were also daily anecdotes concerning interesting donations, and letters from both donors and potential recipients, as well as fictional letters from Santa Claus thanking the donors for their help. These letters created a new home for Santa Claus in fairyland, a place which could be evoked through the charitable gift, where the 'happy child-look' could be brought back to 'little people' in contrast to the 'bitter winds of poverty and neglect'. The often personalised nature of the Christmas charity gift, which characterised much of the giving described earlier in this chapter, was not possible in the context of mass philanthropy. Consequently, Santa Claus became useful in negotiating the gift relationship between donor and recipient which had become disrupted by anonymity. This practice was demonstrated in 1898 when an anonymous donor to the robins' dinner in the Leeds parish of St

Simon's was referred to as Santa Claus. The issue was raised by some *Yorkshire Evening Post* readers, who felt that someone should dress up as Santa Claus when the gifts were being distributed, in order to perpetuate the 'colour and romance of Christmas time'.[34]

Another important factor about this charity was that it encouraged the middle-class child to become a donor. This was the culmination of a process that had been developing for a century. Prochaska reveals how the British and Foreign Bible Society encouraged children's participation in the charitable process in the early nineteenth century, and in 1841 the Methodist missionary society began a children's Christmas appeal, the success of which guaranteed it as an annual event.[35] In the later nineteenth century, children, particularly girls, may also have been influenced by the Christmas examples of selflessness they encountered in popular fiction such as Louisa Alcott's *Little Women* (1868) and Susan Coolidge's *What Katy Did* (1872). The *Yorkshire Evening Post* was keen to testify to the willingness of children to give up their own possessions by printing the notes of goodwill the newspaper received with the toys. Nine-year-old Dorothy E. wrote: '[My] mother told me about the poor little girls and boys who were sure Santa Claus was not coming to their houses. I have sent you all my fairy tale books. Please give them to the little children.' Such acts of selflessness contributed to the ideal picture of middle-class childhood at Christmas, tempering concerns about material desire and acting in ways that suggested an independent 'little person'. However, concern was raised about the nature of the gift. Some readers felt that the 'fund should be devoted to feeding the poor children'. The *Yorkshire Evening Post* was adamant, however, that 'for once the poor children should have what every child in better circumstances regards as a natural right – a luxury – a present from Santa Claus for Christmas'.[36]

The new urban Christmas philanthropy that developed in the late nineteenth century can be seen partly in terms of a continuing concern for the most vulnerable members of society during midwinter. Successive generations of Victorians sentimentalised this concern, though it only reached its apogee at the end of the nineteenth century. Though readers of *A Christmas Carol* may have paused to consider Dickens's explicit call for charitable action, there little evidence for the Victorian period of the novella directly influencing philanthropic action. However, in 1903 the Leeds Dickens Fellowship 'hit upon a very happy and appropriate opening for their surplus energy as well as for the practical expression of their sympathy with the poor and weak which Dickens must infuse into every follower' by providing a tea and entertainment for poor children. In 1905 the York Dickens Fellowship indulged in new heights of sentimentality by providing a similar reception for 'real Tiny-Tims'.[37] Crippled children provided an accentuated example of vulnerability, sanctifying in the context of Christmas the memory of Dickens, who was increasingly seen as the founder of the modern festival. This sentiment also coincided with specific concerns about children's health in the early twentieth century. For example, Sir William Treloar founded his 'little cripples' fund' in 1906 because of his concern over the effects of non-pulmonary tuberculosis on the children of London. However, no matter what the rational basis for intervention was, the public now demanded that the Christmas sentiment be satisfied, as the Leeds Invalid Children's Aid Society found in 1909 when it decided that 'so much had been done for the children during the summer that it was … considered unnecessary to have the usual Christmas treat', and were so overwhelmed with offers of help that the festive event went ahead as usual.[38]

Appropriately for organisations operating in a mass urban society, many of the late-Victorian and Edwardian Christmas charities became obsessed with providing for large numbers of people. Four-figure gatherings were often recorded, such as the 1,500 poor children given Christmas dinner in Southwark by the Ragged School Union and the Shaftesbury Society in 1902, or the 4,000 poor children given Christmas dinner by the Derby robin's Christmas dinner society in 1908.[39] These figures were, however, dwarfed by those found by Stephen Nissenbaum in New York where, in 1902, 20,000 poor people were fed by the Salvation Army. Nissenbaum was struck by the public nature of these events, with large numbers of wealthy New Yorkers paying to watch the poor eat. This led Nissenbaum to develop a theory of 'charity as spectator sport', in which the 'jaded rich', lacking an emotional reciprocity from the gift-giving process they engage in with their own children, turn outwards to the poor for emotionally sustaining gratitude.[40] The theory does not translate well to an English context. Alongside the large public gatherings, considerable efforts were made to allow the poor a Christmas experience in their own homes, provided through distributions of materials. For example, on Christmas Eve 1902, the St Giles Christian mission provided materials for 550 families, the Ham-Yard soup kitchen for 1,000 families, the Vicar of Plaistow for 500 families, and the *Leytonstone Express and Independent* for 4,000 families.[41] Whilst the use of home visit and ticket systems meant that such provisions were means tested, this activity signalled the triumph of the ideal of the hearthside Christmas spent with family, manifested in the vision of a national culture available to *all* classes.

The poor law and the workhouse

The 1834 poor law amendment act aimed to abolish the practice of providing outdoor relief for the able bodied. The only state assistance that would be available to the able bodied was entry into a new generation of workhouses on the principle of 'less eligibility': the workhouse would 'have to be a less acceptable alternative to seeking work at the wages and conditions available to "the independent labourer of the lowest class"'. The new poor law was politically and socially divisive, and was never universally applied, leading to variations both between and within regions.[42] Variations in the application of the new poor law could have a direct impact on the attitudes and practices of Christmas charitable giving, and the distinction between the state provision of welfare and private giving was not clear-cut. Hugh Cunningham demonstrates that the poor law, funded through taxation, was sometimes referred to by contemporaries as 'legal charity' and was 'distinguished from, but not sharply counterposed to, other forms of charity originated by religious and voluntary bodies'.[43]

The first workhouse was established in Bristol in 1698, and by 1831 there were almost 4,800 workhouses in England. The number fell after 1834, but workhouses 'became progressively larger and more grandly constructed'.[44] Before 1834, workhouse paupers were often treated to Christmas fare, but this customary right was subsequently undermined by poor law commissioners who prohibited the provision of extra food on Christmas Day.[45] In *A Christmas Carol*, Dickens made Scrooge the epitome of this sentiment; when pressed for funds to supply the poor with Christmas fare, Scrooge replies that he 'can't afford to make idle people merry'.[46] Again, the rule was never universally implemented; in 1836 the Bridgewater Poor Law Union discontinued the Christmas dinner, but the inmates of the Liverpool Workhouse dined on roast beef and plum pudding on Christmas Day, reflecting the trend in the north of England to resist the implementation of the 1834 act.[47] In 1840 the poor law authorities allowed the supply of extra provisions on Christmas Day, but only if they were supplied by private individuals. This highlighted the need for the authorities to clarify the limits of permissibility in terms of what could be provided by the rates and what was clearly the responsibility of private charity, an issue which accentuated local ideological and political fissures. For example, the Tory *Leeds Intelligencer* attempted to score points against Whig politicians when reviewing the Christmas events at Wakefield Workhouse in 1843: 'Several *Liberal* individuals refused to subscribe on the ground that the inmates of the poorhouse should not be allowed to have a dinner which was to be paid for by charitable contributors'. In 1847 local poor law guardians were granted the discretion to provide extra Christmas food at the expense of the poor rate, and whilst this largely removed the potential for controversy, some chose to continue funding by private subscription or donation in the second half of the nineteenth century.[48] Conversely, there were also local poor law unions which provided additional outdoor relief at Christmas to the most needy; for example, the Leeds Union provided a supplementary grant of one shilling to the over-sixties in Christmas week. By the 1870s and 1880s, however, concerns over indiscriminate giving led to a new crusade against outdoor relief, and supplementary grants for Christmas were forbidden by a local government board ruling in 1878. One consequence was to expand the scope of private charity, as subscriptions were raised in Leeds and other towns to continue the practice.[49]

From the 1850s Christmas treats to the inmates of workhouses began to become more elaborate, and became the main focus of press reports on the civic celebration of Christmas, perhaps only rivalled by hospitals in the latter part of the century. This development was linked to the increasing presence of lady visitors, who, as part of a broader engagement in philanthropic activity, replicated their role in producing the domestic Christmas by introducing some of the character of the expanding festive season to the workhouse, particularly the provision for children. One of the first women to provide for workhouse children at Christmas was Emma Sheppard of Frome, Somerset, whose activities were publicised in the Bristol press and subsequently a pamphlet sentimentally titled *Sunshine in a Shady Place*, which may have inspired the wider participation of middle-class women in this form of philanthropy.[50] The transformation of the dining room at the Liverpool Workhouse with flags and evergreens was typical of developments throughout England, whilst 'benevolent ladies' provided that institution with a Christmas tree in 1857.[51] A variety of entertainments were also introduced; for example, at Bermondsey Workhouse the children watched a magic lantern show on Boxing Day 1853, and during Christmas 1858 the inmates of Birmingham Workhouse were provided with a music band and social dance.[52] By the 1870s, the popularity of the Christmas card and its potential for conveying the meaning and sentiment of the festival inspired philanthropists to form Christmas letter or pillow missions. These organisations sent Christmas cards and letters to paupers in workhouses and hospitals in an attempt to replicate the emotional currents of the middle- and upper-class Christmas amongst the very poorest sections of society. One inmate of a workhouse infirmary stated that a Christmas card 'seemed a message from heaven'. The first letter mission was established by the Rev. E. B. Elliott of St Mark's, Kemp Town, in 1871, and by the 1880s the practice was established in a number of workhouses including Bristol, Liverpool, Manchester and York.[53]

The attendance of poor law guardians and other local dignitaries at workhouses during the festive period made the event a civic spectacle in the later Victorian and Edwardian periods. For example, in 1880, the attendance of the general public at Birmingham Workhouse was so large that entrance on Christmas Day had to be restricted to those accompanied by the board of guardians or who were in possession of a letter of introduction.[54] Christmas meant a respite from the usual routine of hard labour in the workhouse, and in the late Victorian period newspaper reports commented on the mirth and good humour that the festivities produced. There were, however, attacks on the culture and practice of the workhouse Christmas, the most prominent led by George R. Sims (1847–1922), who published *In the Workhouse – Christmas Day* in 1879. Though highly sentimental, Sims's dramatic monologue highlighted the hypocrisy of the seasonal gift in a system which effectively criminalised poverty, especially for the elderly, as well as demonstrating the condescending behaviour of wealthy visitors and the false deference of the paupers.[55]

Despite an increasingly elaborate culture of festivity in workhouses in the later nineteenth and early twentieth centuries, including the appearance of Father Christmas in some workhouses from the 1880s, the central feature of the workhouse Christmas remained the feast. Workhouse regimes were keen to maintain their dietary provision at a level lower than that of the local working classes but adequate enough to stave off accusations that they were starving the paupers in their care. Consequently, monotony of diet was more important than quantity; substantial amounts of food were provided, but elements that might make it more palatable, such as table salt, were removed. Food created considerable interest amongst inmates, making the Christmas meal important.[56] Beef and plum pudding were typically served throughout the nineteenth century, and in the second half of the century it was common for children to be provided with fruit, nuts and sweets. Adults were often allowed a quantity of items such as tobacco and snuff, and more controversially, ale or beer. The provision of alcohol to workhouse paupers became one of the most divisive Christmas issues in Victorian England and needs to be understood with the context of the temperance movement.

Temperance

In the early nineteenth century, contemporaries were well aware that 'good ale and strong beer' were as closely associated with the festive season as mince pies and plum pudding. Alcohol had long been part of the customary fare provided to the poor at Christmas, including workhouse paupers, and, with the exception of the disruption caused by the reformed poor law, the practice continued in the new institutions constructed in the Victorian period. By the 1830s, concerns about the deleterious affects of drink on the health and morals of the population led to the formation of temperance societies, often led by the Anglican clergy or nonconformist ministers. In the 1840s these societies turned their attention to Christmas, offering alternative festive tea parties with speeches by reformed characters on the evils of drink. In 1842 the Rev. W. H. Turner addressed the Christmas Festival of the Bristol total abstinence society, and the *Bristol Mercury* reported his criticism of 'Christmas, as being a time when drunkenness and other vices, were, unhappily, indulged in to a more ordinary extent among all classes of society. It was not among the humbler classes alone that the drinking customs prevailed'.[57] To a certain extent this was a continuation of the sermonising common in the eighteenth century which condemned gluttony and drunken excess during the festive season, but a significant difference was the context of rapid urbanisation and the associated problems of social dislocation.

Despite the rhetoric of a problem affecting all classes, the Christmas activities of the temperance movement were aimed largely at working-class drunkenness. Temperance reformers were particularly concerned to develop the habit of total abstinence in childhood, and in the mid-nineteenth century Band of Hope organisations were formed which offered an alternative Christmas celebration for young people in the decades that followed. It was an alternative to the culture of drunkenness and disorderly behaviour which marked the festive season. In the period between Christmas and New Year, provincial newspapers reported on the violence and drunkenness that had occurred and sometimes contrasted them with the traditional seasonal message of peace and goodwill, and the values of the domestic celebration. In towns and cities with a significant number of Irish immigrants, the reports would also reinforce popular stereotypes. In the 1850s, the *York Herald* called one article reporting on alcohol-related violence the 'Christmas amusements of the Irish' and commented in another that 'they, no doubt, in the true Irish fashion, ... [thought] it was the most "illegant" way of diverting themselves during the general holiday'.[58]

In the last quarter of the nineteenth century, temperance reformers made many appeals to curtail the practice of giving alcoholic Christmas boxes. Whilst reflecting wider beliefs about the moral laxity of the working man, the condemnation was phrased in terms of the threat to home life and the authority of the father figure. One such appeal of 1881 wants the potential benefactor to

> consider that to be in any degree the means of causing a usually sober man to return to his family in a state of drunkenness is not only bringing feelings of shame and self-reproach on the man, but also inflicting unhappiness on his family, who may hitherto have regarded (the head of their cottage home) with respect and admiration.[59]

Since drinking was perceived to be a cause of pauperism, the Christmas provision of ale and beer in workhouses was perceived by some to be dangerous practice, potentially reawakening or reinforcing the problem that had led many paupers to the workhouse in the first instance. During the Christmas season of 1880, George Paddington of Southsea claimed that he witnessed on Boxing Day afternoon a 'dozen persons in several stages of drunkenness … and many other who were queer in vision or in gait'; amongst their number were two paupers whose drunkenness had been prompted by the Christmas half-pint supplied by the workhouse.[60]

With pauperism and alcoholism linked firmly in at least part of the public's imagination, banning the provision of workhouse Christmas beer became a potent (if largely symbolic) course of action. One of the earliest successes took place in 1862, when J. H. Rutherford (1826–90), a Presbyterian minister, persuaded the Newcastle Board of Guardians to provide the paupers with tea and coffee instead of beer on Christmas Day. This success was, however, short lived. The vote had been carried whilst the majority of guardians were absent, and Charles Hamond (1817–1905) commented that during 'the twenty years he had been a member … he had never known so much popular feeling expressed against any motion'. Such was the uproar that Rutherford felt compelled to defend his action in a lecture delivered in Bath Lane Church. When the full Board of Guardians met to discuss the issue, Hamond argued that he 'thought it very harsh to refuse the inmates on Christmas Day what they had enjoyed themselves; he did not think it redounded to the credit of those Guardians who enforced their temperance principles in the manner which they had done last week', whilst Joseph Wilkinson 'urged the teetotaller to try benevolence and charity, instead of forcing their principles down the throats of other people'. Testimonials were presented from the paupers regretting the loss of their Christmas beer, and a large majority of the guardians voted in favour of providing the beer on New Year's Day instead. In April the following year, the *Newcastle Courant* reported that many guardians lost their seats because they had supported the exclusion of Christmas beer.[61] This indicates that in the mid-Victorian period moderate alcoholic consumption continued to play a significant role in the Christmas culture of good cheer, and, despite the activities of temperance reformers, there was widespread support for the continuance of this method of customarily treating the poor.

By the 1870s, however, increased awareness of poverty and the rising expense of poor relief led many more poor law guardians to consider a ban on Christmas beer. Though motions to stop the donation of beer for paupers were easily defeated in Hull and Preston in 1873 and Hartlepool in 1874, the following year the Hull guardians narrowly voted in favour of a ban. Concern over alcoholic consumption was magnified when it was linked to other misdemeanours. In 1876 seven paupers who absconded from Preston Workhouse on Christmas Day attributed their misconduct to the beer they had consumed with their dinner.[62] In the 1880s bans on workhouse Christmas beer were strictly enforced in the northern cities of Leeds, Liverpool and Manchester, partly due to the campaigning of the Workhouse Drink Reform League, which directly lobbied local boards of guardians. The regime at Leeds was so stringent that, when in 1880 the retail firm René, Félix et Cie sent a hamper of rum to add to the plum-pudding sauce, it was returned by the master of the workhouse on the grounds that no alcohol was allowed to enter the premises.[63] In 1890 a member of the Islington Board of Guardians estimated that 200 English workhouses did not allow Christmas beer, though the following year the *Pall Mall Gazette* noted than bans were more noticeable in the 'progressive' north, whilst the practice persisted in southern and western England. There is evidence to support this, as beer continued to be allowed in Birmingham and Bristol, whilst in London the Hackney Union instituted a ban only in 1890.[64] Throughout the 1890s and early 1900s the ban on Christmas beer was gradually, though unevenly, eased throughout England, but the 'beer question' remained a controversial issue. When in 1898 the York Board of Guardians voted to allow the Sheriff of York to supply the paupers with a pint of beer, several letters appeared in the *Yorkshire Herald* reiterating the connection between alcoholism and pauperism, and only one correspondent challenged this view by pointing to a lifetime of low wages and the need for pensions.[65] The proponents of both sides of this argument claimed rational common sense in support of their cause. During a debate amongst the guardians of Birkenhead in 1897, the Rev. Jos. Davies commented that the 'idea that beer gave strength or nourishment was purely sentimental, and it was full time the idea should be banished from the minds of sensible people. That was the opinion of all sober-minded medical men as well'. Equally, there were guardians who, though sympathetic to the cause of temperance, were suspicious of public bodies being used as a platform for teetotalism, and advocated that common sense should make all realise that it was a question of a 'pint of beer versus a ton of disappointment at Christmas time'.[66]

The voluntary impulse

The temperance activists who sought to ban beer in the workhouses and keep the young from seasonal revelries can be seen as part of a long tradition of moral revulsion at Christmas debauchery that had existed since the puritan attempts to suppress the festival in the seventeenth century, though objections on explicitly religious grounds were less marked by the late nineteenth century. In addition, advocates of temperance were willing to exploit the expanding Christmas festival in an attempt to reform working-class morals and behaviour, which could be interpreted as part of a broader trend for middle- and upper-class elites to assert 'social control' over the unruly lower orders. A more subtle and persuasive practice in the nineteenth century was to offer the urban working classes opportunities for 'rational recreation', and the association of Christmas with drinking and revelry made it an important occasion for amusements of a more improving nature.[67] One of the principal means of establishing opportunities for rational recreation in the first half of the nineteenth century was through the establishment of mechanics' institutes, and along with the Christmas festivals of the temperance societies one of the more notable developments in this field was the establishment of the Manchester mechanics' Christmas party in the early 1830s. The early parties were accompanied by lectures on old Christmas customs, such as the boar's head and wassail bowl, which were then performed. These were customs and rituals from the past which had been carefully selected to demonstrate reciprocal bonds between classes, though the emphasis gradually changed to offering a contrast between the unworthy amusements of the past and the progress of the present. Though the parties at Manchester were not typical of mechanics' institutes as a whole, the library holdings of these institutions provided their members with access to important Christmas texts which may have aided the dissemination of middle-class sentiments about the season. For example, the Manchester institute had a copy of Hervey's *Book of Christmas* (1836), whilst the Leeds mechanics' institution acquired *A Christmas Carol* when it was published in 1843, and Irving's *Sketch Book* in 1850, and had two copies of Dickens's 'Christmas Books' and two of 'Christmas Stories' from *Household Words* in 1870. These texts could also be communicated orally. For example, at the York Working Men's Reading Room on New Year's Eve 1856, the members heard the Rev. J. H. Palmer read *A Christmas Carol*.[68]

In the second half of the nineteenth century, some philanthropists sought to abolish the customary practices of the working classes at Christmas, particularly the goose club. The origins of goose clubs can be traced back to the eighteenth century, though their exemption from registration at quarter sessions in Rose's act of 1793 means that little is known about them until the mid-nineteenth century.[69] By the 1840s the practices of goose clubs were being widely reported and condemned by the national and provincial press. As the clubs were often administered by publicans they were subject to the scrutiny of temperance advocates, especially as the goose, or other items of meat, poultry or game on offer, was accompanied by a bottle of gin or other spirits. Furthermore, though subscribers would pay a sum of money, usually six pence in the mid-nineteenth century, some clubs were a lottery with no guarantee of Christmas fare. One club running in Hull in the mid-1850s with 500 subscribers had only 144 prizes, of which four were geese and seventy-two were bottles of brandy, gin, port and sherry. Publicans might not be particularly scrupulous in the quality of their produce either. When a London publican was successfully sued in 1866 for supplying a leg of pork which was unfit for human consumption, a local butcher cast his judgement that 'a quantity of meat being in a bar amidst the heat of the gas might turn bad'.[70] Consequently, goose clubs were perceived not only as a further cause of Christmas intemperance but also as an uneconomic form of saving which provided evidence of the workman's lack of self-denial. In the 1860s attempts to discourage the use of goose clubs became grounded in the language of self-help which had recently been promoted by Samuel Smiles. This rhetoric emphasised the individual responsibilities of working men as breadwinners for their wives and children. A letter published in the *Bristol Mercury* in 1865 by 'a woman's friend' cast the responsibilities of working men in explicitly chivalric terms:

> self-help is the best help ... save your 'tit bits', resign your place at the goose club, let the butcher have your custom henceforth ... Put on your armour of self-denial, let your shield and buckler be patience and perseverance in well doing, and, above all, gird yourself with the bonds of love. Think of your sorrowing wife and neglected children.[71]

Working men were urged to deposit funds in the Post Office savings' bank instead of the goose club, and there were also attempts to reform Christmas boxes in order to promote saving and education. In 1867 a letter in the *York*

Herald called upon the public to follow the example of the York gas company, which gave its apprentices a Christmas box in the form of a ticket for classes at the York Institute, whilst in 1880, A. G. Legard of Headingley recommended giving a Christmas box in the form of stamps attached to savings' bank sheets.[72]

Goose clubs provoked criticisms not only of working-class practices of spending and consumption but also of the 'sharp' business practices of publicans and grocers. Condemnations of goose clubs continued to appear in the late nineteenth and early twentieth centuries, and as the Farepak Christmas hampers scandal of 2006 demonstrates, there remains a culture within the poorer sections of society of saving for Christmas through schemes which offer no interest in exchange for goods which are not competitively priced.[73] However, in the 1880s and 1890s some philanthropists, particularly those connected with temperance, Nonconformist missions and adult schools, attempted to provide goose clubs to tempt the poorer classes away from the pub. Temperance societies and adult schools were running goose clubs in Liverpool and Birmingham in the 1880s, and in York a Wesleyan mission took advantage of the police's suppression of public house goose clubs in 1896 and established its own club with thirty-five members, which had risen to 431 by 1906.[74]

Though some examples of Christmas philanthropy were clearly an attempt to reform the habits and customs of the working classes, it is not clear that all voluntary impulses were so instrumental. Alan Kidd argues that any attempt to analyse philanthropic motives must reject simplistic assertions of social control at one extreme and altruism at the other, and recognise that social intervention often derives from a complex nexus of emotions, needs and values.[75] Victorian and Edwardian Christmas philanthropy rested upon both the continuance of seasonal hospitality and the conditions and practices of a modernising urban society, and consequently duty, obligation and the emotional tug of custom played a role. Individuals may have gained social prestige or political influence from their philanthropic activities, and the publication of names in local newspapers and in subscription lists might have helped to foster reputations, though the mass charitable projects of the late nineteenth and early twentieth centuries meant that anonymity was more likely for the majority of donors. Of continuing importance was the reciprocity or conditionality of the charitable gift. Increasingly, many parents attained emotional satisfaction in exchange for the Christmas presents they gave to their children, and it is likely that emotional satisfaction could be the product of charitable transactions as well, particularly when the gift was informal and personally given. But this satisfaction may well have been combined with the desire for increased status, or a particular agenda such as temperance or merely responding to urgent social need.

Though it varied greatly between denominations, religious feeling may also have played a part in much Christmas philanthropy, as much activity was connected to or organised by members of the churches. Octavia Hill (1838–1912) provides a suitable example of how religious feeling motivated philanthropic action at Christmas. In 1855 she worked at the Christian socialist-promoted Ladies' Guild, helping ragged school children to make toys. Hill wrote very explicit comments about Christmas in her letters at the time. Her priorities were demonstrated in a letter to her mother on 19 December:

> Mr. [F. D.] Maurice tells me that he will preach at Lincoln's Inn on Tuesday morning. Of course I cannot miss that; but I will, if necessary, as a great sacrifice, on one condition, that it is not made a precedent for expecting it again … I very much wish to spend some part of Christmas with you … but I wish very much wish you would be contented, if I spent Christmas Eve with you, as I would value to do so.

Writing to her friend Mary Harris on Christmas Eve, Hill went further: 'I care very little for what is called a merry Christmas … I have renounced parties, above all I have renounced Christmas parties'. Yet at the same time she recognised the value of Christmas to the children in care: 'I must bring home to them some of the gladness which they see around them; their only Christmas trees must not be those in the confectioners' windows, at which they gaze with longing eyes. There is time enough for Christmas to become solemn, when it had become joyful and dear'.[76] Though Hill's decision to choose *between* mirth and duty and *between* her family and the ragged schoolchildren was probably unusual, it nonetheless highlights the significance of the religious impulse to Christmas philanthropy. At the same time, Hill's concern for the happiness of the children demonstrates how one of the most important features of the expanding Christmas could also locate sentimentalism at the heart of social action. Though in many ways the discourses and practices of Christmas philanthropy replicated the broader trends of the philanthropic domain in the long nineteenth century, the sentiments of the festive season also meant that the good deeds of the Christmas season had a logic and purpose of their own.

Conclusion

Christmas philanthropy in nineteenth-century England was based on a combination of old and new practices. The churches continued to play a prominent role in the provision of Christmas charity, and the parish remained an important unit of administration. However, Christmas charity expanded greatly in the second half of the century, as philanthropists and the broader public sought to meet the challenges of mass urban society *and* the emotional demands of a festival celebrating family and childhood. In doing so, philanthropic organisation balanced sentiment and rationality. Though many philanthropic practices were new, the provision of food, drink and warmth to the vulnerable during midwinter has a familiarity to it, suggesting a strong continuity in both obligation and customary expectations. For families and individuals who had fallen into poverty, Christmas helped, however briefly, to support the uneven provision of welfare and on occasion provided treats that were otherwise unaffordable. Often, the price to pay for this was the potentially humiliating processes of means testing and the performance of deference. Unsurprisingly, some poor families learnt to cynically exploit the Christmas charity system, and instrumentalism was also a motivating factor for some philanthropists. Christmas philanthropy replicated the broader concern to distinguish between the deserving and the undeserving poor, and temperance advocates used the festival to attempt to reform the behaviour and customs of the working classes. Yet this is just one dimension of the range of motivations that inspired individuals who participated in the culture of Christmas philanthropy. Naturally, large numbers of people did not contribute, or only made a minimal donation, but the culture of philanthropy during the festive season was extensive, and it expanded as the nineteenth century progressed. It demonstrates that a related public culture of Christmas was just as much a part of nineteenth-century England as the festival of the home. It rested, however, not only on good deeds but also on an increasingly, though not exclusively, commercial culture of entertainment, which is the focus of the Chapter 6.

Notes

1 B. Bushaway, *By Rite: Custom, Ceremony and Community in England 1700–1880* (London: Junction, 1982), p. 180.

2 F. Heal, *Hospitality in Early Modern England* (Oxford: Oxford University Press, 1990), pp. 148–9, 151, 168, 297; R. Hutton, *The Rise and Fall of Merry England: the Ritual Year 1400–1700* (Oxford: Oxford University Press, 1994), pp. 177, 241–2.

3 *The Times*, 28 December 1786; 11 January 1788; 25 December 1789.

4 W. Irving, *The Legend of Sleepy Hollow and Other Stories*, ed. W. L. Hedges (New York: Penguin, 1999), p. 178; Hutton, *Merry England*, p. 243; Bushaway, *By Rite*, pp. 128–30, 240–1.

5 In 1818 parliament instituted the first of four fixed-period Charity Commission enquiries which were active for most of the period until 1837. As Mae Baker and Michael Collins explain, the 'Commissioners were to investigate, highlight abuses and make suggestions for redress', and eventually a permanent Board of Charity Commissioners to supervise all charitable trusts was created by the 1853 Charitable Trusts Act. M. Baker and M. Collins, 'The governance of charitable trusts in the nineteenth century: the West Riding of Yorkshire', *Social History*, 27:2 (2002), 164–5.

6 Bushaway, *By Rite*, pp. 23–4, 253–4; *26th Report of the Charity Commissioners*, British Sessional Papers, 1833, vol. 19, p. 107; *27th Report of the Charity Commissioners*, British Sessional Papers, 1834, vol. 21, pp. 83–4.

7 R. Hutton, *The Stations of the Sun: a History of the Ritual Year in Britain* (Oxford: Oxford University Press, 1996), pp. 58–64.

8 Bushaway, *By Rite*, pp. 188–90.

9 Hutton, *Stations of the Sun*, p. 54.

10 University of York, Borthwick Institute for Archives, Hickleton Papers, A7.4A, diaries of Mary Wood, 1845 and 1876; A7.5, diary of Charles Lindley Wood, 1893; F. W. Cornish (ed.), *Extracts from the Letters and Journals of William Cory* (Oxford: Horace Hart, 1897), pp. 108–9.

11 Isle of Wight Record Office, Oglander Collection, OG/CC/1842, letter from John Wilson Fardell to John H. G. Oglander, 23 November 1894.

12 Bushaway, *By Rite*, pp. 188–90.

13 York City Archives, Acc. 13.

14 *St. Philip and St. James Parish Magazine*, December 1883.

15 M. Sheard, *Records of the Parish of Batley* (Worksop: R. White, 1894), pp. 412–15.

16 D. Owen, *English Philanthropy 1660–1960* (London: Oxford University Press, 1965), p. 324.

17 H. Cunningham, 'Introduction', in H. Cunningham and J. Innes (eds), *Charity, Philanthropy and Reform from the 1690s to 1850* (Basingstoke: Macmillan, 1998), p. 1; M. Daunton, 'Introduction', in M. Daunton (ed.), *Charity, Self-Interest and Welfare in the English Past* (London: UCL Press, 1996), p. 1.

18 N. Evans, 'Urbanisation, elite attitudes and philanthropy: Cardiff, 1850–1914', *International Review of Social History*, 27 (1982), 290–323.

19 F. K. Prochaska, 'Philanthropy', in F. M. L. Thompson (ed.), *The Cambridge Social History of Britain, 1750–1950. Vol. 3: Social Agencies and Institutions* (Cambridge: Cambridge University Press, 1990), pp. 362–6.

20 G. S. Jones, *Outcast London* (Oxford: Clarendon Press, 1971), chapter 13. Alan Kidd argues that Stedman Jones's theory is based upon a misreading of M. Mauss's *The Gift: Forms and Functions of Exchange in Archaic Societies* (New York: Norton, 1967). See A. J. Kidd, 'Philanthropy and the "social history paradigm"', *Social History*, 21 (1996), 187.

21 G. Weightman and S. Humphries, *Christmas Past* (London: Sidgwick and Jackson,

1987), pp. 64–6; P. Mandler, 'Poverty and charity in the nineteenth-century metropolis: an introduction', in P. Mandler (ed.), *The Uses of Charity: the Poor on Relief in the Nineteenth-Century Metropolis* (Philadelphia: University of Pennsylvania Press, 1990), pp. 18–19.

22 E. Ross, 'Hungry children: housewives and London charity, 1870–1918', in Mandler, *Uses of Charity*, p. 173.

23 Weightman and Humphries, *Christmas Past*, p. 66.

24 *York Herald*, 11 December 1888; *Yorkshire Herald*, 31 December 1891.

25 A. J. Kidd, *State, Society and the Poor in Nineteenth-Century England* (Basingstoke: Macmillan, 1999), pp. 99–102; *The Times*, 25 December 1872.

26 R. Porter, 'The gift relation: philanthropy and provincial hospitals in eighteenth-century England', in L. Granshaw and R. Porter (eds), *The Hospital in History* (London: Routledge, 1989), 149–78; *Annual Report of York County Hospital* (York, 1905–1906).

27 K. Waddington, '"Grasping gratitude": charity and hospital finance in late-Victorian London', in Daunton, *Charity, Self-Interest and Welfare*, p. 186.

28 Earl of Halifax, *Fullness of Days* (London: Collins, 1957), pp. 34–6.

29 *Yorkshire Herald*, 24 December 1904.

30 *The Times*, 23 December 1913.

31 G. Buday, *The History of the Christmas Card*, 2nd edn (London: Spring Books, 1964), pp. 100–9.

32 *St. Simon's Parochial Magazine*, December 1880; K. Heasman, *Evangelicals in Action: an Appraisal of their Social Work in the Victorian Era* (London: Geoffrey Bles, 1962), p. 76.

33 *The Times*, 16 December 1891.

34 *Yorkshire Evening Post*, 19 November 1909; 13 December 1909; 17 December 1909; *St. Simon's Parochial Magazine*, January 1898.

35 F. K. Prochaska, *Women and Philanthropy in Nineteenth-Century England* (Oxford: Clarendon Press, 1980), pp. 76, 82.

36 *Yorkshire Evening Post*, 19 November 1909; 3 December 1909.

37 *Yorkshire Post*, 30 December 1903; *Yorkshire Evening Post*, 26 December 1904.

38 *Annual Report of the Leeds Invalid Children's Aid Society* (Leeds, 1909–10).

39 *The Times*, 25 December 1902; 31 December 1908.

40 S. Nissenbaum, *The Battle for Christmas* (New York: Vintage, 1996), pp. 245–53.

41 *The Times*, 25 December 1902.

42 Kidd, *State, Society and the Poor*, pp. 28–9.

43 Cunningham, 'Introduction', p. 2.

44 N. Longmate, *The Workhouse* (London: Pimlico, 2003), p. 23; S. King, *Poverty and Welfare in England 1700–1850* (Manchester: Manchester University Press, 2000), p. 3.

45 *The Times*, 26 December 1838.

46 C. Dickens, *Christmas Books*, ed. R. Glancy (Oxford: Oxford University Press, 1988), p. 11.

47 Longmate, *The Workhouse*, p. 221; *Liverpool Mercury*, 6 January 1837.

48 J. A. R. Pimlott, *The Englishman's Christmas: a Social History* (Hassocks: Harvester, 1978), pp. 81, 90; *Leeds Intelligencer*, 30 December 1843.

49 *Yorkshire Post*, 15 December 1880; Kidd, *State, Society and the Poor*, p. 49.

50 Longmate, *The Workhouse*, pp. 226–8.

51 *Liverpool Mercury*, 26 December 1854; 28 December 1857.

52 *Morning Chronicle*, 26 December 1853; *Birmingham Daily Post*, 27 December 1858.

53 Heasman, *Evangelicals in Action*, p. 231; Weightman and Humphries, *Christmas Past*, p. 56; *Bristol Mercury and Daily Post*, 27 December 1886; *Leeds Mercury*, 26 December 1885; *Liverpool Mercury*, 26 December 1882; *Manchester Times*, 31 December 1881.

54 *Birmingham Daily Post*, 27 December 1880.

55 Longmate, *The Workhouse*, pp. 226–8.

56 M. A. Crowther, *The Workhouse System: the History of an English Social Institution* (London: Batsford, 1981), pp. 193–8, 213–18.

57 L. L. Shiman, *Crusade against Drink in Victorian England* (New York: St. Martin's Press, 1988), pp. 4, 32; *York Herald*, 2 January 1841; *Bristol Mercury*, 31 December 1842.

58 *York Herald*, 31 December 1853; 3 January 1856.

59 *York Herald*, 27 December 1881.

60 *Hampshire Telegraph and Sussex Chronicle*, 1 January 1881.

61 *Newcastle Courant*, 26 December 1862; 2 January 1863; 17 April 1863; J. H. Rutherford, *Beer or No Beer* (London, 1863).

62 *Hull Packet and East Riding Times*, 5 December 1873; 10 December 1875; *Preston Guardian*, 20 December 1873; 30 December 1876; *Northern Echo*, 21 December 1874.

63 *Leeds Mercury*, 24 December 1880; *Liverpool Mercury*, 27 December 1880; *Manchester Times*, 31 December 1881; *Birmingham Daily Post*, 8 December 1890; Weightman and Humphries, *Christmas Past*, p. 67.

64 *Bristol Mercury and Daily Post*, 27 December 1880; *Birmingham Daily Post*, 26 December 1884; *Reynold's Newspaper*, 14 December 1890; *Pall Mall Gazette*, 24 December 1891.

65 *Yorkshire Herald*, 24 December 1898; 27 December 1898; 28 December 1898; 29 December 1898; 30 December 1898; 31 December 1898.

66 *Liverpool Mercury*, 15 December 1897.

67 See A. P. Donajgrodzki (ed.), *Social Control in Nineteenth-Century Britain* (London: Croom Helm, 1977); P. Bailey, *Leisure and Class in Victorian England: Rational Rec-

reation and the Contest for Control, 1830–1885 (London: Routledge, 1978).

68 K. R. Farrar, 'The mechanics' saturnalia', in D. S. L. Cardwell (ed.), *Artisan to Graduate* (Manchester: Manchester University Press, 1974), pp. 99–118; *Annual Report of the Leeds Mechanics' Institution and Literary Society* (Leeds, 1844, 1851, 1871); *York Herald*, 3 January 1857.

69 E. Hopkins, *Working-Class Self-Help in Nineteenth-Century England: Responses to Industrialisation* (London: UCL Press, 1995), p. 14; D. M. MacRaild and D. E. Martin, *Labour in British Society, 1830–1914* (Basingstoke: Palgrave, 1999), p. 125.

70 *Hull Packet and East Riding Times*, 12 October 1855; *Lloyd's Weekly Newspaper*, 21 January 1866.

71 *Bristol Mercury*, 16 December 1865.

72 *York Herald*, 28 December 1867; *Leeds Mercury*, 27 December 1880.

73 *Guardian*, 13 November 2007.

74 *Liverpool Mercury*, 11 November 1882; *Birmingham Daily Post*, 26 December 1884; B. S. Rowntree, *Poverty: a Study of Town Life* (London: Macmillan, 1901), p. 312; *Wesley Mission, Skeldergate, York. Report, 1907* (York, 1907), pp. 11–12.

75 Kidd, 'Philanthropy and the "social history paradigm"', pp. 180–92.

76 C. E. Maurice (ed.), *Life of Octavia Hill as Told in her Letters* (London: Macmillan, 1913), pp. 68–71.

6

Christmas entertainments

This chapter pursues a further dimension of the public culture of Christmas which developed in the nineteenth century. It examines the rise of an entertainment industry focusing on but not restricted to Boxing Day, with an emphasis on theatrical and variety spectacle. In addition, the chapter also explores musical entertainment in the concert halls and in the streets during the festive season. It demonstrates the influence of working-class forms of entertainment such as music hall on the emergence of commercial urban mass cultural forms of leisure, but at the same time reveals the class tensions inherent in the modernisation of society. Sites of leisure became prime locations for viewing childhood as both spectacle and commodity, and more broadly, Christmas holidays magnified contemporary concerns in defining what activities were appropriate for children, and how best the transition to maturity might be negotiated.

Pantomime and the theatre

At the beginning of the nineteenth century there was little in the way of a Christmas leisure industry, with pantomime being the only commercial leisure opportunity associated with the festive season. In the eighteenth century, English pantomime evolved under the influence of the Italian *commedia dell'arte*. It was primarily associated with the Harlequinade and based at the patent theatres of Covent Garden and Drury Lane in London. Harlequinades featured the characters Pantaloon, an old man; Columbine, his beautiful daughter; Harlequin, Columbine's lover; and Harlequin's servant, Clown. Harlequin was at odds with Pantaloon, and usually invisible to him. Clown would play tricks on his master and other members of the cast. Over the course of the eighteenth century Clown gradually became more important, playing

Pantaloon off against Harlequin and carrying out a greater number of tricks. Pantomimes were originally performed throughout the year but gradually became more closely tied to holiday periods and eventually strongly associated with Christmas. The pantomime season opened on Boxing Day, and this contributed to the development of a distinct leisure culture in London on that day. By 1842 pantomimes could also be seen at nine theatres across London, and a statute for the regulation of theatres was passed the following year, ending the restriction on licences to the patent theatres and increasing the availability of pantomime in the following decades.[1] Pantomime was slower to develop in the rest of the country because, in the early nineteenth century, provincial theatres catered principally for landed society, which spent the festive season either in the country or in London. The provincial theatres were gradually realigned as part of a mass urban commercial culture, and pantomime played a part in this process. By the mid-1830s Christmas pantomimes were performed in Brighton and Manchester, though they were not common in provincial theatres until the 1850s.[2]

Before the reign of Victoria, newspaper reports on the London pantomime during the Christmas holidays frequently commented on the composition of the audience being children and 'children of a larger growth'. According to commentators, the pantomime was not only for children: it had the potential to awaken the inner child in adults through the nostalgic tug of memory. In 1816, *The Times'* reporter on the pantomime at Drury Lane commented: '[It] is not unpleasant to be thrown back ... on the scenes of our infancy'. Part of the delight was watching the animated responses of the children in the audience, as one contributor to *Bell's Life in London* noted: '[O]h, the rapture when the pantomime commences! Ready to leap out of the box, the joy and the mischief of the clown, [and the] laugh at the thwacks he gets for his meddling.'[3]

Not everyone was pleased with the influence the pantomime had on children. In 1824 a letter was published in the *Morning Chronicle* complaining of the corrupting influence of the Christmas pantomime, 'which, in one short vacation' was 'calculated to counteract the good lessons implanted in the young mind in a whole twelvemonth's schooling'. This correspondent not only blamed the way in which the Harlequinade ridiculed instead of respected old age but also condemned the immorality of the relationship between the Harlequin and Columbine.[4] By positioning the pantomime in opposition to the qualities of a rational and sober education, comments such as these to some extent pre-empted a perceived decline in children's attendance at the pantomime in the 1830s. Part of the reason for this can be attributed to a shift towards performances later in the evening. 'Theatricus' noted in *The Times* in 1831: 'I have heard many persons regret, that though anxious to treat their children with a sight of the Christmas pantomimes, they are unable to do so owing to the late hour at which they commence'.[5] However, in the early years of Victoria's reign, *John Bull* complained that the declining practice of bringing children to the pantomime is due to 'a churlish feeling prevalent respecting these Christmas entertainments, which is mistaken for wisdom'. The principle of utility now threatened the romantic impulse seen as important to the child's development into a healthy adult. *John Bull* argued that 'to teach a child the *utilitarian* doctrine concerning so glamorous ... an amusement, is to change his humanity with a baboon', and asked: '[P]ray how is the imagination to be awakened in early life, without the aid of pantomime?'[6] By 1846 *The Times* lamented the absence of children's participation in the pantomime audience, especially the 'screams of honest laughter, the shouts of exquisite delight, the beating of hands and stamping of feet ... and the tears of pleasure that glistened from their innocent eyes'. *The Times* suggested that children had been replaced by 'grown-up people, criticising seriously what should be laughed at indiscriminately, or sitting moped up in the embraces of *ennui*'. The pantomime audience also became more rowdy and unsuitable for younger children of the respectable classes. In the 1840s and 1850s it was reported as commonplace for the audience in the pit and gallery to pelt each other with corks, orange peel and nut shells, and in 1852 a piece in *The Times* on the pantomime at Drury Lane highlighted the unsettling heat of the packed theatre and the stand-up fights which took place.[7]

In the second half of the nineteenth century pantomime evolved further. The Harlequinade was marginalised, and the subject matter was increasingly drawn from a small pool of fairy tales; casts were expanded; and greater expense was lavished on scenery. The 1860s saw the appearance of music-hall performers, which led some pantomimes to become gigantic variety shows.[8] The prevalence of fairy tales has led some scholars to argue that pantomime changed from the rowdiness of the mid-nineteenth century to being an increasingly moralising form of children's entertainment, especially in the context of theatre's growing respectability amongst the middle classes after 1870.[9] Brian Crozier challenges this idea, arguing that pantomime audiences remained largely restricted to the upper-working and lower-middle classes. His argument is based partly on upper-middle-class revulsion towards the vulgarity of music-hall elements within pantomime and partly on the 'lack of interest among pantomime audiences in the development of fairyland as a metaphor for childhood'. For Crozier, the very presence of music-hall stars and the magnificence of the staging are evidence that the material was being addressed primarily to an adult audience. In 1882 the theatre critic W. Davenport Adams complained: '[I]t is nevertheless to the music-hall element that we owe the main portion of that propriety of word, gesture, and "business" which makes so much of our pantomimes unsuited to youthful ear and eye and not only unsuited to the youthful ear and eye, but unpleasant to all people of whatever age who possess good taste and feeling'.[10] Later in 1904 the *Daily Mail's* attack on the suitability of Drury Lane's *The White Cat* prompted a torrent of supportive letters condemning its vulgarity. Many pantomimes were also considered to be too long. In 1902, *The Times* appealed to theatre managers to put on pantomimes where 'instead of drooping heads and over-tired faces, a bright and unexhausted interest and a still undimmed delight' were apparent in the child.[11] Crozier does offer some qualifications. He demonstrates that children were being taken to the pantomime in greater numbers than ever before; and that some theatre managers were responding to the needs of child audiences through the offer of half-price seats for children. There was also 'evidence of a degree of identification between children and fairy roles in the appearance of child stars as major figures within the fairy tale which was part, but only part, of the pantomime as a whole', including Addie Blanche as *Mother Goose* at Drury Lane in 1880, and Minnie Terry in *Cinderella* at the Lyceum in 1893. There is also evidence of whole pantomimes being performed by children. For example, at London's Avenue Theatre, a company of around 80 children, with ages ranging from eight to fifteen, performed *Dick Whittington* on Christmas Eve, 1882.[12]

To compensate for their revulsion towards music-hall inspired pantomime, Crozier argues that upper-middle-class audiences turned towards a new form of child-oriented theatrical entertainment, instigated by the first production of *Alice in Wonderland* in 1886, and reaching its apogee with *Peter Pan* in 1904. J. P. Wearing states that '*Peter Pan* very rapidly became a permanent feature of the Christmas scene', and every revival was attended 'with almost cultish fanaticism'. For Crozier, such productions embodied 'an intensified interest in alternative worlds and fantasy of all kinds, [and] an association between these and childhood', and from 1899 he has found a 'marked increase in the numbers of non-pantomime Christmas productions for both child and adult audiences'.[13] During Christmas 1912 *Peter Pan* embarked upon its ninth revival at the Duke of York's theatre, and *The Times* celebrated the performance of the child-actress Ivy Sawyer as Betty, declaring: '[The] child actress is becoming a vogue at Christmas', and 'there is a capriciously lurking poetry about her acting which assures us that at bottom she understands all about fairies, just as the author said she did'.[14]

The increasing presence of children on stage during the festive season can be seen as part of broader adult desire to watch children perform, representing the extent to which Christmas had become a celebration of childhood. As we have seen, the child-centred Christmas developed out of children's performances of delight and gratitude during the family celebration, and by the Edwardian period was also embodied in the emergence of children's Christmas concerts in schools. However, children's public performances also highlighted the tensions between encouraging the child to be both spectacle and commodity, and increasing concerns for child welfare which were partially dependent on notions of vulnerable innocence. By the 1880s some philanthropists were concerned that the pantomime and other Christmas theatricals both exploited and sexualised children, especially young girls. The theatre historian Michael Booth argues that the 'female physique, and the feminine domination of fairyland were linked in a sexual, pictorial, and spectacular combination of ideal purity and handsome flesh'.[15] The exploitation and sexualisation of children were brought to public attention by Ellen Barlee's *Pantomime Waifs, or a Plea for our City Children* (1884). Barlee highlights the practice of theatres hiring children between the ages of three and fifteen, 'generally drawn from a very low class, and selected more for beauty and agility than intellectual powers'. The corrupting nature of the theatre on young girls is made clear, as the process of training involves the 'testing [of] their straightness of limb, and here the necessary critical examination they have to undergo would rob any respectable girl of her modesty'. There were also complaints concerning the 'clothing of children [which] was of the scantiest kind, and many were in flesh-coloured tights'. Barlee displayed particular concern for female acrobats, where the 'degradation of such feminine exposure of life and limb' became an 'outrage ... to morality and decency'. Barlee believed that the 'daily contact with sin' hardened young girls to vice, left them vulnerable to men buying them beer and spirits, engendered 'a dissatisfied and discontented mind in matters of every-day life' and provoked 'much competitive jealousy amongst themselves'. The biggest problem, then, was that in adulthood the girls would be 'totally unfitted for any domestic calling', after the 'shipwreck of their innocence and purity'.[16] The implication of denying these young girls the conventional expectations of motherhood and housekeeping was, for Barlee, a slide into prostitution.

Urban sites and spectacles

Beyond pantomime and theatrical productions, many other entertainments and spectacles developed in nineteenth-century towns and cities. In the early decades of the nineteenth century choral societies began performing selections of sacred music immediately before or during the festive season, such as the Derby Choral Society's concert on Christmas Eve 1829. On Boxing Day 1832 the Newcastle and Gateshead Choral Society performed parts of Haydn's *Creation* and selections from Handel's *Messiah*, and by mid-century the latter oratorio had become firmly associated with the Christmas season. The music historian Dave Russell argues that performances of *Messiah* became an important source of profit, and most northern choirs performed it 'virtually every Christmas'. In larger towns it became possible to attend several performances in a week, as chapels, churches and Sunday schools also performed the work.[17] Simon Gunn argues that classical music played an important role in the 'foundation of a public high culture' in the provincial cities of the second half of the nineteenth century, mainly the reserve of the middle and upper classes, with the exception of special events such as the Christmas *Messiah*, which were attended by the 'popular classes'.[18] This created a potential conflict of expectations of conduct at these events. In 1869 the *York Herald* published a letter which complains about the behaviour of the audience during the performance of *Messiah* that Christmas, notably the stamping of feet to the time of the music, loud talking during the performance, and the disturbance caused by 'a large portion of the audience vulgarly disturbing the other portion by leaving their seats before the performance is over'. This correspondent also felt that this behaviour offered a 'heathenish insult' to the Archbishop of York who was present at the performance. This sentiment demonstrates that whilst sacred concerts were a form of entertainment, members of the audience could experience the music in explicitly religious terms, and that the public celebration of Christmas was problematic in that it disrupted the spaces which local elites had striven hard to establish as respectable. The concerts increasingly became a matter of civic pride, but also of commercial responsibility. Another complaint about the Christmas *Messiah* at York focused on the narrow entrance to the festival concert room, where the 'crushing, squeezing, and struggling of both sexes for entrance were equally discreditable to the city and those who let the hall for such entertainments'. 'The time has evidently arrived', the writer continued, 'when the city authorities should take seriously the question of providing a suitable building.'[19]

By the Edwardian period the provincial choral societies had begun a long process of decline as potential participants and audiences were provided with an ever-increasing range of leisure opportunities.[20] Other music concerts remained a part of the leisure opportunities available during the festive season. For example, in Leeds William Spark's organ recitals in the 1870s and 1880s were an important part of that city's Boxing Day culture.[21] In the Victorian period Boxing Day was also promoted as a time to visit attractions. In 1852 *The Times* promoted a number of sites and institutions which might tempt the 'country cousin' or *blasé* Londoner on Boxing Day, including St Paul's Cathedral, the Tower of London, and the Zoological Gardens. Some of the attractions were of a rational and improving nature. The British Museum began opening its doors to visitors on public holidays in 1837, and by 1842 attracted 30,000 visitors on Boxing Day. As the nineteenth century progressed, the British Museum remained open on Boxing Day, though it failed to retain the same level of interest as rival museums and galleries became available. By the 1880s and 1890s, South Kensington Museum usually attracted between 9,000 and 10,000 visitors and the Natural History Museum between 4,000 and 6,000 visitors, and by 1912 all the major museums and galleries welcomed between 1,000 and 3,000 visitors each on Boxing Day.[22]

In the second half of the nineteenth century, the Boxing Day crowds at the London museums and galleries were easily overshadowed by those at the relocated Crystal Palace at Sydenham, its success based on an ability to create 'a gigantic variety entertainment'. On Boxing Day 1862 its entertainments included gymnasts, champion vaulters, stump orators, 'negro' minstrels, clowns, character songs and dances, as well as a pantomime, all situated in an environment of 'fancy-fair stalls, evergreens, banners, illuminations, pictures, and Christmas trees'. The illumination of the lamps at dusk added to the spectacle, as did the appearance of a sixty-five foot Christmas tree, described by *The Times* as the most extensive ever seen. Initially, the Crystal Palace faced competition from the Royal Polytechnic Institution, which combined its mechanical and scientific exhibits with a similarly eclectic mix of Christmas entertainments. However, whilst the Polytechnic attracted crowds of around 5,000 on Boxing Day in the late 1850s, and struggled financially before eventually becoming solely an educational institution, the Crystal Palace quickly drew crowds of around 40,000, rising to over 50,000 in the early 1870s. Though the numbers declined steadily from this point, in the Edwardian period the Crystal Palace was still attracting over 20,000 Boxing Day visitors, and the provision of spectacular variety was still very much evident.[23]

Other entertainments included circuses, typically focusing on equestrian displays but also providing variety. Astley's Amphitheatre was a prominent feature of Boxing Day in London from the 1840s until the 1870s, and in the second half of the nineteenth century circuses were also a part of bank holiday culture in the major provincial cities. The equestrian displays of the circuses are one of the few examples of public entertainment which were not a more elaborate version of activities available in the home. Connections can be made between private theatricals and public theatre; minstrel shows were another popular destination on Boxing Day but were also performed domestically. For example, the Moore and Burgess minstrels performed in London every Christmas season from the mid-1860s until the early twentieth century.[24] Michael Pickering argues that minstrelsy had a flexibility of form that allowed it to be extended 'by the amateur performance of blackface songs, acts and routines in community and domestic milieu'. For example, John Coker Egerton (1829–88), rector of Burwash in Sussex, recorded in his diary of 1880 that a 'nigger' band had performed at his house on Christmas Eve, comprised of local parishioners.[25]

Throughout the nineteenth century there was also a culture of domestic Christmas slide shows, thanks to magic lantern devices. In the first half of the century, William Hone (1780–1842) recalled an instance on Twelfth Night, 1818, when Joshua Leverge called at his house crying 'Gallantee show' and proceeded to show his children images of the prodigal son, Noah's ark, and the judgement on a baker who 'sold short of weight, and was carried to hell in his own basket', whilst Harriet Martineau (1802–76) recalled from her childhood how a magic lantern would be exhibited on Christmas Day and on one or two other occasions in the year, the terror of which caused a bowel-complaint.[26] In the second half of the nineteenth century, magic lanterns continued to be used as entertainment for children both in the home and by philanthropic organisations, and some scenes promoted particular agendas such as temperance. However, as visual spectacle they were quickly surpassed by the panorama and diorama displays which had been developing since the late eighteenth century. Richard Altick argued that panoramas and dioramas were a combination of commerce and high culture, providing a show-business equivalent of the 'romantic literature of art and travel', as well as an opportunity to display the latest news from overseas. When, for example, 'London learned in late November 1827 of Admiral Codrington's destruction of the Turkish and Egyptian fleets at Navarino, the scene designers at both Drury Lane and Covent Garden quickly created appropriate pictures to insert into their Christmas pantomimes'. By the mid-nineteenth century the panorama and diorama shows had become an important part of Boxing Day culture in London and could be seen at venues such as Burford's Panorama, the Colosseum, the Cosmorama and the Egyptian Hall. Altick argued that by the 1860s panorama and diorama shows ceased to be 'a major genre of popular art' in London, though they did not entirely disappear until the Edwardian period. However, companies were able to maintain interest in their displays by touring the provinces. For example, Banvard's panorama of the Mississippi and Missouri rivers was available in London during Christmas 1848, and transferred to Leeds for one week during the Christmas season of 1850.[27]

By the late nineteenth century touring companies such Hamilton's Excursions continued to provide panorama and diorama shows in the provincial cities. The showmen had often used the terms panorama and diorama interchangeably, and by this stage they conjured expectations of 'a slapdash mixture of wide-screen or moving paintings, dissolving views, music and talk'.[28] Further confusion was caused by the introduction of the cinematograph in 1896. Cinematograph pictures were quickly established during the festive season in a variety of contexts. In 1897 there was a cinematograph display at Reynolds's Gallery in Liverpool, and the following year the Zala variety entertainment, largely a troupe of acrobats, included pictures of the recent Sudan campaign at the Public Hall in Ipswich. The same year the women's weekly *Home and Hearth* suggested that the cinematograph was a popular entertainment at children's Christmas parties, and in 1900 it was available at the Crystal Palace and used on Christmas Day by the Spennymoor Methodist New Connexion.[29] In the early twentieth century variety continued to be the order of the day, and the Edwardian panorama shows were a combination of the exotic, foreign, comic, banal and curious. In 1904, one Boxing Day show in York featured scenes of cowboy and Indian life; Canadian, Norwegian and Swiss winter sports; the saving of a shipwrecked crew by lifeboat; battleship scenes from the Russo-Japanese war; an illustrative tour of Italy; and a comic series of scenes concerning a family holiday, amongst many others.[30] A similarly eclectic mix could be found in the early cinematic theatres that appeared throughout England in the late Edwardian years. The temptations of variety were so strong that relatively few films appeared that represented Christmas itself. George Albert Smith's *The Vision of Santa Claus* appeared in 1898, depicting Santa Claus on a snowy housetop before disappearing out of view as he descended down the chimney, and then reappearing in a children's bedroom to fill their stockings. This film lasted for only approximately one minute and was probably not seen much beyond the producer's pleasure garden in Hove.[31] Mark Connelly has uncovered the existence of more Christmas films from this period, including *A Christmas Card* (1906); *The Old Folks' Christmas* (1913); and *The Christmas Strike* (1913), films which used Christmas to reinforce a paternalist vision of class harmony.[32] There were also attempts to bring religious representations of Christmas to the screen, though the film depicting the life of Christ entitled *From Manger to Cross*, shown at the Albert Hall on Christmas Eve 1912, attracted only a small audience.[33]

The triumph of variety entertainment during the festive season suggests the development of a commercial mass culture in which working-class culture, particularly the music hall, played an important role, demonstrating that forms of leisure were disseminated up as well as down the social scale. These processes did not operate completely free from tension, and there were always cultural elites that sought to distance themselves from popular entertainment, whilst some leisure pursuits remained class-specific, particularly public houses. The origins of the music hall lay in the informal amateur sing-song culture of the 'free and easy' which developed in the 1830s into a more formalised and licensed form of concert entertainment. The same period witnessed the rise of the penny gaffs, which featured a mixture of melodrama, singing and dancing but also included pantomime-style material at Christmas.[34] The first proper music halls emerged in the 1850s, and their influence on other forms of seasonal theatrical and spectacular entertainment was frequently acknowledged in the press in the following decades, though sometimes as a vulgar point of comparison designed to highlight a performance of quality. Newspapers and periodicals also increasingly included some halls in their reports on Boxing Day festivities in the cities and towns, and by the 1890s the seasonal performances at the London Pavilion were even reported in *The Times*.[35]

Despite the increasing acceptance of music hall, distinctions were sometimes made. For example, in 1872 the *Daily News* chose to mention only the 'music-hall entertainments of the better class'.[36] Concerns persisted that the halls were a site for the corruption of youth. In 1871 Henry Day published a letter in the *Liverpool Mercury* complaining that he had found the Parthenon Music Hall open on Christmas Day, in the evening, and whilst the hall did not sell alcohol, there 'were youths of both sexes, seeming to be out for the evening, determined to enjoy themselves, and, thinking that intoxication was the height of happiness, were gone in that direction, having … brought bottles of spirits with them', resulting in a 'pandemonium' of catcalls and whistling, obscene language addressed to young women, and violent conflicts.[37] Whilst these scenes were horrifying enough to the 'respectable' classes, the fact that they took place on Christmas Day was potentially a further insult to both religious sensibility and the sanctification of the hearthside celebration of family and childhood. Consequently, many local authorities explicitly refused halls and public houses a licence to open on Christmas Day, and in other locations such as Leeds an informal agreement was made between police and licence holders not to open. However, there is evidence of a more pragmatic attitude developing in the early twentieth century. When it was reported to the Leeds Watch Committee in 1901 that some premises were ignoring the existing informal arrangement with the police an attempt to formalise the licences was defeated on the grounds that it was better to contain the local 'roughs' in licensed premises than to leave them free to cause disturbances elsewhere.[38]

Christmas in the streets

The concern to contain the 'roughs' demonstrates that the Christmas culture of the pubs and halls often spilled over onto the streets, sometimes bringing with it drunkenness and violence, and often song. The tradition of Christmas music being played in the streets dates back to at least the fourteenth century. The waits, as they were known, were small bands of professional musicians employed by corporations to play music for civic ceremonies. During the festive season, the waits became particularly associated with perambulating the streets in the early hours of Christmas morning. The formal connection to the civic authorities was severed, however, by the Municipal Corporations Reform Act of 1835, though in some places, such as Westminster, warrants were issued for authorised waits until at least 1871. In other places, such as York, groups of musicians managed to maintain continuity and tradition until, in the case of the York waits, they were finally disbanded in 1902. There was, however, no shortage of groups of musicians, of varying and often dubious quality, parading the streets in the early hours of Christmas morning. They were regularly condemned in the national and provincial press as a nuisance, and from the 1840s to the 1930s were frequently mocked in the pages of *Punch*, particularly when they made claims for being an authentic survival of a time-immemorial custom. The attack was supported by antiquarians such as William Sandys and Robert Chambers. Sandys claimed that instead of performing traditional music, they generally drew from a repertoire consisting of 'a polka or galope, with some of the latest opera airs'.[39]

In the second half of the nineteenth century, groups of carol singers increasingly performed in the build-up to Christmas and throughout the festive season, and often the terms carol-singing and waits were used interchangeably. Whilst some groups were connected to the Anglican and Nonconformist churches, many churchmen were wary of the practice. For example, in 1892 the vicar of St Saviour's in Leeds comments that 'rough and noisy activities ... are none the better for being joined to carols sung in no devotional spirit'.[40] More specifically, contemporaries dreaded the appearance of bands of unruly youths in the guise of carols singers. In 1872 'a quiet man' left the readers of the *Derby Mercury* in no doubt as to 'what sort of depth Christmas carolling had descended', describing the 'rabble of young ruffians whistling, hooting and shouting' as a 'dozen tom-cats screaming in a nocturnal scrimmage'.[41] Two years later J. Duthie of Preston elaborated on the connection between youth, the practice of late-night carolling and the potential for moral degradation. In an address to 'Ministers, Sunday School teachers and parents, he identified the main participants as Sunday scholars, who were 'encouraged to tramp the streets all night, and use the words of devotion and praise as a means of begging, not for *need* but for *feasting* and *drinking*. Consequently, 'the free companionship of the sexes ...at the age when the passions are ripening' meant that young girls and boys were 'exposed to the strongest influence of vice'. Duthie concluded by asking how many 'poor fallen women and the inmates of prisons and lunatic asylums could date their first downward step to a Christmas Eve street rambling and carol singing'.[42] His comments no doubt exaggerated the dangers but demonstrate how easy it was for some Victorians to link immorality with popular culture, particularly when a corruptible child was involved. More often, commentators were concerned with the destructive capacity of gangs of young males. For example, in 1857 a York resident complains about the 'disgraceful acts which are invariably committed on Christmas morning by a set of young lads', in particular damage to property, and in 1860 a letter appeared in the *Birmingham Daily Post* bemoaning a local New Year custom: '[Y]oung rascals commence disturbing your rest immediately after midnight by fiendish yells of "open the door, and let the New Year in", amusing themselves at the same time by destroying your door; and well for you if any trees or shrubs you possess escape spoliation'.[43]

In the later nineteenth century new spectacles appeared on the streets at Christmas time. Shops and the Christmas crowds of shoppers provided an increasingly elaborate spectacle (discussed in Chapter 7), and a culture of celebrating New Year in England was gradually adapted to the needs of a mass urban culture. Throughout the nineteenth century the New Year was potentially a time for reflection and taking stock. For many evangelicals, particularly Nonconformists, the practice of seeing in the New Year had a spiritual significance akin to repentance, vigil and being prepared for Christ's second coming, and an increasing number of chapels had late-night services on New Year's Eve.[44] The idea of seeing out the old year and welcoming in the new had a broader place in English culture as well. In 1874 the *Liverpool Mercury* described the practice of welcoming the New Year by venturing out to hear church bells at midnight as an old custom in most northern towns, yet in Liverpool the celebration of New Year came to feel distinctly modern. St Peter's Catholic Church became the focal point of gatherings of large crowds on New Year's Eve, and the following year the *Mercury* described the mixed nature of the crowd, which revealed the different strands that came together to make the modern celebration of New Year a reality. There were young gentlemen out for 'rollicking fun', 'singing concert-hall strains and negro melodies'; another group chanted revival hymns, and Scotsmen celebrated hogmanay through a rendition of 'Auld Lang Syne', demonstrating how the presence of the Scottish in England was important in disseminating a secular celebration of the New Year. The biggest group, however, understood New Year in traditional terms, 'waiting stolidly, and many of them seemingly sadly, for the first note of the bells that would ring the death knell of the expiring year – the indication, as one of them expressed it, that another milestone in the journey of life had been passed'. A decade later and the *Liverpool Mercury's* tone had changed significantly. When the clock struck twelve to welcome 1885, 'there was a general scene of congratulations and well wishes for the New Year. The multitude did not, however, confine their expressions of joyful greetings to their friends, but very roughly insisted upon foisting their wishes indiscriminately into the ears of everyone who had come in their way'. According to the *Mercury*, scenes of the 'wildest excitement' featured 'the dregs of society in Liverpool', and the availability of refreshments at every street corner meant that many were 'far advanced in intoxication'. Three years later, amongst the chaos and confusion, the *Mercury* reporter highlighted the matches 'producing coloured lights [which] were thrown into the air in every direction', the 'young women and girls [who] went about in groups with bare heads on with hats and bonnets tipped back', and told how 'here and there a young fellow pounced down on a group of girls and kissed one of them'.[45]

Large crowds were reported in other northern cities during this period, though they were not reported in as much depth as in Liverpool. In the 1880s, gatherings began to take place in London outside St Paul's Cathedral, and in 1890 the *Daily News* declared that the event appeared 'to have become an established function', and estimated that between 5,000 and 6,000 had attended. In 1893 the event garnered further attention through being illustrated by the *Graphic*, and was well publicised by the turmoil that accompanied New Year's Eve. According to the *Birmingham Daily Post*, an 'intensely exciting' scene developed as the large and 'well dressed' crowd, stimulated by 'a considerable indulgence in whisky', faced a co-ordinated attempt by the unemployed of London to seize the steps of the Cathedral and sing 'The Starving Poor of Old England'. The unemployed were defeated by a force of over 300 policemen, the crowd alternately cheering the police and singing 'music-hall ditties', the national anthem, 'Rule Britannia' and 'Auld Lang Syne'. By the turn of the century, the London press was describing these gatherings as 'echoes' of the Scottish New Year celebration, especially as bagpipe music could be heard, though it increasingly had to contend with the sound of hooters and steamers on the Thames blowing their sirens.[46] In the provinces, meanwhile, the celebration of the New Year became even more the preserve of the young in thrall to consumer culture. In York for example, crowds of young people amassed in the chief thoroughfares, singing the popular songs of the year just passed, the *Yorkshire Herald* noting how '"you made me love you" rose from the throats of various youths on the left pavement, and their fellows on the right responded "I didn't want to do it"'.[47]

Christmas balls and parties

Away from the boisterous atmosphere of the Christmas streets, social elites attended balls and parties throughout the festive season. At the beginning of the nineteenth century a well-established culture of Christmas, New Year and Twelfth Night balls took place at the residences of the landed classes as part of the annual calendar of elite sociability. For example, the Duchess of Bedfordshire's Twelfth Night masquerade ball was held at Woburn Abbey in the early 1800s, 'attended by all the beauty and fashion for twenty miles around', as well as all the gentry of the town of Bedford.[48] Entertainments at country houses continued throughout the nineteenth century and beyond. As the previously discussed example of the 2nd Viscount Halifax demonstrates, the aristocracy often held servants' balls which were open to other leading families in the county and allowed aristocrats to forge charitable networks with local business elites, and from the mid-nineteenth century both the landed and business classes would also appear at fund-raising balls held at infirmaries and asylums. Balls were also held in association with military regiments, such as the Twelfth

Night ball of the Fifth Hampshire Engineers, active in Southampton in the 1860s.[49] Whilst the balls of the landed classes were by invitation only, there were an increasing number of events which utilised public spaces and took on a slightly more commercial character. For example, in the 1820s, New Year balls took place at Congdon's Hotel in Exeter and at the Derby Assembly Rooms. By the mid-nineteenth century, festive balls were a fixed part of the calendar or were annual or irregular entertainments in many small and county towns, and though they were often observed to have been 'fashionably attended', even in the 1840s there were problems for the organisers in maintaining the desired social exclusivity. In 1845 the York Assembly Rooms kept the New Year ball 'as a *private assembly*, and we have no doubt that the attendance will not only be large, but highly respectable'.[50]

By the early Victorian period, a fashion had developed amongst the upper middle classes of providing 'juvenile parties' during the festive season. Whilst these gatherings were satirised as 'costly vanities' in the pages of *Punch* throughout the remainder of the century, more immediately the conduct of Christmas parties drew criticism from those of a serious Christian disposition. These objections are exemplified in a letter from 'Laura' to the *British Mothers' Magazine* in 1850. According to Laura, whilst there were practical concerns over exposing younger children 'to the evening air, and by unrestrained indulgence in the tempting feast', the real danger of the parties threatened the elder children. For them, an evening spent dancing and 'acting charades', too much like theatricals if performed publicly, encouraged the manifestation of the 'evils of dissipation': 'The love of display, the passion for the admiration of the other sex, are prematurely excited; and while those who receive flattery and attention are flushed with vanity, feelings of a sadder but not less unwholesome character too often occupy the minds of their less distinguished companions'.[51] These complaints had been common to evangelical middle-class reformers of manners and morals since the eighteenth century, and though the potential dangers were less pronounced and explicit, they have much in common with Duthie's concerns about young people carolling noted earlier. Despite differences in class status, Christmas amusements were important and formative moments determining the boundaries of childhood and the point at which innocence was lost.

'Laura' did not object to Christmas parties for children in principle, and in the second half of the nineteenth century they became a fixture of the festive season, especially as evangelical objections to dancing and performance gradually lessened. Tips for recipes and games to make parties a success were a frequent feature in women's and children's periodicals, as the practice also became a must for the socially aspirant classes. Concerns persisted, however, about what was appropriate for children, and later in the century this intensified as the romanticisation of childhood reached its apogee. Reflecting on Christmas 1868, a sentimental Mrs Punch noted: '[F]ashionable young ladies and fashionable young gentlemen there are of all ages, from four years upwards; but the children – where are all the children gone to?' She continued:

> [S]upposing that Mr. Punch and I were to deck a Christmas tree for them, would they enjoy it, would they care for our sixpenny toys, would they play blind-man's buff, and be content to go home at eight o'clock, after partaking of your mother's home made cakes and goodies? I fear not. I fear they would criticise us, and think us shabby, and declare they would never enter such a dull house again.[52]

A generation later, in a Christmas editorial the *Leeds Mercury* bemoaned the 'growing loss of simplicity in all our social functions':

> Our social life from top to bottom has become artificial … Is it quite beyond the powers of boys and girls to entertain one another? … Nothing will satisfy them now but gloves and collars, programmes and hired bands, unlimited waltzes, and champagne-cup for supper. My young lords' and ladies' carriages must come at midnight or after, like the carriages of grown-up people. Nor does the well-intentioned performance of an amateur – musician, conjurer or reciter – any longer satisfy audiences accustomed to be entertained by professional artists.

With the little children turning 'up their noses at a plum-cake and nursery romps', the innocence of childhood was imperilled, at exactly the time when it was supposed to be celebrated.[53] However, this discourse was undoubtedly exaggerated. In 1898 *Hearth and Home* commented that the 'blasé London child who goes to three or four entertainments every week during the Christmas holidays, misses the ecstasy which is felt by unsophisticated infants when an invitation to a Christmas party arrives … and mother and nurse know not a peaceful moment until the children are dressed and away'.[54]

In the mid-Victorian period, children's Christmas parties were also staged in a civic context. They often took place on Twelfth Night, as the traditional association of that date with cakes led confectioners to promote that date as another occasion in which to indulge children. Inspiration may also have been taken from Queen Victoria's select gatherings at Windsor Castle in the 1840s and 1850s featuring an elaborate 'royal twelfth cake', a custom which was continued by the Prince and Princess of Wales as a 'juvenile party' in the 1860s.[55] In 1867 the *Ladies' Treasury* described Twelfth Night as 'a pleasant festival of happy meetings, rejoicing all the little people's hearts with merriment', and bringing 'a golden harvest to the confectioners'.[56] The 1860s also saw the establishment of a Twelfth Night fete at the Drill Hall in Derby, and in the following decades a 'select audience of juveniles' received cake from the Lord Mayor.[57] Much more elaborate, however, were the Twelfth Night fancy dress balls for children that became a regular event at the Mansion House in London from the 1870s. Lady Mayoresses of London had regularly held fancy dress balls at the Mansion House in the preceding decades, as well as balls for juveniles, but a Twelfth Night ball was not instituted until 1876, when Caroline Cotton organised a pseudonymous ball in which all costumes had to be made from calico. During the same period the other remaining Mansion Houses also organised juvenile parties in the New Year, though the event at Bristol usually took place in mid-January. At the York Mansion House in early January 1873, the Lord Mayor and Lady Mayoress received a party of around 200 children who where entertained by a magic-lantern and quadrille band. At the London event, the guests included the children of the aldermen and members of the Court of Common Council, along with 'distinguished and private friends', and by the late 1890s more than a thousand guests attended, two-thirds of whom were between the ages of six and fourteen. Though the ball featured a wide diversity of entertainers, including the band of the Coldstream Guards, performing dogs, and ventriloquists, reports made it clear that the real spectacle was the children in costume, making it part of the practice of watching children at Christmas time. As the *Daily News* commented in 1886, 'for the most part the grown up folks were too absorbed in the children to watch one another'. Later in 1898, the reporter of the same publication elaborated on why the event was so appropriate to prevailing expectations of children: '"dressing up" comes naturally to childhood; it is one of its chief delights; and perhaps for that reason, children in fancy dress are less self-conspicuous and more charming than men and women of riper years, who fear either that they may seem ridiculous or that they may not appear to advantage'.[58]

The festive mayoral balls for juveniles attempted to instil a sense of civic identity, ritual and tradition in their young guests, and by the Edwardian period this was combined with the modern and commercial practices of Christmas, as is well illustrated by the York balls which, by this time, took place at the Guildhall. In 1907 the Lord Mayor of York took on the role of Santa Claus, entertaining an audience of over 500 children by emerging from a 'wide, old-fashioned fire place' at the Guildhall, wearing a 'civic, crimson gown, which served to identify the wearer with the state and circumstance of the ancient city [and] harmonised thoroughly with the traditional garb of St. Nicholas'. The

Guildhall was promoted to the children as the 'Castle of Santa Claus', with banners declaring that fact: a tree covered in cotton wool to indicate snow, and a Yule log in, and stockings surrounding, the fire place. The Lord Mayor was accompanied by the Sword and Mace Bearers, informed the children that they were gathered in the 'York House of Parliament', and asked them to write a short essay on the civic insignia of the city. After an interval, and the mayor's withdrawal, the back of the chimney gave way, and Santa Claus appeared, followed by the Snow Queen (the mayor's daughter) on a pony-drawn sleigh, and finally two 'polar bears'.[59] This scene was remarkably similar to the Christmas displays in the department stores at the time, whose development will be discussed in Chapter 7.

Conclusion

This survey has only been able to convey a small flavour of the increasingly commercial leisure activities, aimed at the masses for profit, of which people in the nineteenth century partook from Boxing Day until Twelfth Night. It does, however, demonstrate the extent to which a public culture of Christmas existed away from the home, but nonetheless connected to it, although for many people the former domain may have been more important and meaningful than the latter. The connections between the private and public lay in the importance of spectacle and performance, particularly in relation to childhood. Children were increasingly indulged away from home as well as within it, and became a potent spectacle themselves. At the same time, the greater concern for children's welfare heightened an already existing awareness of the influence of entertainment and leisure on the maturation process, which was accentuated at Christmas time.

Notes

1 M. Connelly, *Christmas: a Social History* (London and New York: I. B. Tauris, 1999), p. 45; A. E. Wilson, *Christmas Pantomime: the Story of an English Institution* (London: George Allen and Unwin, 1934), chapter 4 and p. 142; *The Times*, 27 December 1842.

2 *Brighton Patriot and South of England Free Press*, 3 January 1837; *Manchester Times and Gazette*, 31 December 1836.

3 *The Times*, 27 December 1816; 28 December 1830; *Bell's Life in London and Sporting Chronicle*, 25 December 1825.

4 *Morning Chronicle*, 29 December 1824.

5 *The Times*, 29 December 1831.

6 *John Bull*, 23 December 1838.

7 *The Times*, 27 December 1843; 27 December 1845; 28 December 1846; 28 December 1852.

8 Connelly, *Christmas*, p, 46.

9 N. Auerbach, *Private Theatricals: the Lives of the Victorians* (Cambridge, Mass., and London: Harvard University Press, 1990), pp. 13–15.

10 Cited in Wilson, *Christmas Pantomime*, p. 172.

11 *Daily Mail*, 29 December 1904; *The Times*, 27 December 1902.

12 B. Crozier, 'Notions of Childhood in London Theatre, 1880–1905' (PhD dissertation, University of Cambridge, 1981), pp. 204–10; *The Times*, 25 December 1882.

13 Ibid., pp. 213, 228–34; J. P. Wearing, 'Edwardian London west end Christmas entertainments 1900–1914', in J. L. Fisher and S. Watt (eds), *When they weren't doing Shakespeare* (Athens: University of Georgia Press, 1989), p. 236.

14 *The Times*, 25 December 1912.

15 M. R. Booth, *Victorian Spectacular Theatre* (Cambridge: Cambridge University Press, 1991), p. 79.

16 E. Barlee, *Pantomime Waifs, or a Plea for our City Children* (London, 1884), pp. 30–1, 52–4, 58, 72, 77–8, 113; see also C. Steedman, *Strange Dislocations: Childhood and the Idea of Human Interiority 1780–1930* (London: Virago, 1995).

17 D. Russell, *Popular Music in England, 1840–1914*, 2nd edn (Manchester: Manchester University Press, 1997), pp. 192–6, 263.

18 S. Gunn, *The Public Culture of the Victorian Middle Class: Ritual and Authority in the English Industrial City 1840–1914* (Manchester: Manchester University Press, 2000), p. 144.

19 *York Herald*, 24 December 1869; 20 December 1875.

20 Russell, *Popular Music*, pp. 292–8.

21 *Leeds Mercury*, 27 December 1870; 27 December 1880.

22 *The Times*, 27 December 1842; 28 December 1852; 27 December 1912; *Reynold's Newspaper*, 30 December 1888; 29 December 1889; *Lloyd's Weekly Newspaper*, 31 December 1893. The South Kensington Museum was subsequently renamed the Victoria and Albert Museum.

23 R. D. Altick, *The Shows of London* (Cambridge, Mass., and London: Belknap Press, 1978), pp. 388, 485, 504–5; *The Times*, 27 December 1862; 27 December 1872; 27 December 1902.

24 Hugh Cunningham, *Leisure in the Industrial Revolution c.1770–c.1880* (London: Croom Helm, 1980), p. 33; *The Times*, 27 December 1872; 24 December 1901.

25 M. Pickering, 'White skin, black masks: "nigger" minstrelsy in Victorian England', in J. S. Bratton (ed.), *Music Hall: Performance and Style* (Milton Keynes: Open University Press, 1986), p. 78; R. Wells (ed.), *Victorian Village: the Diaries of the Reverend John Croker Egerton, Curate and Rector of Burwash, East Sussex 1857–1888*

(Stroud: Sutton, 1992), p. 257.

26 W. Hone, *Ancient Mysteries Described* (London: J. M'Creery, 1823), pp. 230–1; H. Martineau, *Autobiography* (London: Smith Elder, 1877), vol. 1, pp. 15, 20.

27 Altick, *Shows of London*, pp. 174–5, 180–1, 482; Booth, *Victorian Spectacular Theatre*, pp. 5–7; *Leeds Mercury*, 21 December 1850.

28 Altick, *Shows of London*, pp. 174, 506.

29 *Liverpool Mercury*, 28 December 1897; *Hearth and Home: an Illustrated Weekly Journal for Gentlewomen*, 8 December 1898; *Ipswich Journal*, 31 December 1898; *Leeds Mercury*, 26 December 1900; *Northern Echo*, 29 December 1900.

30 *Yorkshire Herald*, 27 December 1904.

31 F. Gray, 'George Albert Smith's visions and transformations: the films of 1898', in S. Popple and V. Toulmin (eds), *Visual Delights: Essays on the Popular and Projected Image in the Nineteenth Century* (Trowbridge: Flick Books, 2000), pp. 171, 177.

32 Connelly, *Christmas*, pp. 159–62.

33 *The Times*, 25 December 1912.

34 P. Bailey, *Leisure and Class in Victorian England: Rational Recreation and the Contest for Control, 1830–1885* (London: Routledge, 1978), p. 29; Cunningham, *Leisure in the Industrial Revolution*, pp. 166–7.

35 *The Times*, 27 December 1892.

36 *Daily News*, 26 December 1872.

37 *Liverpool Mercury*, 27 December 1871.

38 *Leeds Mercury*, 3 January 1901.

39 J. Merryweather, *York Music: the Story of a City's Music from 1304–1896* (York: Sessions Book Trust, 1988), pp. 7–13, 131, 174–5; J. A. R. Pimlott, *The Englishman's Christmas: a Social History* (Hassocks: Harvester, 1978), p. 142; *Yorkshire Herald*, 8 December 1909.

40 *St. Saviour's Monthly Paper*, December 1892.

41 *Derby Mercury*, 1 January 1873.

42 *Preston Guardian*, 5 December 1874.

43 *York Herald*, 26 December 1857; *Birmingham Daily Post*, 7 December 1860.

44 L. E. Schmidt, *Consumer Rites: the Buying and Selling of American Holidays* (Princeton: Princeton University Press, 1995), pp. 119–21.

45 *Liverpool Mercury*, 1 January 1974; 1 January 1875; 1 January 1885; 2 January 1888.

46 *Lloyd's Weekly Paper*, 1 January 1888; 1 January 1899; *Daily News*, 1 January 1890; *Reynold's Newspaper*, 31 December 1893; *Birmingham Daily Post*, 1 January 1894; *The Times*, 1 January 1903; 1 January 1913.

47 *Yorkshire Herald*, 1 January 1914.

48 *Morning Chronicle*, 10 January 1804; *Derby Mercury*, 12 January 1804.

49 *Hampshire Telegraph and Sussex Chronicle*, 9 January 1867.

50 *Derby Mercury*, 19 December 1827; *Trewman's Exeter Flying Post*, 8 January 1824; *York Herald*, 27 December 1845.

51 *British Mothers' Magazine*, 1 December 1850.

52 *Punch*, 26 December 1868.

53 *Leeds Mercury*, 29 December 1888.

54 *Hearth and Home: an Illustrated Weekly Journal for Gentlewomen*, 8 December 1898.

55 *John Bull*, 8 January 1842; *John Bull and Britannia*, 9 January 1858; *Sporting Gazette*, 9 January 1864.

56 *Ladies' Treasury*, 1 January 1867.

57 *Derby Mercury*, 13 January 1875, 11 January 1882.

58 *York Herald*, 4 January 1873; *Daily News*, 7 January 1876; 7 January 1886; 5 January 1895; 7 January 1898.

59 *Yorkshire Herald*, 5 January 1907.

7

Christmas shopping and advertising

At the heart of the public and commercial culture of Christmas that developed in the nineteenth century lay the experience of Christmas shopping, though like the entertainment industry it was in many ways connected to domestic festivities. This chapter maps the expansion of Christmas consumerism, demonstrating how retailers, manufacturers and advertisers gradually came to exploit the sentiments of the festive season. Whilst it demonstrates several continuities of practice, I emphasise the emergence of a distinctive Christmas shopping culture in the late-Victorian and Edwardian periods. Increasingly elaborate Christmas displays in the shops and the crowds of people who were drawn to them were a feature of this period's modernity. The late Victorians and Edwardians responded with ambivalence to the modernity of new technologies, democratisation and above all mass consumer society, and a combination of excitement and misgiving are evident in the festive shopping culture at the turn of the century.[1]

Christmas fare

The association of Christmas with eating is as old as the festival itself. Pimlott argued that food retained the highest position in the volume of Christmas trade, and highlighted that a trade in turkeys for the London market was already highly organised in the eighteenth century; in 1788 *The Times* noted that 30,000 turkeys had been 'martyred' that season.[2] The turkey was first introduced to England in the mid-sixteenth century, gradually replacing the swan as a feasting food. By the late eighteenth century it had become the fashionable Christmas bird of choice in London, which was supplied by turkey farms in Cambridgeshire and Norfolk and sent to London by stage coach.[3] It had also long been customary for country people to send parcels of turkeys and other produce to friends and relatives in the cities. This custom persisted for much of the nineteenth century. At Christmas 1824 the *Worcester Herald* declared: '[O]ur coaches to London for the last three or four days have been almost exclusively laden with those solid and acceptable remembrances to our metropolitan friends, a profusion of game, the luscious chine, and the choicest cullings of the poultry-yard'; whilst on Christmas Day 1825, Robert Sharp of South Cave wrote to his son William in London: 'we are preparing a Box with Christmas cheer for you'.[4] As tokens of remembrance of the ties of family, kin and friendship, gifts of food were both the material and symbolic heart of the Christmas feast, and were used to celebrate social bonds when family and friends were absent.

In the Victorian period, press coverage of the traffic of Christmas fare indicated both the growth in demand and the sophistication of organisation. In 1840 the *Bury Post* noted that seventy tons of meat and poultry had been sent to London from Bury St Edmunds in a six-day period. The following year turkeys were transported to London from Suffolk by steamer. In the Victorian age, traders had to look further afield for supplies, as the business of Christmas became increasingly globalised. In 1843 turkeys were being supplied from Belgium, France and the Netherlands, and by the 1880s the Christmas supply of meat was being supplemented by companies such as the Australian Frozen Meat Company.[5] By 1896 turkeys were being imported from Germany, Italy and Canada in sufficient quantity to lower their price by up to fifty per cent, making them affordable to a much wider range of people.[6] Pimlott noted that England drew upon 'most of the world' for its Christmas supplies. This was particularly the case in the supply of Christmas fruits and nuts. As luxury items, fruit and nuts were strongly associated with Christmas in the nineteenth century, though, as Michael Winstanley argues, evidence points to the development of a substantial market for fresh produce having developed by the Edwardian period.[7] In 1852 *Chambers's Edinburgh Journal* described the apples, pears, hothouse grapes, pineapples, pomegranates, soft medlars, Kent cob-nuts, filberts and foreign nuts available at Covent Garden market on the Saturday before Christmas Day.[8] By 1898 *The Times's* description of the fruit markets referred to nuts from Turkey; grapes from Belgium, Spain and France; pineapples from the Azores; pears from Canada; tomatoes from France, Italy, Spain and Belgium; chestnuts from Italy, France, and Spain; apples from California and Canada; and bananas from the Canary Islands and Madeira.[9]

Throughout this period, Christmas markets were an important means of distributing poultry and other fare, through they increasingly coexisted with a wider array of shops and shopping practices. Shops played a crucial role in the supply of Christmas provisions, and the descriptions of the poulterers', fruiterers' and grocers' shops in *A Christmas Carol* indicate how far the practice of 'vying' with each other for Christmas trade had developed by the 1840s.[10] Butchers also played an important role in the Christmas trade. In most market towns cattle shows took place a week before Christmas, and butchers would then display the prize carcasses at market and in shops. Displays of Christmas meat were a potent local spectacle, signifying that the Christmas season was close at hand. In 1838 the *Bristol Mercury* declared that if 'there was nothing else to remind to us of the approach of Christmas, we have abundant evidence in the butchers' shops'.[11] Whilst turkeys were mainly the preserve of the higher classes, beef had strong connotations as a national dish, and its provision at Christmas time was invested with the authority of tradition. In 1848 the *Era* reported on the Prize Cattle Bazaar in Lambeth, noting how one proprietor decorated his premised with evergreens, and 'caused a brilliant gas Georgian crown to be illumined upon the occasion', inspiring the neighbourhood 'with spirit at this festive season'. The *Era* continued: 'In a word, he kept up the character of the old English charter. Roast beef in plenty at Christmas appeared to be the theme of his enterprise, for masses of the same were exhibited on large dressers, on the road side, whilst the band was playing the tune of "the roast beef of old England"'. In the following decade, the butchers of York subscribed for a gas banner declaring 'Hurrah! for the roast beef of old England', which was suspended across the Shambles.[12]

The Christmas retail trade was not only concerned with fresh and natural foodstuffs. Along with supplies of dried fruits, an increasingly important part of the grocers' Christmas trade was based upon sales of confectionery. In 1843 Dickens described the way in which 'French plums blushed in modest tartness from their highly-decorated boxes', and in 1852 *Chambers's Edinburgh Journal* noted 'boxes of foreign confections, adorned with admirable specimens of the lithographic art'.[13] By the 1870s, trade magazines such as the *Grocer* were helping to promote branded products. In 1870 this trade publication declared: '[Cadbury's] have shown that we can compete with continental makers in the production of boxes if we try.' Highlighting Cadbury's 'Mexican' chocolate, the journal continued: '[At] Christmas time the demand is always larger than usual for such articles, and this will be a good opportunity for our readers to "push" the Mexican chocolate.' The sending of samples to a trade journal, which in turn recommended it to their readers, was an important indicator that the Christmas trade was becoming more organised and commercial, and it remained a prominent feature of the trade press in the weeks before Christmas for the rest of the period. In 1900 the *Grocers' Journal* recommended the 'very pretty fancy boxes of chocolates' manufactured by Fry's and urged readers to obtain one of Fry's illustrated catalogues, whilst in 1910 it notes that 'there is nothing more readily saleable at Christmas time than a good half-a-crown's worth [of chocolates], and Messrs. Rowntree offer a number of attractive novelties at this price.' The inclusion of gift items with the chocolates, such as 'a jewel casket, in red leatherette, with tray; a photo frame in imitation beaten copper; glove and handkerchief boxes in leatherette', demonstrates how elaborate Christmas marketing had become, though Rowntree's were also producing cheaper lines at a shilling, and as the *Grocers' Journal* comments, 'every class of trade is catered for'.[14]

Christmas crackers and decorations

In the mid-nineteenth century the long-established custom of decorating at Christmas, principally with evergreen materials, began to take on a more commercial aspect. This was partly due to the innovations of Tom Smith and Co., who developed the first Christmas cracker, which became an important part of the ephemeral material culture of the festive season. Tom Smith was a London confectioner who established his own company in Clerkenwell, producing wedding cakes and sweets around 1840. During a trip to Paris in the 1830s he conceived the idea of manufacturing bonbons with lucky mottoes, and initially experimented with putting love notes in the wrapping. According to company legend, Smith was inspired by the cracking sound made by his fire at Christmas, which was incorporated into the design. In 1847 the cracker was patented, though it was not until 1860 that the 'crack' was perfected with the addition of saltpetre. The conventional wisdom of the development of the Christmas cracker has it that the sweet was replaced by a small gift, but whilst small gifts were introduced, confectionery crackers continued to coexist with more elaborate crackers. Christmas crackers were a great commercial success, and Tom Smith and Co. experienced an increasing amount of competition as the nineteenth century progressed. In 1880, for example, the *Grocer* carried an advertisement for over ten different designs produced by Batger and Co.; whilst in the 1890s Tom Smith and Co. sent the following warning to the trade: '[I]t is deemed important to caution the trade against the incalculable injury that is being done by small manufacturers in putting forth monster boxes of gaudy and vulgar crackers lacking appreciable contents.' By the Edwardian period, large department stores such as Gamage's were also producing their own lines of crackers.[15]

The commerciality of late-Victorian and Edwardian Christmas crackers can be demonstrated by the wide range of themes and novelties they contained, as manufacturers sought to capture children's imaginations. Tom Smith and Co. alone offered a bewilderingly wide choice. Some of their crackers represented Christmas themes, such as the 'Father Christmas box of fun' produced in 1881, and others like the 'Twelfth Night cosaques' were designed with nostalgic images of Christmases past on the packaging. However, many crackers represented contemporary interest in foreign cultures and often featured racial stereotyping. 'Nigger's delight' crackers were common, and in 1881 it was possible to buy South African crackers, Russian 'Cossack' crackers, crackers from Japan, and India 'cosaques'. The crackers came in extremely elaborate packaging, and in another product of 1881, 'Parnell's portmanteau', the crackers were 'ornamented with Irish characters, containing grotesque Irish costumes and head dresses, such as Paddy's hat, peasant shawls and aprons trimmed with shamrock leaves … packed in trunk-shaped boxes with a label of Mr Stewart Parnell on his way from Cork to Westminster'. Some crackers represented current affairs or prominent cultural themes, such as the Darwinian crackers, containing miniature monkeys, of 1890; the Chino-Japanese war crackers of 1895; the suffragette crackers of 1908 (which featured an illustration of a suffragette holding a banner saying 'Vote for Tom Smith'); and the general election crackers of 1910. Other crackers captured the excitement of modernity, including the cinematograph crackers, motor car crackers, and the 'marvels of the x rays' crackers produced in 1898. There were also crackers that represented the growing currents of militarism, including the gatling gun repeating crackers of 1895, and 'regulars and volunteers' in 1908. In 1913 Gamage's range of crackers included dreadnought crackers, which came in a box the shape of a battle ship. These elaborate thematic crackers were the preserve of the middle and upper classes, but by the end of the nineteenth century even a purveyor of luxury goods like Tom Smith and Co. were offering many boxes at a retail price of 6d and 9d, indicating an intention to supply the mass market.[16]

From the mid-nineteenth century the evergreen materials used for Christmas decorations received new attention from women's magazines, which promoted a design aesthetic that was partly connected to an interest in the seasonal decoration of church interiors. The supply of evergreen materials, and from the mid-nineteenth century, Christmas trees, was another major feature of the Christmas markets. In 1862, *Once a Week* reported that bundles of holly and mistletoe were being sold at Covent Garden, Farringdon and other vegetable markets in London, a process carried out by regular traders and irregular costermongers. At the beginning of December, between six and seven hundred men and boys, mainly from the St Giles and Seven Dials areas of London, gathered evergreens from the countryside surrounding London, though some were gathered illegally from suburban gardens. Later, in 1896, the *Daily Mail* reported that just one Covent Garden wholesale firm alone distributed £12,000's worth of holly and mistletoe to its customers.[17]

In additional to the large trade in evergreens, an increasing number of artificial decorations became available in the second half of the nineteenth century. The popularity of the Christmas tree in the 1850s quickly established a market for tree ornaments, with one of the earliest advertisements for them appearing in 1853.[18] In the following decades firms like Tom Smith and Co. developed their own lines in Christmas decorations. In 1875 they offered gelatine wreaths, coloured sprays and festoons, and banners and flags bearing mottoes such as 'Compliments of the season'. By 1909 Tom Smith and Co. sold tissue-paper decorations, including bells and garlands. Ronald Hutton suggests that commercially produced paper hangings had become commercially available in the 1880s in urban areas, and being convenient and reusable, spread to country areas and down the social scale. The prohibitive cost of decorations in some instances did not necessarily mean that poorer households were not decorated. As Weightman and Humphries demonstrate, the rural poor might be able to collect evergreen materials locally, whilst in urban areas home-made paper chains, stuck together with flour paste were common in working-class homes from the 1850s onwards. Evidence of this can be found in the memoir of John Blake (born 1899), who recalled: 'Mum made up some paper chains, with a festive bell hanging in the middle, and had them stretched across the top of the room from wall to wall.'[19]

From New Year gifts to Christmas presents

Before the nineteenth century seasonal gift giving was a common occurrence at New Year. In the Tudor and Stuart period the New Year gift was 'a vital symbol of relationships at the heart of the body politic' and also existed throughout society, though political gifts were dying out by the eighteenth century. Advertisements in eighteenth-century newspapers and periodicals indicates that New Year gifts were also being given to children, primarily for educational purposes, and Pimlott noted that many gifts 'probably usually took the form of produce and home-made articles'.[20] In the nineteenth century there was, according to Pimlott, 'transference' in the practice of seasonal giving from New Year to Christmas, which was 'essential to the establishment of present-giving on its modern scale'.[21]

This change in seasonal gift customs placed increasing importance on benevolence towards family members, especially children, and contributed toward the gradual development of a mass market for Christmas presents. However, there were also continuities between New Year and Christmas gift customs, particularly in the role played by gift books. For the sixteenth century, Edwin Haviland Miller identified the custom of authors presenting gift books to patrons on New Year's Day, and the practice of giving highly personalised and decorated books that were blank inside continued for a considerable time after this. By the eighteenth century, however, books were becoming more commercially available, and special children's books were offered for sale during the Christmas and New Year period, as well as 'pocket books, pocket ledgers, diaries and almanacks'.[22] However, it was advances in printing technology in the nineteenth century which allowed an increasingly literate population to obtain a much wider range of books at an affordable price, and these came to be heavily marketed at the Christmas season, particularly by London and Edinburgh publishing firms which advertised in the national and provincial presses.[23] Books remained an important part of the Christmas trade throughout the period, and reviews of Christmas books were a prominent feature in the pages of national and provincial newspapers throughout December. Simon Eliot demonstrates that the Christmas publishing season, from October to December, became the largest book publication period of the year in the 1840s, and 'the size and importance of the Christmas season grew dramatically in the period from 1850 to 1890'.[24] An important part of this trade was the Christmas annual, aimed at children. Though festive publications aimed at children had existed since the eighteenth century, emphasis has been placed upon the importance of *The Christmas Box; an Annual Present for Children*, published in 1828, as heralding the beginning of the Christmas annual. Edited by Thomas Crofton Croker, the *Christmas Box* contained items of history and poetry, including contributions from Sir Walter Scott and Maria Edgeworth.[25] Following this, hundreds of Christmas annual titles appeared throughout the nineteenth century, including *Ainsley's Christmas Annual*, which ran from 1875 to 1890; and *Pears' Christmas Annual*, running from 1891 to 1903. Added to the contents of the *Christmas Box* were stories, indoor games and puzzles.

The Christmas annuals were also an important influence on another nineteenth-century publishing phenomenon, the magazine and newspaper Christmas number. Pimlott highlighted the role *Punch* played in producing a special Christmas number, and writing in the 1890s, Arthur Pask believed that the form of the Christmas number had been perfected in 1855 when the *Illustrated London News* published its Christmas number with coloured pictures.[26] Though much of the content followed the form of the Christmas annuals, it did not have to be specifically festive. For the illustrated newspapers, stories and colour prints were the main selling points. In 1895 the editor of the *Graphic* mused that 'perhaps the *Graphic* was the first to depart from the usual line of roast beef and plum pudding' when it featured in its Christmas number 'a complete story, by Anthony Trollope, of Australian bush life, illustrated by Luke Fildes'. The importance of the Christmas number can be illustrated by the fact that the *Graphic* paid over £1,000 for a single story, and a similar amount for a picture. Similarly, by 1887, the editor of the *Lady's Pictorial* noted: 'I thought the public had had enough of Santa Claus, children and dogs ... and ours being a woman's paper, I determined to experiment with a picture of a pretty woman'. The first product of this experiment was 'Sweet Seventeen' by Corcos, resulting in sales of 80,000 copies.[27] This allowed the national illustrated papers to distinguish themselves from the standard Christmas material being presented by the provincial newspapers. In 1892, for example, the *Yorkshire Herald's* Christmas number contained a 'thrilling Christmas story' entitled 'That Terrible Christmas Eve' by Lucy Hardy; legends and anecdotes of Christmas; Christmas riddles; a 'Christmas column for the young'; Christmas poems; and 'Yuletide lore'.[28]

One of the most distinct trends in the growth of present-giving in the nineteenth century was the increase in importance of gifts for children. This has been linked to the expanding role the nursery played in Victorian and Edwardian middle-class life, which significantly developed the market for toys.[29] Kenneth Brown argues that toy distributors were quick to recognise the commercial potential of Christmas, and he highlights the prominent role that Germans played in the trade, since they 'were instrumental in organising Christmas trade fairs and their influence was equally apparent in the arcades and bazaars'.[30] Advertisements for toys as Christmas presents first appeared in the 1850s, and in 1856 Nathaniel Hawthorne noted that the London toy shops were amongst those showing 'some tokens of approaching Christmas', whilst the Lowther Arcade in the capital became a major destination for toy shopping.[31] From the 1870s the link between toys and Christmas was strengthened by the new department stores. Lewis's Bon Marché in Liverpool introduced its first Christmas 'fairyland' in the 1870s, and when in 1887 Whiteley's was gutted by fire, it reopened with a toy section in 1888, making sales worth £12,000. After a successful Christmas season selling toys in 1901, Cockaynes of Sheffield tried to sell toys all year round, but quickly abandoned the experiment.[32] In the Edwardian period the demand for toys also led to the creation of the giant toy emporium, notably Hamley's (then located in Oxford Street), and Gamage's of Holborn.[33]

A large number of toys were available at Christmas by the Edwardian period. Amongst the toys being offered by Gamage's at Christmas 1913 were toy trains and accessories; electrical novelties; wireless stations; chemistry sets; model boats, aeroplanes and cars; kites; mechanical toys; cowboy and Indian outfits; 'harmless guns, pistols, swords, bows and arrows'; drums and other toy musical instruments; garden games; balls; board games; bricks and cubes; constructional toys; stuffed toys; dolls, dolls' houses, prams and tea sets; and jokes.[34] Of particular popularity in the Edwardian period were toy soldiers and martial themes, part of the growing militarism of British society in this period. This militarism was linked to patriotism, which Mark Connelly demonstrates was also manifested in desire for the toy to be home-made, with *The Times* commenting in 1911 that British-made toys were 'to be preferred to German and American importations'.[35] There is also evidence to suggest that boys caught some of this patriotic fervour. In his autobiography Cyril Beaumont (1891– 1976) recorded: '[O]f all the various kinds of presents that I received during the birthdays and Christmases of my childhood I can recall none that afforded me greater delight than a box of toy soldiers, especially of Britain's make.'[36]

Weightman and Humphries highlight the 'craze toys' that were being marketed at Christmas from the 1880s, and in 1911 *The Times* commented that it was 'a pity that cat-faced dolls and missing links, and other more objectionable monstrosities [we]re now appearing in the big toy bazaars'.[37] In 1913 the *Lady's Pictorial* went further:

> Baby ... does not choose for himself. Mothers, fathers, aunties, and god-parents make choice for him, and these are all influenced consciously or unconsciously, by Futurists, Cubists, artists with pencils that run wild and imaginations that are still wilder. They are the humour of pantomime phenomena, of beasts that suggest nightmares and creatures which out-rival in grotesqueness the gargoyles to be seen upon cathedral fronts, on ancient church towers and choir stalls. It is to satisfy their own sense of humour and their own modern craze for the eccentric that grown-ups buy these 'hideosities' for little folks.[38]

Whilst this reaction to the 'modern' suggests a tension between the cultural manifestations of modernity and the haven of the home that Christmas symbolised and idealised, others were excited by the possibilities of modern consumer culture. R. G. Studd (born 1889) commented: 'Our Christmas holidays were unorthodox. In the early years of the century they were the most up-to-date of Christmases, as modern as the miraculous animated pictures which were a feature of them.'[39]

The large number of toys given away by middle-class children to the Christmas charities who supplied the poor were discussed in Chapter 5, but charity was the not the only means for working-class children to obtain toys. Children's presents were available from penny bazaars and street traders who congregated in urban centres in the week before Christmas.[40] In 1911 *The Times* declared that it was 'astonishing what a penny w[ould] buy in some of the toy shops in the poorer districts', describing, for example, 'a muslin "Christmas stocking" which contained a cracker, a small but soul-stirring trumpet, a tin oystershell, a wooden whistle..., a wooden beat, a paper cap, an assortment of sweets, and a match-box out of which a small mouse popped when it was opened'. John Bennett (born 1902), recalling his childhood in Walworth, noted receiving 'a cheap shop-purchased Christmas stocking'. *The Times* also noted that in the 'mean streets' reasonably elaborate toys could be purchased for a halfpenny or a farthing. These items were not directly profitable to small shopkeepers but instead provided an increase in the 'ordinary business'. Displays of cheap toys also attracted the attention of poor children who gazed longingly but could afford nothing.[41] Not all working-class children were so unfortunate, however. Kenneth Brown shows how many working-class families in the period 1850–1914 made a special effort to obtain toys for their children at Christmas. Recalling her Edwardian childhood in London, Grace Foakes noted that her father obtained dolls for her and her sister on Petticoat Lane for the cost of 1s 11d.[42]

In 1887 the *Drapers' Record* declared that the stocking of toys was the first stage of a 'novel fashion', in which 'fancy articles, foreign to the regular ones kept in stock by drapers ... [we]re sold under the name of "Christmas goods"', and argued that retailers recognised the power of Christmas sentiments to overcome 'a dull season of the year when the regular trade is flat'. Display practices included removing regular items from the shop windows and replacing them with fancy goods, and also displaying those goods on tables in the middle of the shop. Such displays would 'cause considerable attraction to the passers-by, and purchasers of the nic-nacs when once in a shop [we]re ... often induced to buy other things'. These retail practices were not uniformly adopted, however, and could cause tension with other shopkeepers who felt that tradesmen 'ought to confine themselves to their own line'. The *Drapers' Record* also noted regional differences in this practice, commenting that it was 'not a new feature with many of the large concerns in the North of England, Scotland and Ireland'. Following on from toys, the *Drapers' Record* stated that 'pretty articles' such as accessories of the 'toilet table' and fancy boxes of haberdashery were being presented in this way, as well as 'art-pottery and Wedgwood' and 'articles of ladies' dress in the form of ties, neckerchiefs, handkerchiefs, and scarves'. The latter of these gift items receive particular praise from the *Drapers' Record* for their usefulness, revealing an awareness of the importance of Christmas gift relationships, where items 'remain in some instances as lasting souvenirs of the good will that has prompted the donors, and on which account ought to claim precedence over those "good things" that are provided for the table at this annual festival', signalling a shift from food to gifts as the heart of the emotional experience of Christmas.[43]

Despite the expansion of the consumer opportunities related to Christmas in the late nineteenth century, some retailers benefited more than others. In 1896 the *Daily Mail* reported that furniture dealers were complaining of 'an almost utter stagnation of trade', and similar complaints were heard from tailors and dressmakers, though the latter did receive an increase in orders for evening dresses.[44] A decade later this situation was remedied by development of ready-to-wear lines. As part of the trend 'in many departments other than those chiefly concerned to get something "Christmassy" to show and talk about', the *Drapers' Record* reported that ready-to-wear items were being exhibited for Christmas around the beginning of December – a practice that 'was quite new two or three years ago'.[45]

By the Edwardian period there were very few consumer goods which were not marketed as Christmas presents. The press played an important role in this process, as elaborate guides to shops and goods became the norm in December issues of national and provincial newspapers. In 1893, for example, the *Lady's Pictorial* featured a 37-page guide to potential Christmas presents available in London's West End; whilst an eight-page 'Christmas Presents Supplement' covered similar territory in the *Daily Mail* in 1904, demonstrating collaboration between retail firms and newspapers, as the guides were interspersed with formal advertisements.[46] Provincial newspapers also introduced this feature to review the Christmas shopping opportunities in their own localities. In 1900 the *Yorkshire Herald* introduced a Christmas review of the shops in York, featuring the chief attractions of thirty-nine retail outlets. A wide range of goods was covered, including furniture, drapery and hosiery, millinery, toys, books, musical instruments, wines and spirits, and chemists' products. Modern devices such as the gramophone were contrasted with more traditional products of the grocery and 'fancy goods' genres.[47]

The increased range and volume of Christmas presents being purchased at the beginning of the twentieth century demonstrates a corresponding growth in the number of Christmas-present relationships between family, kin and friends. An important factor in widening the scope of Christmas presents was the popularity of the Christmas card after 1870. As was noted in Chapter 2, Christmas cards encompassed a wide range of subject matter and simplified the process of sending written Christmas greetings that had become common in the eighteenth century, while also allowing correspondents to contact a wider circle of people. Pimlott argued that the Christmas card 'provided a release for emotions which were normally inhibited. It also served as a vehicle for often unconscious self-expression'.[48] In 1883 *The Times* declared that the Christmas card 'fulfil[led] a high end' in the process of conveying Christmas wishes, which was 'a happy means of ending strifes, cementing broken friendships and strengthening family and neighbourly ties'. Not everyone agreed, however. In 1877, one resident of Bristol writes to complain that in the sending of Christmas cards, people are bringing 'up from the depths of their inner consciousness the names of people they know little, and for whom they care less ... in order to swell out the total number they may despatch as forming a ground of boasting'; whilst the number received were being 'recounted with a zest and pride'. This Bristol resident concludes that when 'Mary Ann the maid can boast of as many Christmas cards as her mistress or the young ladies, it will soon go out of favour.'[49] Whilst the Christmas card did not, of course, go out of fashion, a belief that it would persisted for the rest of the period. The Bristol residents' comments revealed that snobbery could be a factor in the consumption of Christmas cards, and Pimlott highlighted how they became less popular in high society in 1880s and 1890s as production shifted to the needs of the mass market.[50] By this point Christmas cards became available in a wide range of shops. In 1881 the *York Herald* reported: '[N]ever before was there such an abundance of Christmas cards exhibited in the shop windows. Formerly those presents were only to be had of the booksellers, but so prevalent has the custom become of purchasing these artistic productions that nearly every draper and dealer in ornamental and fancy goods has a large and conspicuous display of them'.[51] New ways to commercially exploit the Christmas card were also found. In 1882, Chapman's Christmas Bazaar in York was offering free Christmas cards with purchases above 6d, whilst in 1884 Walter Henry Bacon's Kensington Fine Art Distribution used a coupon in his advertisements with which customers could obtain free cards.[52]

The ease with which Christmas cards could be sent in the mail may also have encouraged the sending of packages, which was made more convenient by the introduction of the parcel post in 1883, and the subsequent reduction of the parcel rate from 1s for seven pounds to 11d for eleven pounds in 1900.[53] The expansion of Christmas shopping was also aided by the growth of mail order facilities. Alison Adburgham has shown how important mail order was to department stores such as Marshall and Snelgrove by the 1880s, and further expansion came with the utilisation of the telephone in the 1890s. By the Edwardian period most of the large West End stores in London were producing extensive Christmas catalogues that were sent out to customers as early as October.[54] Mail-order shopping at Christmas may have also received a boost from the weather conditions in Edwardian London. In the week before Christmas in 1904, an 'unprecedented fog' deterred many people from making a pre-Christmas shopping trip to London, leading to what the *Daily Mail* called a 'disastrous effect on trade'. A by-product of this situation was a large increase in the mail order business. Whiteley's were receiving nearly 1,000 orders a day by telephone, for which purpose eight full-time staff were engaged, whilst 11,000 letters were received a day, where forty staff were employed to open them.[55] The mail-order catalogues featured the whole range of items available in store, and in 1913 Gamage's Christmas catalogue was 470 pages long.[56] These catalogues undoubtedly contributed to the lengthening of the Christmas shopping season, and also encouraged children's aspirations to more elaborate and expensive gifts. For example, John Scupham of Market Rasen in Lincolnshire, who grew up in the 1900s, recalled poring over the Gamage's catalogue and conjuring up 'romantic visions of huge model yachts, train sets that would fill our biggest room, and resplendent regiments equipped with canon which could fire rubber shells', adding also: 'I generally got what I wanted for Christmas; I had about two or three pounds to spend on things in the catalogue, and the order would go in around late November'.[57] This narrative signals a developing tension between the forces of consumerism and the sentiments of the family Christmas, a relationship that for the most part had been complementary. Christmas was meant to promote family unity, not foster selfish individualism through consumer desire. Though desire and individualism were inherent in the romantic spirit which contributed to the middle-class ideal of childhood which developed in the nineteenth century, it also sat uneasily with the notion innocence which contemporaries sought in children both as an innate quality and as the foundation of a healthy adulthood.

The growth of a Christmas shopping culture

Descriptions from the 1840s and 1850s of shops during the Christmas season imply, particularly in the case of purveyors of foodstuffs, that retailers were already aware of the need to create spectacle through special Christmas displays. Often this involved the use of evergreens, and light also played an important role in the creation of spectacle. The illumination of the shops at Christmas was a regular feature of press reports from the 1850s, and in 1882 the *York Herald* declared: 'Last night in a blaze of light, the shop windows of the butchers, poultry dealers, grocers, confectioners, drapers, and booksellers in this city were brilliant in their displays of those commodities which combine to make "merry" the Christmas festival.'[58] In 1900 the *Grocers' Journal* elaborated on the importance of lighting: '[T]he shops themselves should be kept brilliantly lighted; this is particularly necessary when gloom and fog outside have so depressing an effect. To get people outside the shop is halfway to success.' By the Edwardian period shopkeepers were able to draw upon a range of products to boost Christmas displays. In 1910, for example, J. Watson Ltd were offering a free working model aeroplane to grocers in return for them stocking a range of Indian and Ceylon teas: 'Bringing Tea direct from the PLANTATION will make your Xmas Display the TALK of the TOWN and greatly increase your XMAS TAKINGS'. In 1913 the firm of Dudley & Co. were advertising in the *Drapers' Record*, offering retailers 'over 100 of the most novel and attractive "Xmas Present" window tickets and window posters ever produced', and 'everything necessary for the embellishment of your Xmas window [to] make it redolent of the festive season'.[59]

The growth of a Christmas shopping culture also depended upon making shops a comfortable environment to be in, and historians have rightly highlighted the role played by the department stores that developed in the second half of the nineteenth century. By the 1870s and 1880s shopping in the West End of London had become a safe and pleasurable experience for women, and also a means for them to gain access to public space. Consequently, the West End became the focus of press representations of Christmas shopping in the late nineteenth and early twentieth centuries, though the culture was replicated on a smaller scale throughout England. Chris Hosgood demonstrates how female shoppers were portrayed in the press as cunning and duplicitous, particularly during the January sales period that developed as a response to the problems of remaindered stock after the Christmas period. During the Christmas shopping season, however, Hosgood found that female shoppers were portrayed as selflessly promoting the happiness of their families.[60] This is ably demonstrated by an article that appeared in the *Daily Mail* in 1904. It attempted to construe the motivations behind the 'women of every age and of every degree staring at the glittering windows'. Normally, according to the *Mail*, these women are thinking 'of themselves alone; others perhaps of the youths on whom they have set their hearts; others, very surely of the husbands whose waning admiration they would pitifully strive to keep by the frail tie of frill and ribbon. The lonely woman is there, the gentle old soul is there, the soft-eyed girl is there, the managing mother is there, and each heart brings a different hunger to the gay windows.' At Christmas, by contrast, 'there is greater unanimity of expression ... and Christmas shopping makes the whole world of women kin. Everybody today seems to be buying things for somebody else; the expression of the bargain hunter is swept away, and an unselfish joy sits in the eyes of the shoppers.'[61]

At the same time that female Christmas shoppers were constructed as virtuous, male Christmas shoppers were either ridiculed, or removed from the domain of fashionable consumption altogether.[62] In 1880, for example, the Christmas number of the *Penny Illustrated Newspaper* featured a present-laden father, entering his home, welcomed by wife and children. By 1907 the *Sphere* had placed the mother in this central position. Those men who did go Christmas shopping were portrayed as bungling incompetents. In 1888 the *Lady's Pictorial* featured a cartoon in which a man purchases a walking stick for his wife, has a series of mishaps on the way home, and is greeted by an indignant wife who complains that the item is out of fashion and comments on man's 'stupidity'. This attitude was still apparent in 1912 when the *Lady's Pictorial* declared that men 'sally forth out in the hope that they will find something, with the result that they rarely buy satisfactorily'.[63] With the home and Christmas perceived as feminine worlds, shopping was seen as an extension of the domestic Christmas, and this attitude to male participation within it clearly reflects the masculine ambiguity towards domesticity reflected in what John Tosh has identified as the 'flight from domesticity'.[64] Hosgood uses the spirit of inversion associated with Christmas and forms of carnival to explain these representations of male and female Christmas shoppers in late-Victorian and Edwardian England. Christmas shopping represented a temporary release from the norms of patriarchal authority, transferring authority to the wife and mother, before stripping her of symbolic authority when the January sales arrived.[65] Whilst the spirit of inversion is undoubtedly an important strand in the culture of Christmas, its importance may have been exaggerated, particularly in terms of overstating the cultural currency of pantomime in society at large. Despite this, Christmas shopping may have been one of a whole range of activities in which subtle tensions of household authority were played out between husband and wife.

In the late nineteenth century children were encouraged to participate in the Christmas shopping culture. Bill Lancaster attributes the first Santa's Grotto to J. R. Robert's store in Stratford, London, in December 1888, when it was reported that 17,000 children visited Santa Claus.[66] The creation of shopping arenas for children at Christmas spread rapidly in the 1890s and 1900s, aiding the quick assimilation of Santa Claus and associated festive rituals into society. Children's shopping areas comprised elaborately designed in-store displays, often called 'Christmas bazaars', though this term had much wider connotations. Michael Moss and Alison Turton argue that it Walter Wilson's Colosseum in Glasgow that pioneered the first department-store style Christmas bazaar in the mid-1880s.[67] The department stores reified the discursive domain of fairyland that was already well established as a site for the fostering of childhood innocence and imagination. At one Leeds department store in 1905, a scene featured a snow-covered old English village at Christmas, suddenly interrupted by the appearance of Father Christmas in a motor car. At Peter Robinson's, in London's Oxford Street in 1913, in what the *Lady's Pictorial* termed the 'children's dreamland realised', the spectacle began with a miniature recreation of Hendon Aerodrome, where airships delivered presents. This was followed by the 'children's dream train', which children boarded for the cost of sixpence per ticket, or one shilling first class, to be taken 'off on a tour through an enchanted land, and round a great golden Spanish galleon laden with treasures. A stop [wa]s eventually made at a castle door, which opening, disclose[d] none other than Father Christmas himself'. By this stage Christmas Bazaars had become so intrinsically associated with children that the *Lady's Pictorial* reported that 'objection was recently taken to grown-ups frequenting the Christmas Bazaars'.[68]

These displays drew children into a shopping culture. Reporting on the 'crowds of enraptured children' at the Christmas shops, the *Daily Mail* notes that 'children are beginning to flock to the great centres, with their mothers and aunts and governesses and nurses, with money in their purses and joy in their hearts'. The *Daily Mail* also comments: '[T]hey are mostly the smaller children who go shopping now; their elder brothers and sisters will come later, when examinations and breaking-ups are over.' In 1903 the breaking up of school prompted the *Daily Telegraph* to report that Monday 22 December had been the 'children's day' at the shops where whole windows that the previous week had been 'given up to furs, dressing-cases, costly items in silver, and so forth were now filled with pretty, inexpensive wares that would appeal to more juvenile tastes and purses'.[69] Despite receiving gifts themselves from store-employed Santa Clauses, the implication is that middle- and upper-class children were buying for other people, and further represented the expansion of Christmas gift relationships.

The culture of Christmas perpetuated by the shops in late-Victorian and Edwardian England inevitably spilled over into the streets. Weightman and Humphries emphasise how the lavish displays of the Christmas shops highlighted the gap between rich and poor and caused resentment amongst poorer children.[70] There is evidence to show how children were drawn to these displays of spectacle and consumption. In 1906 one York resident complained about the appearance of a store Santa Claus: 'Almost before school closing, the pavement is made impassable by a small army of children, struggling to obtain a favourable position against the appearance of "Santa", and totally oblivious to the appeals of a burly but good-natured policeman'. This correspondent made clear that this Santa Claus was handing out goods free of charge and made the point that 'barely one word of thanks or gratitude was accorded to the donor'. This was attributed to free school board education, which the York resident blamed for a decline in good conduct and respect for authority.[71] There was also a more general concern about the crowds generated by Christmas shopping. In 1909 the police were called to Swan and Edgar in London because the crowds at the corner of Great Marlborough Street and Regent Street had entirely blocked the roads and brought traffic to a standstill.[72] In 1913 *The Times* complained: '[E]very year at this season the streets of London grow more tumultuously crowded, and the mere physical difficulty of making one's way through the throng to do one's Christmas shopping becomes greater.' This was a situation which, according to *The Times*, threatened the message of universal goodwill associated with the festival:

> even the mortality caused by motor-omnibuses is not ultimately as socially destructive as the moral degradation of our chaotic pavements, with the loss of self-respect, the fraying of the temper, and, above all, the dislike of one's fellow-beings which they engender. Even at the season of peace and goodwill he must be a democrat indeed who can feel any real affection for his fellow-citizens in the mass after an hour amid the hurly-burly of the streets.

Images of crowds were one of the defining features of the perception of modernity in late-Victorian and Edwardian England. It is important, however, not to overemphasise the ways in which modernity created tensions at Christmas.

Running parallel with these complaints was an excitement about the crowds of Christmas shoppers. In 1908 the *Daily Mail* described the 'Christmas crowd' as 'the crowd that enjoys itself'; whilst in 1910 the *Lady's Pictorial* commented on how women were 'not likely to abate one jot or tittle of the exquisite delight of Christmas shopping', where there would be 'just the same exciting and excited crowds in the shops'. After suggesting in 1913 that travelling would become more difficult because of the Christmas crowds, the *Lady's Pictorial* noted: 'the fun has begun'.[73]

Advertising in the press

Advertisements for gifts for the Christmas and New Year season have appeared in newspapers and periodicals since the eighteenth century. In 1728 an advertisement for 'Famous Anodyne Necklaces' appeared in the *Country Journal*; an item aimed at children described as 'very proper for a present at Christmas or for a New Year's gift'. Pimlott commented on the 'bias towards the improvement rather than the entertainment of the young' in these items, a factor also apparent in advertisements for children's books, such as the edition of *Aesop's Fables* published in 1739, described as 'a very proper New-Year's Gift to the Youth of both sexes'.[74] These advertisements remained sporadic and limited to a small range of products well into the nineteenth century. This can partially be attributed to the way in which advertising was perceived in the first half of the nineteenth century, since in the minds of middle-class readers it was associated with fraudulent and false claims, particularly in the case of patent medicines.[75] However, it was patent medicines, and other associated items such as beauty products, that offered the most innovative advertising. In 1825 an advertisement for Rowland's macassar oil suggested: 'Congratulations at this festive season are – a merry Christmas, and a happy New Year; and every auxiliary is eagerly sought after for the embellishment of the person'. The exploitation of the sentiments of Christmas in advertising became more explicit in the early Victorian period. In 1840 the same manufacturer offered a range of toilet articles in the following terms: 'CHRISTMAS SOUVENIR. At a period when the social sympathies are most prominent, and the genial influence of "HOME" is felt in the highest degree … the most appropriate present becomes the first subject of consideration'; and in 1846 Rowlands declared: '[The] present season is hallowed by one of the most delightful offices of friendship and affection; the interchange of gifts as remembrances of the donors, and tokens of their esteem for the receivers.'[76]

Christmas sentiments were also used to sell patent medicines. In 1857 Mr Page Woodcock of Lincoln advertised wind pills as a Christmas gift, reminding readers that 'the memories which each returning Christmas festival awakens within us, are dear to each of our hearts, and indelibly engraved there'; though a more pragmatic advert appeared on Boxing Day, offering the product as a cure for the 'Christmas Ghost', indigestion, suffered by those who 'indulge too freely in the good things so bountifully spread forth'. Patent medicines also seized upon the imagery of Christmas when illustrated Christmas advertisements became common in the Edwardian period. In 1904 a Beecham's pills advertisement featured Father Christmas with a Christmas pudding, turkey and goose, advising a 'healthy Christmas' with the verse

> Old Christmas comes, and in his train
> Come turkey, pudding, goose – and pain!
> Which last folks dodge, e'er it can reach 'em
> By turning in good time to Beecham.

In 1906 Coleman's used an image of Santa Claus for their Wincarnis product for relief from influenza.[77]

In the early nineteenth century advertisements began to appear that emphasised the range of Christmas goods available at a single retailer's. At this point retailers and wholesalers used standard advertising techniques which attempted to secure a regular clientele and emphasised the respectability of the enterprise. In 1818 for example, Edward Loder of Woodbridge in Suffolk advertises 'foreign fruit for Christmas', returning 'sincere thanks to his friends and the public for past favours, and begs leave to inform them that he has now on sale for the present season' a range of fruit, nuts, sweets, spices and beverages. Two years later Dunnett's Toy and Tunbridge Ware Repository in London's Cheapside offered foreign and English toys and various 'fancy articles' as Christmas presents, qualified by the statement that the 'nobility and gentry [we]re respectfully informed'. As the nineteenth century progressed, these statements gradually disappeared from textual advertisements, though in the early Victorian period, shopkeepers still needed to reassure potential customers. In 1839, John Brown and Sons of Newcastle offered a range of Christmas presents, including magic lanterns, ladies' dressing cases and work boxes, and a 'variety of useful and ornamental goods', advising that parties were 'respectfully invited to visit show rooms, whether as purchasers or not'.[78] After 1840 there was a steady growth in the number of Christmas advertisements appearing in the press. A wide range of items came to be advertised, including fancy goods, food and drink, books, toys, clothes, stationery, sheet music, and Christmas cards and decorations. The expansion of Christmas advertising by local retailers has been demonstrated by Beverley Ann Tudor's study of the Leicester press between 1855 and 1871. Tudor found that advertisements for food and drink were especially prominent at Christmas, and that some grocers only placed advertisements for the festive season.[79] As a broader trend, festive advertising became more focused on the build-up to Christmas Day, instead of appearing in a somewhat random fashion throughout the twelve days of the season as had happened earlier in the century. Christmas advertising also began to appear earlier in the year, with November advertisements for Christmas goods common in the second half of the nineteenth century. This signalled a gradual lengthening of the Christmas shopping period, though pinpointing the beginning of the season is very difficult. As the *Lady's Pictorial* commented in 1913, 'each year we find earlier and earlier signs of it, yet there is never any actual beginning to it'.[80]

For much of the nineteenth century Christmas advertisements, particularly in text-based newspapers, were presented as a block of text, often accompanied by a bold header. Despite examples of advertisers who appealed to the sentiment of the domestic Christmas, including Farrars, a wine and spirits merchant in York, who advertised using the theme of the 'pledging cup' being passed around at a Christmas family reunion, many Christmas advertisements relied on informing rather than persuading the public, referring to utility, quantity and price. Roy Church stresses, however, that it is an oversimplification to assume that advertising before 1880 was directed towards a rational consumer, whilst advertising at the end of the century was aimed at non-rational impulses. Church argues that the 'need to persuade as well as to inform was acknowledged long before', and also that persuasion was not a substitute for information.[81] Advertisements often included phrases such as 'suitable for presents', or 'acceptable presents'. In the second half of the nineteenth century the spacing of the text in some advertisements improved, with bold phrases highlighting the most important information. In the late Victorian period it became common for advertisements to repeat words in bold on successive lines to make their message stand out, as in the advertisement for the Alsop's Fancy Furniture which appeared in the *Bristol Mercury* in 1890.[82]

By the Edwardian period small and basic textual advertisements for Christmas goods continued to be placed in newspapers alongside more elaborate illustrated announcements, which owed their origins to the illustrated papers. Illustrated newspapers aimed at the middle classes began in the 1840s and soon incorporated pictorial advertisements, though it was only in the late nineteenth century that they addressed the Christmas market, and even then they tended to be generic illustrations of luxury items with the phrase 'Christmas presents' added, like the Mappin & Webb advertisement that appeared in the *Graphic* in 1893. These advertisements suggest that it was relatively late in the nineteenth that Christmas gift giving expanded to routinely include expensive items. In the Edwardian period illustrated advertisements of luxury goods dominated the *Lady's Pictorial*, including the Liberty and Maple & Co. advertisements which appeared in 1903. As a cultural form, the illustrated advertisement of luxury goods was strong enough to resist the growing pull of the Christmas imagery that was being deployed elsewhere. However, fashionable women's shopping and consumption were gradually becoming an important part of the festive season, a factor illustrated by the many advertisements for fur coats that appeared at Christmas in the Victorian period, including from the International Fur Store of Regent Street, London, which advertised 'Lovely Furs for Christmas Presents and New Year's Gifts' in 1903.[83]

By the Edwardian period, the mass-circulation daily newspapers increasingly used the emergent iconography of Christmas to embellish advertisements. As was discussed in Chapter 2, an unstable image of Santa Claus was employed to sell a range of different products, including fancy goods, tobacco, ale, toys and chocolate.[84] The last of these items raises the question of whether these advertisements were speaking directly to children. For most of the Victorian period, the Christmas advertising of goods for children was aimed at mothers. In 1857 the York County Outfitting Depot advertised 'Christmas presents for Juveniles' through an appeal to the 'Ladies of the City and County'; whilst in 1879 T. and H. Chapman declared: 'Ladies are invited to buy their children's toys at the wholesale toy shop'. Whilst Edwardian advertisements did encourage more participation on the part of children, Gamage's repeatedly used the phrase 'come yourselves and bring the children', suggesting that it was still the adult being addressed.[85] There were exceptions to this, however. A 1904 advertisement for a 'grand free & spectacular bazaar' at C. S. Broadbent Ltd., Leeds, contained the following caveat: 'NOW, A WORD TO THE CHILDREN ... Dear old Father Christmas has also brought his LARGE PILLAR BOX, for he whispered to the general manager that he is anxious to send one hundred presents away, to arrive at their destination Christmas Eve, to all good little boys and girls not over eight years of age, who write him the nicest letters'.[86]

The numerous Christmas advertisements placed on behalf of individual retailers often emphasised variety and an ability to cater for a range of different people and tastes. These advertisements might differentiate the appeal of products on grounds of gender, tapping into preconceived notions of the gendered nature of consumer goods, though not aggressively so. As Lori Loeb shows, it was advertisements placed by manufacturers that had the greatest potential for drawing upon gendered meanings, particularly in terms of an idealised image of the female consumer. Loeb argues that advertising played upon commercial interpretations of domestic ideology.[87] Advertisements aimed at women often emphasised their domestic role and the creation of a family experience. This was apparent in the advertisement for the Apollo Piano-Player which asked the question 'What were Christmas without an Apollo?' This was one of a series of advertisements featuring new technologies to enhance the musical experience of Christmas in the home, which might help foster feelings of *communitas*. In advertising a similar device, the combination autopiano, Kastner & Co. declared: '[At] Christmas time, social gatherings would be incomplete and dull if harmony and music did not produce the right joyful spirit, but how much more can you enhance your own pleasure and that of your family and friends by becoming master of the world of music'. These manufacturers faced stiff competition from the gramophone, and many advertisements for gramophones and records appeared at Christmas during the Edwardian period. J. G. Graves Ltd of Sheffield declares in 1911 that the 'Graves Gramophone brings the best of everything right into the midst of the family circle'; whilst a 1912 Christmas advertisement for HMV records contains the advice 'that *personal* selection is very important'. The mass market was well attuned to the dynamics of gift relationships.[88]

The association between Christmas and the home was also exploited by furnishing companies. Waring & Gillow Ltd, for example, recreates rooms originally shown at the Ideal Home Exhibition, but places in each room a suggestion for a Christmas present, the idea being that 'further warmth and intimacy has been given them by adding those dainty, personal etceteras with which we so love to surround ourselves at home'. In 1907 the same company stresses this link by declaring that 'Waring's is pre-eminently the place for Christmas Gifts, because Waring's is pre-eminently the place for everything for the complete furnishing of the Home'. Their message, however, cuts across gendered lines of consumption: 'The most beautiful gift that a husband can give to his wife, or that a wife can give to her husband, is something for the home'. Other advertisers play upon the feminine need to respond to masculine desire. In 1910 Gillette is telling women: 'He wants a Gillette safety razor', and encourages them to 'Buy "Him" one this Xmas'. The power of suggestion now becomes an important factor in gift giving, something that contemporary commentators recognised. In 1913 the *Lady's Pictorial* notes that 'in the trading as well as in the medical world it is becoming more and more recognised that a great deal can be affected by the power of suggestion. The mind largely controls the body, the patient can be persuaded out of pain and ills which are very often due to the imagination. So can the Christmas shopper be persuaded to make choice'.[89]

The power of suggestion was undoubtedly aided by the illustrated Christmas advertisements of the Edwardian period, but also by the increasing trend towards whole-page advertisements, and here a significant contribution was made by both the *Daily Mail* and Boots the Chemists. Originally based in Nottingham, Jesse Boot expanded the sales of his herbalist and grocer's shop in 1874 to include proprietary medicines. National expansion followed his conversion to a limited liability company in 1883, and by 1914 Boots had 560 branches. In 1904 Boots began advertising in the national press, and to boost the Christmas-shopping trade took whole front-page advertisements in the *Daily Mail* for ten consecutive days. This was followed by eight full-page advertisements in *The Times*, and similar insertions in the provincial dailies of Nottingham, Sheffield, Birmingham and other cities.[90] Jesse Boot realised the power of the sentiments of the home Christmas, and on 23 December 1904 he placed another front-page advertisement in the *Daily Mail*, thanking customers for their response, and wishing them a 'merry Christmas and a prosperous New Year'. This message was repeated on Christmas Eve 1908, and captured the flag-waving imperial character of the *Daily Mail* by calling the advertisement 'a message to the world' with the verse

> Where'er the British Flag flies in the breeze
> There, presents from OUR STORES have found their way
> Sent from kind friends, whose sole wish is to please
> And cheer their absent friends on Christmas Day.[91]

From 1904 Boots was the heaviest Christmas advertiser in both the national and provincial press. At Christmas 1907 it boasted on the front page of the *Daily Mail* that it had 'branches in all the principal towns' and they were 'the largest gift sellers in the country', and in 1913 it declared itself on the front page of the *Leeds Mercury* to be 'The Largest Christmas Present Emporium in the World!' Boots used the common feature of illustrating gift items but provided innovative frameworks within which to situate them. In 1907, two Boots advertisements featuring Santa Claus appeared in the *Leeds Mercury*, the first of which sees Santa Claus piloting a hot air balloon on which the gift items are illustrated; in the second he sits on top of a large present-laden Christmas tree. Another innovation was a campaign in *The Times* in 1913, where a series of small advertisements asked the question 'How many days till Christmas?' and revealed the answer, encouraging a distinct culture of Christmas shopping in the run-up to the festival proper.[92]

The dominant presence of Boots in Edwardian Christmas advertising reflects the growing significance of the multiple-shop firms. The Edwardian period also saw Christmas advertisements on behalf of chains such as Lipton's, Stead and Simpson, and W. H. Smith. Earlier than this, the Singer Sewing Machine Company, which had nearly 400 branches by 1900, was targeting female recipients in Christmas advertisements in the 1860s. Hamish Fraser argues that these firms had a common willingness to adopt new selling techniques, and 'vigorous and frequently spectacular advertising' that placed an emphasis on the cheapness of their goods. They were rewarded by significant increases in market share, which Fraser has interpreted as a 'rebellion by consumers against the high costs of traditional shopping'.[93] Though more traditional forms of shopping and advertising were still present in the Christmas market in the early years of the twentieth century, the commercial practices of the multiples were in line with the advice given to retailers by the *Grocers' Journal* in 1900 'that an absolutely cash trade be the order of the day; selling goods to the masses for cash, not the classes on credit, is the sure and easy way to a good turnover'.[94]

Conclusion

Christmas shopping in the late-Victorian and Edwardian era featured an unprecedented number of excitable but also fractious crowds, elaborate in-store display and urban spectacle. It demonstrated the extent to which the culture of Christmas presents had become embedded in the national culture of England, a celebration and indulgence of childhood, but also of much broader relationships in the spectrum of family, kin and friendship. This shopping culture became an essential prerequisite to the domestic celebration of Christmas which had become firmly established earlier in the century, though inevitably the inversion of the binary between home and market which underpinned the early formation of domestic ideology unsettled some contemporaries who felt the sanctity of the festival, sacred and/or secular, was tarnished by excessive commercialism. This culture remained class-specific, with many of the more elaborate sites of consumption beyond the grasp of the poorer classes. However, much of the spectacle was visible in the streets and available to all, but it was experienced differently. Though the extent of the Christmas shopping culture was unprecedented, there were continuities in form and practice throughout the nineteenth century. The spectacle of Christmas shops and crowded thoroughfares was not unknown to the early Victorians, and rudimentary and unsophisticated selling techniques coexisted with the self-consciously modern wonders of Edwardian England.

Notes

1 B. Rieger and M. Daunton, 'Introduction', in M. Daunton and B. Rieger (eds), *Meanings of Modernity: Britain from the late-Victorian Era to World War II* (Oxford and New York: Berg, 2001), pp. 1–21.

2 J. A. R. Pimlott, *The Englishman's Christmas: a Social History* (Hassocks: Harvester, 1978), pp. 127, 130; *The Times*, 26 December 1788.

3 G. Weightman and S. Humphries, *Christmas Past* (London: Sidgwick and Jackson, 1987), pp. 124–5.

4 Reprinted in *The Times*, 28 December 1824; J. E. Crowther and P. A. Crowther (eds), *The Diary of Robert Sharp of South Cave: Life in a Yorkshire Village 1812–1837* (Oxford: Oxford University Press, 1997), p. 29.

5 *The Times*, 25 December 1840; 27 December 1841; 16 December 1843; 20 December 1843; 23 December 1881.

6 *Daily Mail*, 22 December 1896.

7 M. J. Winstanley, *The Shopkeeper's World 1830–1914* (Manchester: Manchester University Press, 1983), pp. 152–3.

8 *Chambers's Edinburgh Journal*, 18, 1852, p. 410.

9 *The Times*, 22 December 1898.

10 C. Dickens, *Christmas Books*, ed. R. Glancy (Oxford: Oxford University Press, 1988), pp. 48–9.

11 *Bristol Mercury*, 22 December 1838.

12 *Era*, 24 December 1848; *York Herald*, 22 December 1855.

13 Dickens, *Christmas Books*, p. 49; *Chambers's Edinburgh Journal*, 18, 1852, p. 410.

14 *Grocer*, 3 December 1870; *Grocers' Journal*, 24 November 1900; 19 November 1910.

15 Victoria and Albert Museum Archive of Art and Design, records of Tom Smith Group Ltd, AAD/1998/3; AAD/1998/3/16, catalogue of Christmas novelties 1895–96; Pimlott, *Englishman's Christmas*, p. 130; Weightman and Humphries, *Christmas Past*, p. 43; C. Lalumia, 'Scrooge and Albert. Christmas in the 1840s', *History Today*, 51 (2001), 28; *Grocer*, 27 November 1880; *Gamage's Christmas Bazaar 1913*, ed. A. Adburgham (Newton Abbot: David and Charles, 1974), pp. 158–61.

16 Victoria and Albert Museum, Tom Smith Group, AAD/1998/3/6, 14, 16, 18, 22, 24, catalogue of Christmas novelties 1881–82, 1890–91, 1895–96, 1898–99, 1908–09, 1909–10; *Gamage's Christmas Bazaar 1913*, p. 160.

17 *The Times*, 27 December 1862; *Daily Mail*, 22 December 1896.

18 *Morning Chronicle*, 25 November 1853.

19 Victoria and Albert Museum, Tom Smith Group, AAD/1998/3/1, Descriptive Catalogue 1875; AAD/1998/3/24, Catalogue of Christmas Novelties 1909–10; R. Hutton, *The Stations of the Sun: a History of the Ritual Year in Britain* (Oxford: Oxford University Press, 1996), p. 120; J. Blake, *Memories of Old Poplar* (London: Stepney Books, 1977), p. 12; Weightman and Humphries, *Christmas Past*, pp. 112–16.

20 Hutton, *Stations of the Sun*, p. 22–3; Pimlott, *Englishman's Christmas*, p. 73–4.

21 Pimlott, *Englishman's Christmas*, p. 122.

22 E. H. Miller, 'New Year's Day gift books in the sixteenth century', *Studies in Bibliography*, 15 (1962), 233–41; Pimlott, *Englishman's Christmas*, pp. 74–5.

23 M. Harrison, *The Story of Christmas: its Growth and Development from the Earliest Times* (London: Odhams Press, 1951), p. 181.

24 S. Eliot, 'Some trends in British book production, 1800–1919', in J. O. Jordan and R. L. Patten (eds), *Literature in the Marketplace: Nineteenth Century British Publishing and Reading Practices* (Cambridge: Cambridge University Press, 1995), pp. 33–4.

25 T. C. Croker (ed.), *The Christmas Box and Annual Present for Children* (London: W. H. Ainsworth, 1828).

26 Pimlott, *Englishman's Christmas*, p. 129.

27 A. T. Pask, 'The evolution of Christmas annuals', *Windsor Magazine*, 2 (1895), 679–709.

28 *Yorkshire Herald*, 17 December 1892.

29 Ibid., pp. 159–60.

30 K. D. Brown, *The British Toy Business: a History Since 1700* (London: Hambledon, 1996), pp. 20–1, 38.

31 A. Fraser, *A History of Toys* (London: Spring Books, 1972), p. 211; Pimlott, *Englishman's Christmas*, p. 121.

32 Brown, *British Toy Business*, pp. 63–4.

33 Weightman and Humphries, *Christmas Past*, p. 160.

34 *Gamage's Christmas Bazaar 1913*, pp. 1–177.

35 *The Times*, 23 December 1911; M. Connelly, *Christmas: a Social History* (London and New York: I. B. Tauris, 1999), pp. 202–3; Fraser, *History of Toys*, pp. 178–95.

36 C. W. Beaumont, *Flash-Back: Stories of my Youth* (London: C. W. Beaumont, 1931), p. 101; Brown, *British Toy Business,* p. 58.

37 Weightman and Humphries, *Christmas Past*, p. 164; *The Times*, 23 December 1911.

38 *Lady's Pictorial*, 13 December 1913.

39 R. G. Studd, *The Holiday Story* (London: P. Marshall, 1950), p. 21.

40 Weightman and Humphries, *Christmas Past*, pp. 164–5.

41 *The Times*, 23 December 1911; H. J. Bennett, *I Was a Walworth Boy* (London: Peckham Publishing Project, 1980), p. 6.

42 Brown, *British Toy Business*, p. 60; G. Foakes, *Between High Walls: a London Child-*

hood (London: Shepheard-Walwyn, 1972), p. 57.

43 *Drapers' Record*, 17 December 1887.

44 *Daily Mail*, 22 December 1896.

45 *Drapers' Record*, 23 November 1907.

46 *Lady's Pictorial*, 2 December 1893; *Daily Mail*, 6 December 1904.

47 *Yorkshire Herald*, 18 December 1900.

48 Pimlott, *Englishman's Christmas*, pp. 75, 106.

49 *The Times*, 28 December 1877; 25 December 1883.

50 Pimlott, *Englishman's Christmas*, p. 106.

51 *York Herald*, 24 December 1881.

52 *York Herald*, 2 December 1882; 6 December 1884.

53 Pimlott, *Englishman's Christmas*, p. 124.

54 A. Adburgham, *Shops and Shopping 1800–1914: Where, and in What Manner the Well-Dressed Englishwoman Bought her Clothes* (London: Allen and Unwin, 1964), pp. 233–4; Weightman and Humphries, *Christmas Past*, p. 160.

55 *Daily Mail*, 23 December 1904.

56 *Gamage's Christmas Bazaar 1913*.

57 Cited in Weightman and Humphries, *Christmas Past*, p. 164.

58 *York Herald*, 24 December 1852; 23 December 1882.

59 *Grocers' Journal*, 8 December 1900; 19 November 1910; *Drapers' Record*, 15 November 1913.

60 C. P. Hosgood, '"Doing the shops" at Christmas: women, men and the department store in England, c. 1880–1914', in G. Crossick and S. Jaumain (eds), *Cathedrals of Consumption: the European Department Store, 1850–1939* (Aldershot: Ashgate, 1999), pp. 98–9, 107–13; 'Mrs Pooter's purchase: lower-middle class consumerism and the sales, 1870–1914', in A. Kidd and D. Nicholls (eds), *Gender, Civic Culture and Consumerism. Middle-Class Identity in Britain 1800–1940* (Manchester: Manchester University Press, 1999), pp. 146–63.

61 *Daily Mail*, 22 December 1904.

62 Hosgood, 'Doing the Shops', pp. 104–6.

63 *Penny Illustrated Newspaper*, 11 December 1880; *Sphere*, 23 November 1908; *Lady's Pictorial*, 29 December 1888; 21 December 1912; Hosgood, 'Doing the Shops', pp. 105–6.

64 J. Tosh, *A Man's Place: Masculinity and the Middle-Class Home in Victorian England* (New Haven and London: Yale University Press, 1999), pp. 170–94.

65 Hosgood, 'Doing the Shops', pp. 107–13.

66 W. Lancaster, *The Department Store: a Social History* (Leicester: Leicester University Press, 1995), pp. 23–4; Connelly, *Christmas*, p. 192.

67 M. Moss and A. Turton, *A Legend of Retailing. House of Fraser* (London: Weidenfeld and Nicolson, 1989), p. 72.

68 *Leeds Mercury*, 11 December 1905; *Lady's Pictorial*, 22 November 1913; 20 December 1913.

69 *Daily Mail*, 16 December 1908; *Daily Telegraph*, 23 December 1903.

70 Weightman and Humphries, *Christmas Past*, p. 165.

71 *Yorkshire Herald*, 20 December 1906.

72 Connelly, *Christmas*, pp. 194–5.

73 *The Times*, 23 December 1913; *Daily Mail*, 18 December 1908; *Lady's Pictorial*, 26 November 1910; 6 December 1913.

74 Pimlott, *Englishman's Christmas*, p. 74.

75 R. Church, 'Advertising consumer goods in nineteenth-century Britain: reinterpretations', *Economic History Review*, 53:4 (2000), 633.

76 *The Times*, 24 December 1825; *York Herald*, 26 December 1840; 12 December 1846.

77 *York Herald*, 3 December 1857; 26 December 1857; *Daily Mail*, 24 December 1904; *Leeds Mercury*, 31 December 1906.

78 *Ipswich Journal*, 19 December 1818; *Morning Chronicle*, 27 December 1820; *Newcastle Courant*, 6 December 1839.

79 B. A. Tudor, 'Retail trade advertising in the *Leicester Journal* and the *Leicester Chronicle* 1855–71', *Journal of Advertising History*, 9 (1986), 42–3.

80 *Lady's Pictorial*, 6 December 1913.

81 *York Herald*, 2 December 1865; Church, 'Advertising consumer goods', pp. 639–42.

82 *Bristol Mercury and Daily Post*, 19 December 1890.

83 *Graphic*, 16 December 1893; *Lady's Pictorial*, 5 December 1903.

84 *Daily Telegraph*, 1 December 1913; *The Times*, 2 December 1908; 23 December 1912; *Leeds Mercury*, 23 December 1902; 17 December 1907; *Daily Mail*, 4 December 1908; *Illustrated London News*, Christmas number 1901.

85 *York Herald*, 12 December 1857; 20 December 1879; *Daily Mail*, 24 November 1904; *The Times*, 13 December 1906.

86 *Leeds Mercury*, 1 December 1904.

87 L. Loeb, *Consuming Angels: Advertising and Victorian Women* (Oxford: Oxford University Press, 1994), pp. 16–45, 180.

88 *Graphic*, 26 December 1903; *The Times*, 16 December 1909; *Leeds Mercury*, 16 December 1911; *Daily Mail*, 10 December 1912.

89 *Graphic*, 6 December 1913; *The Times*, 18 December 1907; 16 December 1910; *Lady's Pictorial*, 6 December 1913.

90 W. H. Fraser, *The Coming of the Mass Market, 1850–1914* (London: Macmillan, 1981), pp. 119–20; S. Chapman, *Jesse Boot of Boots the Chemist: a Study in Business History* (London: Hodder and Stoughton, 1974), pp. 31–85.

91 *Daily Mail*, 23 December 1904; 24 December 1908.

92 Chapman, *Jesse Boot*, p. 85; *Leeds Mercury*, 13 December 1907; 17 December 1907; 19 December 1913; *The Times*, 13 December 1913.

93 *Leeds Mercury*, 19 December 1907; *York Herald*, 3 January 1863; 11 December 1869; *Yorkshire Herald*, 18 December 1909; 12 December 1912; Fraser, *Coming of the Mass Market*, pp. 118, 121.

94 *Grocers' Journal*, 8 December 1900.

8

Conclusion

By the beginning of the twentieth century, the idea of spending Christmas at home with the family had an essential place in the English national culture. However, just as many people travelled long distances to spend the festive season with loved ones, a significant number of wealthy people took the decision to spend Christmas away from home. The origins of going away for Christmas lay in the culture of wealthy invalids searching for a mild winter climate to mitigate the lung diseases aggravated by the polluted atmosphere of large urban centres. By the 1830s, coastal resorts were competing for business with the more traditional spa towns as a place of winter retreat and regular residence.[1] The growth of Christmas travel was also dependent on the expansion and development of the railways. Festive excursions by rail had become common in the 1850s, and one calculation in 1912 estimated that Christmas passenger traffic had, since 1861, increased by over 400 per cent on a number of the major lines.[2] In the Edwardian period, a distinct culture of visiting seaside hotels at Christmas had developed. In December 1903 the *Daily Telegraph* ran a column entitled 'Christmas by the Sea', featuring reports on a number of resorts including Brighton, Blackpool, Margate and Torquay. Emphasis was placed on the entertainments provided by the hotels, including dinners, pantomimes, concerts and dances.[3] By 1912, several pages of advertisements appeared in the *Daily Mail* under the heading 'Christmas from Home'.[4] A similar culture also developed in London. In 1910 *The Times* ran a large feature on 'Christmas at the hotels', which included reports on events at the Savoy, the Carlton and the Waldorf. The hotels made a strong distinction between Christmas activities for children and New Year events for an older audience. On Christmas Eve at the Savoy there was a Punch and Judy show followed by a toy distribution, whilst the Carlton featured a 32-foot Christmas tree. Alternatively, New Year was an occasion for the spectacle of fashion and crazes. As *The Times* notes in 1910, the hotels 'are booked months ahead. The custom of ushering in the New Year, with a blare of trumpets and lowered lights has become popular'.[5] Three years later, the same newspaper comments that 'few will be unaffected by the craze for Tango', and the aspirational magazine *Home Chat* shows its readers how to dance the Tango in preparation for Christmas parties.[6]

Both *The Times* and the *Lady's Pictorial* saw hotel festivities as evidence of the decline of the family Christmas. Excuses were offered, however, suggesting that the traditional Christmas had become incompatible with modern living. *The Times* highlighted problems of expense, the worry of organisation, and the desire of 'relief from the cares of housekeeping' caused by the 'stress of life in cities'.[7] The *Lady's Pictorial* developed this argument: 'vast numbers of people live in flats, wherein it is impossible to entertain save on a very limited scale, [and] domestic service has ceased to be what it was'. Furthermore, spending Christmas in a hotel could have advantages, as the *Lady's Pictorial* asked why the 'spirit' of Christmas could not be recreated in a restaurant, and may actually be improved because nobody had 'time or opportunity nor the inclination amid such thoroughly cheerful surroundings to feel disagreeable or rake up family squabbles'. The following year the same publication argues that restaurants and hotels are performing an additional service because they 'prevent the middle-aged and old folk, those who have no special ties, the flotsam and jetsam of social life, the lonely strangers within our gates, and those who find the domestic circle dull at such a time, from regarding Christmas as a time of sad memories and depression'.[8]

Christmas travel was not restricted to the shores of England. There had been a long tradition of the social elite visiting the Mediterranean as part of the Grand Tour, but whilst the Grand Tourists of the eighteenth century were 'strangers on a unique excursion', the Victorians and Edwardians became regular visitors to what became regarded as a home from home. As the nineteenth century progressed, the minority of Britons who travelled for leisure grew steadily as rising incomes and the decrease in the cost of travel made foreign holidays accessible to most of the middle classes, aided by companies like Thomas Cook and Sons.[9] By 1880 *Cook's Excursionist* advertised trips to the south of France for Christmas and New Year, and in 1902 *Cook's Traveller's Gazette* featured a three-page guide to Christmas in Bethlehem, Rome and Seville, marketed as cultural and religious experiences. By 1912, the range of excursions had been extended to include 'Xmas in the High Alps'.[10] English travellers had begun to visit the Alps for winter sports in the 1860s, and Christmas gradually came to be a part of a growing trend. In 1890 over forty visitors spent Christmas in

Grindelwald, and on Christmas Eve 1896 over 2,000 visitors of all nationalities had arrived in Davos, with more expected on Christmas Day. The gradual dominance of English guests can be demonstrated by statistics from St Moritz, where 328 of the 531 guests staying in hotels on Christmas Day in 1901 were English.[11] In the Edwardian period the winter sports phenomenon was a prominent feature in the press. In December 1903 the *Daily Telegraph* reported on the 'record bookings' of the 'rush to Switzerland', a decade later the fashionable nature of the holiday was confirmed by features advising women on the trip, including 'The Sportswoman's Luggage' in the *Daily Mail* and 'travel hints' for 'Christmas in the High Alps' in the *Lady's Pictorial*.[12]

In concert with the Christmas hotel culture, the fashion for vacationing during the festive season caused concern in the later-Edwardian period. In 1911 *The Times* comments that 'Christmas is losing its family character' and is particularly worried that 'children must remain in the nest while their parents are flying towards the south and sun'. The discussion is not only framed by the place that the child has come to assume in the festive season, but also in terms of modernity and reactions against Victorianism. *The Times* highlights the 'many' who feel 'that family gatherings at Christmas are humdrum, banal, *bourgeois*, even mid-Victorian, [from] which we take it there are no more crushing epithets in the vocabulary of our modern smart folk'. However, it is not only the power of hindsight which reveals that the threat to the family Christmas was being grossly exaggerated. Within the same article, *The Times* recognises 'how many of us there are who insist on taking our world with us wherever we go or else on making it where we go if we cannot take it with us. We go to the Alps in troops for "winter sports" of our own importation. We go to the Riviera for golf, tennis, pigeon-shooting, gambling … and the charms of the society we find there, which after all, is largely a replica of that which we enjoy at home'.[13] This sentiment is confirmed by the activities of the Swiss resorts in the 1890s and 1900s. At St Moritz in 1892, the Hotel Kulm provided a Christmas tree and distribution of presents on Christmas Eve, followed by a shadow pantomime and carol singing, whilst in Davos Father Christmas appeared at the Hotel Belvedere. The local English-language newspaper, the *Alpine Post*, readily discusses the meaning of Christmas in its editorials, declaring in 1897 that there is 'a glorious opportunity for making this Christmas-tide … a pleasure to look back upon for the rest of our lives, and above all we can each do our best that the "little ones", long after we are gone, may keep up a happy recollection of a Christmas spent in the High Alps', and its report on the events of Christmas Day at the Hotel Kulm in 1908 recalls the spirit of Irving in describing 'a carnival of colour, a feast of beauty, a mine of mirth. Everyone felt happy and looked so; everywhere good-fellowship prevailed; and everything contributed in some way or another to the festival of merry-making'.[14] By the end of this period the English press also began describing the Swiss resort Christmases in similar terms. In 1913 the *Lady's Pictorial* commented on how the Christmas dinner served 'to unite guests into a huge family party', and the familial metaphor was extended in the practice of Christmas visiting: 'Parties are rapidly made up for visits to other hotels, and the joys of a return visit are eagerly anticipated.'[15]

The discussions of the impact of hotels and resorts on the English Christmas display the characteristics of the modernity of the late nineteenth and early twentieth centuries. They reveal an ambivalence that weighed the exciting possibilities of modern commercial leisure opportunities against the possibility that something essential to the national culture, of Christmas being spent in the family home, was possibly under threat. The Christmas of home, hearth and family was now regarded as the traditional and authentic celebration under threat from social change, just as hospitality had once been. Yet deep down these commentators knew that the domestic Christmas had developed a remarkable sentimental and emotional resonance almost guaranteeing that large numbers of people would seek to replicate festive rituals, no matter what location or situation they found themselves in. Though developed as part of a domestic ideology conceived partly in opposition to the corrupting influence of the public sphere, the festive rituals of the home went hand in hand with the consumer and commercial transformations of the Christmas festival embodied in the shopping, advertising, leisure and travel cultures of the decades immediately prior to the First World War.

By this time Christmas loomed exceedingly large in the public imaginary, the most important festival in England, and as Mark Connelly has shown, was often envisaged as an expression of English national identity and character. The evidence in this book, however, suggests that the hegemonic role of Christmas in the national culture was at least open to question. The extensive coverage of Christmas in a rapidly expanding press in the Victorian and Edwardian periods always had a tendency to amplify the idea of a nation uniformly celebrating a festival partly in terms of an 'imagined community'.[16] The people who spent their Christmases at Swiss ski resorts, for example, represented only a tiny minority of English people, and to some extent this reflects part of an early phase of the press's fascination with the young and rich which would increase significantly over the course of the twentieth century. The incorporation of increasing numbers of people into a national culture of Christmas depended on a variety of factors, including the religious opposition of Protestant dissenters to at least some aspects of the festival, and whilst this was largely overcome by the Edwardian period, class difference and poverty were not. However, despite the significant social problems of the Edwardian period, it is fair to assume that Christmas had an association for everybody, whether that meant spending Christmas with family, entertainment, having to work harder, riotous excess, or opportunities for seasonal employment, begging or the receipt of charity. Despite the emphasis on home and hearth, Christmas remained highly *visible*, and even the 'have nots' could experience the spectacle of the festive street culture.

It would be unwise to view these developments in terms of the triumph of middle-class values. Whilst there were certainly elements of working-class emulation of those higher up the social scale, and much festivity seemed to be lavish pursuits for the wealthy only, in the longer term the commercial dimensions of Christmas seemed to have more of an inclusive effect on the festival as the beginning of mass production brought potential gifts within the range of more and more people. Furthermore, the development of commercialised leisure associated with the festive season promoted a populist culture that was not class-specific in origin. This did not, however, mean that Christmas escaped the censure of moral reformers who often employed preconceived ideas of the character of the working classes when articulating their outrage. Concerns about alcoholism, begging and the corruption of children during the Christmas season were all conceived of as having the potential to undermine propriety, independence and, often not least, the proper celebration of the birth of Christ. They were often informed by the middle-class ideal of childhood, but here the wealthier sections of society had to come to terms with the consequences of their own culture as well. As Christmas became increasingly a celebration of childhood, both public and private festivities often focused on the child as a visual spectacle and by extension as a commodity. This only complicated the definition of and distinctions within childhood and the proprieties which children must observe. That the child came to signify Christmas went far beyond the association with the infant Saviour, because, as the *Alpine Post* noted above, it helped the adult recollect their own childhood and its associations and renewed the commitment to providing children with the memories which would fortify them in later life. Given the tradition of the Christmas lament, the capacity of the child to provoke reminiscence only increased the nostalgic and sentimental associations of the season, reifying the perception of social change and the passage of time and intensifying the modernity of the present.

It would be tempting to conclude that all the essential components of the modern Christmas were in place by 1914, yet future research on Christmas in the twentieth century is still needed in order for us to fully understand the history of this annual ritual that most people in the Western world pay homage to in some shape or form. Though I have placed considerable emphasis on the consumer and commercial aspects of Christmas, these processes were far from complete. The decline of domestic service (already hinted at here) and the rapid growth of television in the post-war era would have meant significant change for the family celebrations of the well-to-do, whilst the general pattern of rising income and increased leisure time may well have collapsed class distinctions in the way Christmas was celebrated. Whilst charity remains prominent at Christmas, tracing changes in both the civic and philanthropic contours of the festival may be possible. Other longer-term processes, including secularisation and the rise of new communities in suburbs and housing estates and the decline of others, will also have to be considered, and changing work and leisure cultures offer the opportunity to study new Christmas phenomena such as the office party and the problem and regulation of drunken driving during the festive season. It seems inevitable, however, that these changes will have kept the tradition of the Christmas lament alive and well.

Notes

1 J. K. Walton, *The English Seaside Resort: a Social History 1750–1914* (Leicester: Leicester University Press, 1983), pp. 18–20.

2 H. MacFarlane, 'What the railways owe to Charles Dickens', *Railway Magazine*, 1912, p. 140.

3 *Daily Telegraph*, 8 December 1903.

4 *Daily Mail*, 30 November 1912.

5 *The Times*, 23 December 1910.

6 *The Times*, 13 December 1913; *Home Chat*, 29 December 1913.

7 *The Times*, 23 December 1910.

8 *Lady's Pictorial* 21 December 1912; 20 December 1913.

9 J. Pemble, *The Mediterranean Passion: Victorians and the Edwardians in the South* (Oxford: Clarendon Press, 1987), pp. 2–3; J. A. R. Pimlott, *The Englishman's Holiday* (London: Faber and Faber, 1947), pp. 168–70; 191–4.

10 *Cook's Excursionist and Tourist Advertiser*, 16 December 1880; *Cook's Traveller's Gazette*, November 1902; 2 December 1912.

11 P. B. Bernard, *Rush to the Alps: the Evolution of Vacationing in Switzerland* (Boulder: East European Quarterly, 1978), pp. 99, 117–22, 151; J. A. R. Pimlott, *The Englishman's Christmas: a Social History* (Hassocks: Harvester, 1978), p. 132; *Daily Mail*, 25 December 1896.

12 *Daily Telegraph*, 25 December 1903; *Daily Mail*, 19 December 1912; *Lady's Pictorial*, 22 November 1913.

13 *The Times*, 11 December 1911.

14 *Alpine Post*, 31 December 1892; 18 December 1897; *Alpine Post and Engadin Express*, 29 December 1908.

15 Lady's Pictorial, 22 November 1913.

16 B. Anderson, *Imagined Communities: Reflections on the Origins of the Spread of Nationalism* (London: Verso, 1983).

Bibliography

Unpublished primary sources

Bodleian Library Broadside Ballads, University of Oxford
Cadbury Family Papers, Birmingham City Archives
Hickleton Papers, Borthwick Institute for Archives, University of York
Hunter Archaeological Society Records, Sheffield Archives
Marrington Collection, Shropshire Archives
Oglander Collection, Isle of Wight Record Office
Records of Tom Smith Group Ltd, Victoria and Albert Museum Archive of Art and
    Design, London
Simpson, A., 'All in a Worker's Lifetime: the Autobiography from the late Victorian
    times', unpublished typescript, York Reference Library (1972)

Annual reports

Charity Commissioners, British Sessional Papers, 1833–34
Leeds Invalid Children's Aid Society, 1909–10
Leeds Mechanics' Institution and Literary Society, 1844–71
Wesley Mission, Skeldergate, York, 1907
York County Hospital, 1905–6
York Penitentiary Society, 1865–1910

Newspapers and periodicals

Alpine Post and Engadin Express
Bell's Life in London and Sporting Chronicle
Birmingham Daily Post
Brighton Patriot and South of England Free Press
Bristol Mercury and Daily Post
British Mothers' Journal
British Mothers' Magazine
Chambers's Edinburgh Journal
Cocoa Works Magazine

Cook's Excursionist and Tourist Advertiser
Cook's Traveller's Gazette
Daily Mail
Daily News
Daily Telegraph
Derby Mercury
Drapers' Record
East London Observer
Era
Examiner
Gentleman's Magazine
Graphic
Grocers' Journal
Guardian
Hampshire Telegraph and Sussex Chronicle
Hearth and Home: an Illustrated Weekly Journal for Gentlewomen
Home Chat
Household Words
Hull Packet and East Riding Times
Illustrated London News
Ipswich Journal
John Bull
Ladies' Treasury
Lady's Newspaper
Lady's Pictorial
Leeds Intelligencer
Leeds Mercury
Liverpool Mercury
Lloyd's Weekly Paper
Magazine of Domestic Economy
Manchester Times
Morning Chronicle
Newcastle Courant
New Monthly Magazine
Northern Echo
Pall Mall Gazette
Penny Illustrated Newspaper
Preston Guardian
Punch
Railway Magazine
Reynold's Newspaper
St. Philip and St. James Parish Magazine
St. Saviour's Monthly Paper
St. Simon's Parochial Magazine
Sphere
Sporting Gazette
Sun
The Times

Trewman's Exeter Flying Post
Yorkshire Evening Post
Yorkshire Herald

Books and pamphlets published before 1914

Allen, R., *The Autobiography of Rose Allen: Edited by a Lady* (London: Longman, 1847).
Ashton, J., *A Righte Merrie Christmasse!!! The Story of Christ-tide* (London: Leadenhall Press, 1894).
Barlee, E., *Pantomime Waifs, or a Plea for our City Children* (London, 1884).
Bourne, H., *Antiquitates Vulgares; or the Antiquities of the Common People* (Newcastle: J. White, 1725).
Brand, J., *Observations on Popular Antiquities* (Newcastle: T. Saint, 1777).
Browne Owen, H. M., 'Memoir of the life and writings of Mrs. Hemans', in F. D. Browne Hemans, *The Works of Mrs. Hemans, with a Memoir by Her Sister* (Philadelphia, 1840), vol. 1.
Chambers, R. (ed.), *The Book of Days* (London and Edinburgh: W. and R. Chambers, 1832).
Coleridge, S. T., 'Christmas within doors, in the north of Germany', in *The Friend: a Series of Essays to and in the Formation of Fixed Principles in Politics, Morals, and Religion* , 3rd edn (London, 1837).
Collyer, R., *Some Memories* (Boston: Boston American Unitarian Association, 1908).
Cornish, F. W. (ed.), *Extracts from the Letters and Journals of William Cory* (Oxford: Horace Hart, 1897).
Croker, T. C. (ed.), *The Christmas Box and Annual Present for Children* (London: W. H. Ainsworth, 1828).
Dawson, W. F., *Christmas: its Origins and Associations* (London: Elliot Stock, 1902).
Dickens, C., *Christmas Books*, ed. R. Glancy (Oxford: Oxford University Press, 1988).
Gamage's Christmas Bazaar 1913, ed. A. Adburgham (Newton Abbot: David and Charles, 1974).
Gatty, H. K. F., *Julian Ewing and Her Books* (London: SPCK, 1887).
Gilbert, D. (ed.), *Some Ancient Christmas Carols*, 2nd edn (London: John Nichols and Son, 1823).
Gissing, G., *The Odd Women* (Oxford: Oxford University Press, 2002).
Hervey, T. K., *The Book of Christmas*, ed. S. Roud (Ware: Wordsworth Editions, 2000).
Hone, W., *Ancient Mysteries Described* (London: J. M'Creery, 1823).
Hone, W., *Every-Day Book* (London: William Tegg, 1825–26).
Ireland, A. E. (ed.), *Selections from the Letters of Geraldine Endsor Jewsbury to Jane Welsh Carlyle* (London: Longmans, Green, and Co., 1892).
Irving, W., *The Legend of Sleepy Hollow and Other Stories*, ed. W. L. Hedges (New York: Penguin, 1999).
Kemble, F. A., *Records of Late Life* (London: Richard Bentley and Sons, 1882), vol. 1.
Martineau, H., *Autobiography* (London: Smith Elder, 1877), vol. 1.
Maurice, C. E. (ed.), *Life of Octavia Hill as Told in her Letters* (London: Macmillan, 1913).
Panton, J. E., *Leaves from a Life* (London: Eveleigh Nash, 1908).

Pask, A. T., 'The evolution of Christmas annuals', *Windsor Magazine*, 2 (1895).

Platts, J., *The Manners and Customs of all Nations* (London, 1827).

Romaine, W., *The Necessity of Receiving Christ in our Hearts, set forth in a Sermon Preached at St. Dunstan's in the West, London, on Christmas-Day… 1757* (London, 1758).

Round About our Coal-Fire (London: J. Roberts, 1730).

Rowntree, B. S., *Poverty: a Study of Town Life* (London: Macmillan, 1901).

Rutherford, J. H., *Beer or No Beer* (London, 1863).

Sandys, W., *Christmas Carols Ancient and Modern* (London: Richard Beckley, 1833).

Sandys, W., *Christmastide: its History, Festivities and Carols* (London: John Russell Smith, 1852).

Schmid, J. C. von, *Christmas Eve, or Antony Kronor. The Orphan Wanderer. A German Tale. Translated by a Lady* (Oxford and London: Darton & Co., 1849).

Sheard, M., *Records of the Parish of Batley* (Worksop: R. White, 1894).

Southey, R., *Letters from England*, 3rd edn (London: Longman, 1814).

Taylor, J., *The Complaint of Christmas and the Teares of Twelfetyde* (London: James Boler, 1631).

The Vindication of Christmas (London: G. Horton, 1653).

Autobiographies, diaries and memoirs published after 1914

Ayres, J. (ed.), *Paupers and Pig Killers: the Diary of William Holland, a Somerset Parson, 1799–1818* (Stroud: Sutton, 2003).

Bamford, S., *The Autobiography of Samuel Bamford: Volume One, Early Days* (London: Frank Cass, 1967).

Bankes, V., and P. Watkin, *A Kingston Lacy Childhood* (Wimborne: Dovecote Press, 1986).

Baring, M., *The Puppet Show of Memory* (London: William Heinemann, 1922).

Beaumont, C. W., *Flash-Back: Stories of my Youth* (London: C. W. Beaumont, 1931).

Bennett, H. J., *I Was a Walworth Boy* (London: Peckham Publishing Project, 1980).

Blake, J., *Memories of Old Poplar* (London: Stepney Books, 1977).

Burnett, J., *Useful Toil: Autobiographies of Working People from the 1820s to the 1920s* (Harmondsworth: Penguin, 1977).

Cameron, C., *Rustle of Spring: an Edwardian Childhood in London's East End* (London: Skilton and Shaw, 1979).

Chorley, K., *Manchester Made Them* (London: Faber and Faber, 1970).

Church, R., *Over the Bridge: an Essay in Autobiography* (London: William Heinemann, 1955).

Crowther, J., and P. Crowther (eds), *The Diary of Robert Sharp of South Cave: Life in a Yorkshire Village 1812–1837* (Oxford: Oxford University Press, 1997).

Foakes, G., *Between High Walls: a London Childhood* (London: Shepheard-Walwyn, 1972).

Halifax, Earl of, *Fullness of Days* (London: Collins, 1957).

Harvey, W. F., *We Were Seven* (London: Constable, 1936).

Hudson, D., *Munby, Man of Two Worlds: the Life and Diaries of Arthur J. Munby 1828–1910* (London: J. Murray, 1972).

Hughes, M., *A London Family 1870–1900* (Oxford: Oxford University Press, 1991).

Knightley, L. M., *The Journals of Lady Knightley of Fawsley 1856–1884*, ed. J, Cartwright (London: J. Murray, 1915).

Lubbock, S., *The Child in the Crystal* (London: Jonathan Cape, 1939).

Morgan, R. (ed.), *The Diary of a Bedfordshire Squire* (Bedford: Bedfordshire Historical Record Society, 1987).

Palmer, H. E., *The Mistletoe Child: an Autobiography of Childhood* (London: J. M. Dent, 1935).

Roberts, R., *The Classic Slum: Salford Life in the First Quarter of the Century* (Manchester: Manchester University Press, 1971).

Sandeman, P. E., *Treasure on Earth: a Country House Christmas* (London: National Trust, 1995).

Shepard, E. H., *Drawn from Memory* (London: Methuen, 1957).

Stanley, L. (ed.), *The Diaries of Hannah Cullwick, Victorian Maidservant* (London, 1984).

Studd, R. G., *The Holiday Story* (London: P. Marshall, 1950).

Sturt, G., *William Smith, Potter and Farmer 1790 1858* (London: Chatto and Windus, 1920).

Thomas, G. O., *Autobiography, 1891–1941* (London: Chapman and Hall, 1946).

Wells, R. (ed.), *Victorian Village: the Diaries of the Reverend John Croker Egerton, Curate and Rector of Burwash, East Sussex 1857–1888* (Stroud: Sutton, 1992).

Secondary works

Adburgham, A., *Shops and Shopping 1800–1914: Where, and in What Manner the Well-Dressed Englishwoman Brought her Clothes* (London: Allen and Unwin, 1964).

Altick, R. D., *The Shows of London* (Cambridge, Mass., and London: Belknap Press, 1978).

Anderson, B., *Imagined Communities: Reflections on the Origins of the Spread of Nationalism* (London: Verso, 1983).

Armstrong, N., 'Father(ing) Christmas: fatherhood, gender and modernity in Victorian and Edwardian England', in T. L. Broughton and H. Rogers (eds), *Gender and Fatherhood in the Nineteenth Century* (Basingstoke: Palgrave, 2007).

Arscott, C., 'Childhood in Victorian art', *Journal of Victorian Culture*, 9:1 (2004).

Auerbach, N., *Private Theatricals: the Lives of the Victorians* (Cambridge, Mass., and London: Harvard University Press, 1990).

August, A., *The British Working Class 1832–1940* (Harlow: Longman, 2007).

Bailey, P., *Leisure and Class in Victorian England: Rational Recreation and the Contest for Control, 1830–1885* (London: Routledge, 1978).

Baker, M., and M. Collins, 'The governance of charitable trusts in the nineteenth century: the West Riding of Yorkshire', *Social History*, 27:2 (2002).

Barnett, J. H., *The American Christmas: a Study in National Culture* (New York: Macmillan, 1954).

Belk, R., 'Materialism and the making of the modern American Christmas', in D. Miller (ed.), *Unwrapping Christmas* (Oxford: Oxford University Press, 1993).

Bella, L., *The Christmas Imperative: Leisure, Family and Women's Work* (Halifax: Fernwood Publishing, 1992).

Benson, J., *British Coalminers in the Nineteenth Century: A Social History* (Dublin: Holmes and Meier, 1980).

Benson, J., *The Rise of Consumer Society in Britain, 1880–1980* (Harlow: Longman, 1994).

Bernard, P. B., *Rush to the Alps: the Evolution of Vacationing in Switzerland* (Boulder: East European Quarterly, 1978).

Bienefeld, M. A., *Working Hours in British Industry: An Economic History* (London: Weidenfeld and Nicolson, 1972).

Booth, M. R., *Victorian Spectacular Theatre* (Cambridge: Cambridge University Press, 1991).

Bradley, L., 'From Eden to empire: John Everett Millais's *Cherry Ripe*', *Victorian Studies*, 34:2 (1991).

Bratton, J. S. (ed.), *Music Hall: Performance and Style* (Milton Keynes: Open University Press, 1986).

Brockliss, L. W. B., and D. Eastwood (eds), *A Union of Multiple Identities: the British Isles, 1750–1850* (Manchester: Manchester University Press, 1997).

Broughton, T. L., and H. Rogers (eds), *Gender and Fatherhood in the Nineteenth Century* (Basingstoke: Palgrave, 2007).

Brown, K. D., *The British Toy Business: a History Since 1700* (London: Hambledon, 1996).

Buday, G., *The History of the Christmas Card*, 2nd edn (London: Spring Books, 1964).

Bushaway, B., *By Rite. Custom, Ceremony and Community in England 1700–1880* (London: Junction, 1982).

Callow, S., *Dickens' Christmas: a Victorian Celebration* (London: Francis Lincoln, 2003).

Cardwell, D. S. L. (ed.), *Artisan to Graduate* (Manchester: Manchester University Press, 1974).

Carrier, J. G., 'The rituals of Christmas giving', in D. Miller (ed.), *Unwrapping Christmas* (Oxford: Oxford University Press, 1993).

Chapman, S., *Jesse Boot of Boots the Chemist: a Study in Business History* (London: Hodder and Stoughton, 1974).

Cheal, D., *The Gift Economy* (London and New York: Routledge, 1988).

Church, R., 'Advertising consumer goods in nineteenth-century Britain: reinterpretations', *Economic History Review*, 53:4 (2000).

Clark, A., *The Struggle for the Breeches: Gender and the Making of the British Working Class* (Berkeley: University of California Press, 1995).

Connelly, M., *Christmas: a Social History* (London and New York: I. B. Tauris, 1999).

Crippen, T. G., *Christmas and Christmas Lore* (London: Blackie and Son, 1923).

Crossick, G., and S. Jaumain (eds), *Cathedrals of Consumption: the European Department Store, 1850–1939* (Aldershot: Ashgate, 1999).

Crowther, M. A., *The Workhouse System: the History of an English Social Institution* (London: Batsford, 1981).

Crozier, B., 'Notions of Childhood in London Theatre, 1880–1905' (PhD dissertation, University of Cambridge, 1981).

Cunningham, H., *Children and Childhood in Western Society since 1500* (Harlow: Longman, 1995).

Cunningham, H., 'Introduction', in H. Cunningham and J. Innes (eds), *Charity, Philanthropy and Reform from the 1690s to 1850* (Basingstoke: Macmillan, 1998).

Cunningham, H., *Leisure in the Industrial Revolution c. 1780–c. 1880* (London: Croom Helm, 1980).

Cunningham, H., and J. Innes (eds), *Charity, Philanthropy and Reform from the 1690s to 1850* (Basingstoke: Macmillan, 1998).

Daunton, M. J., *House and Home in the Victorian City: Working-Class Housing 1850–1914* (London: Edward Arnold, 1983).

Daunton, M., 'Introduction', in M. Daunton (ed.), *Charity, Self-Interest and Welfare in the English Past* (London: UCL Press, 1996).

Daunton, M. (ed.), *Charity, Self-Interest and Welfare in the English Past* (London: UCL Press, 1996).

Daunton M., and B. Rieger (eds), *Meanings of Modernity: Britain from the Late-Victorian Era to World War II* (Oxford and New York: Berg, 2001).

Davidoff, L., 'Class and gender in Victorian England: the diaries of Arthur J. Munby and Hannah Cullwick', *Feminist Studies*, 5:1 (1979).

Davidoff, L., *Worlds Between: Historical Perspectives on Gender & Class* (New York: Routledge, 1995).

Davidoff, L., and C. Hall, *Family Fortunes: Men and Women of the English Middle Class 1780–1850*, 2nd edn (London and New York: Routledge, 2002).

Davidoff, L., and others, *The Family Story: Blood, Contract and Intimacy, 1830–1960* (Harlow: Longman, 1999).

Davis, D., *A History of Shopping* (London: Routledge and Kegan Paul, 1966).

Davis, P., *The Lives and Times of Ebenezer Scrooge* (New Haven and London: Yale University Press, 1990).

Davis, S., '"Making night hideous": Christmas revelry and public order in Philadelphia', *American Quarterly*, 34 (1982).

Dellheim, C., 'The creation of a company culture: Cadbury's, 1861–1931', *American Historical Review*, 92 (1987).

Donajgrodzki, A. P. (ed.), *Social Control in Nineteenth-Century Britain* (London: Croom Helm, 1977).

Eliot, S., 'Some trends in British book production, 1800–1919', in J. O. Jordan and R. L. Patten (eds), *Literature in the Marketplace: Nineteenth Century British Publishing and Reading Practices* (Cambridge: Cambridge University Press, 1995).

Englander, D., and R. O'Day (eds), *Retrieved Riches: Social Investigation in Britain, 1840–1914* (Aldershot: Scolar Press, 1995).

Evans, N., 'Urbanisation, elite attitudes and philanthropy: Cardiff, 1850–1914', *International Review of Social History*, 27 (1982).

Farrar, K. R., 'The mechanics' saturnalia', in D. S. L. Cardwell (ed.), *Artisan to Graduate* (Manchester: Manchester University Press, 1974).

Finnegan, F., *Poverty and Prostitution: a Study of Victorian Prostitutes in York* (Cambridge: Cambridge University Press, 1979).

Fisher, J. L., and S. Watt (eds), *When they Weren't Doing Shakespeare* (Athens: University of Georgia Press, 1989).

Fraser, A., *A History of Toys* (London: Spring Books, 1972).

Fraser, W. H., *The Coming of the Mass Market, 1850–1914* (London: Macmillan, 1981).

Funnell, P., and others, *Millais: Portraits* (London: National Portrait Gallery, 1999).

Gillis, J. R., *A World of their Own Making: Myth, Ritual and the Quest for Family Values* (New York: Basic Books, 1996).

Golby, J., 'A history of Christmas', in *Popular Culture: Themes and Issues* (Buckingham: Open University Press, 1981).

Golby, J. M., and A. W. Purdue, *The Making of the Modern Christmas*, 2nd edn (Stroud: Sutton, 2000).

Granshaw, L., and R. Porter (eds), *The Hospital in History* (London: Routledge, 1989).

Gray, F., 'George Albert Smith's visions and transformations: the films of 1898', in S. Popple and V. Toulmin (eds), *Visual Delights: Essays on the Popular and Projected Image in the Nineteenth Century* (Trowbridge: Flick Books, 2000).

Gunn, S., *The Public Culture of the Victorian Middle Class: Ritual and Authority in the English Industrial City 1840–1914* (Manchester: Manchester University Press, 2000).

Hall., C., K. McClelland and J. Rendall, *Defining the Victorian Nation: Class, Race, Gender and British Reform Act of 1867* (Cambridge: Cambridge University Press, 2000).

Hamlin, D., 'The structures of toy consumption: bourgeois domesticity and the demand for toys in nineteenth-century Germany', *Journal of Social History*, 36 (2003).

Harris, J., *Private Lives, Public Spirit: Britain 1870–1914* (Harmondsworth: Penguin, 1994).

Harrison, M., *The Story of Christmas: its Growth and Development from the Earliest Times* (London: Odhams Press, 1951).

Heal, F., *Hospitality in Early Modern England* (Oxford: Oxford University Press, 1990).

Heasman, K., *Evangelicals in Action: an Appraisal of their Social Work in the Victorian Era* (London: Geoffrey Bles, 1962).

Higonnet, A., *Pictures of Innocence: the History and Crisis of Ideal Childhood* (London: Thames and Hudson, 1998).

Higgs, M., *Christmas Cards from the 1840s to the 1940s* (Princes Risborough: Shire Publications, 1999).

Hobsbawm, E., and T. Ranger (eds), *The Invention of Tradition* (Cambridge: Cambridge University Press, 1983).

Holcombe, L., *Victorian Ladies at Work: Middle-Class Working Women in England and Wales, 1850–1914* (Newton Abbot: David and Charles, 1973).

Hopkins, E., *Working-Class Self-Help in Nineteenth-Century England: Responses to Industrialisation* (London: UCL Press, 1995).

Horn, P., *Life Below Stairs in the 20th Century* (Stroud: Sutton, 2001).

Hosgood, C. P., '"Doing the shops" at Christmas: women, men and the department store in England, c. 1880–1914', in G. Crossick and S. Jaumain (eds), *Cathedrals of Consumption: the European Department Store, 1850–1939* (Aldershot: Ashgate, 1999).

Hosgood, C. P., '"Mercantile monasteries": shops, shop assistants and shop life in late-Victorian and Edwardian Britain', *Journal of British Studies*, 38 (1999).

Hosgood, C. P., 'Mrs Pooter's purchase: lower-middle class consumerism and the sales, 1870–1914', in A. Kidd and D. Nicholls (eds), *Gender, Civic Culture and Consumerism. Middle-Class Identity in Britain 1800–1940* (Manchester: Manchester University Press, 1999).

Hubert, M. (ed.), *Jane Austen's Christmas: the Festive Season in Georgian England* (Stroud: Sutton, 1996).

Hutton, R., *The Rise and Fall of Merry England: the Ritual Year 1400–1700* (Oxford: Oxford University Press, 1994).

Hutton, R., *The Stations of the Sun: a History of the Ritual Year in Britain* (Oxford: Oxford University Press, 1996).

Jones, G. S., *Outcast London* (Oxford: Clarendon Press, 1971).

Jordan, J. O., and R. L. Patten (eds), *Literature in the Marketplace: Nineteenth Century British Publishing and Reading Practices* (Cambridge: Cambridge University Press, 1995).

Joyce, P., *Work, Society and Politics: The Culture of the Factory in Later Victorian England* (Brighton: Harvester Press, 1980).

Kidd, A., and D. Nicholls (eds), *Gender, Civic Culture and Consumerism. Middle-Class Identity in Britain 1800–1940* (Manchester: Manchester University Press, 1999).

Kidd, A. J., 'Philanthropy and the "social history paradigm"', *Social History*, 21 (1996).

Kidd, A. J., *State, Society and the Poor in Nineteenth-Century England* (Basingstoke: Macmillan, 1999).

Kincaid, J., *Child-Loving: the Erotic Child and Victorian Culture* (London and New York: Routledge, 1992).

King, S., *Poverty and Welfare in England 1700–1850* (Manchester: Manchester University Press, 2000).

Kuper, A., 'The English Christmas and the family: time out and alternative realities', in D. Miller (ed.), *Unwrapping Christmas* (Oxford: Oxford University Press, 1993).

Lalumia, C., 'Scrooge and Albert. Christmas in the 1840s', *History Today*, 51 (2001).

Lancaster, W., *The Department Store: a Social History* (Leicester: Leicester University Press, 1995).

Lockhart, J. G., *Charles Lindley, Viscount Halifax: Part Two 1885–1934* (London: Geoffrey Bles, 1936).

Loeb, L. A., *Consuming Angels: Advertising and Victorian Women* (Oxford: Oxford University Press, 1994).

di Leonardo, M., 'The female world of cards and holidays: women, families and the work of kinship', *Signs*, 12 (1987).

Löfgren, O., 'The great Christmas quarrel and other Swedish traditions', in D. Miller (ed.), *Unwrapping Christmas* (Oxford: Oxford University Press, 1993).

Longmate, N., *The Workhouse* (London: Pimlico, 2003).

MacRaild, D. M., and D. E. Martin, *Labour in British Society, 1830–1914* (Basingstoke: Palgrave, 1999).

Malcolmson, R. W., *Popular Recreations in English society 1700–1850* (Cambridge: Cambridge University Press, 1973).

Mandler, P., '"In the olden time": romantic history and English national identity, 1820–1850', in L. W. B. Brockliss and D. Eastwood (eds), *A Union of Multiple Identities: the British Isles, 1750–1850* (Manchester: Manchester University Press, 1997).

Mandler, P., 'Poverty and charity in the nineteenth-century metropolis: An introduction', in P. Mandler (ed.), *The Uses of Charity: the Poor on Relief in the Nineteenth-Century Metropolis* (Philadelphia: University of Pennsylvania Press, 1990).

Mandler, P., *The Fall and Rise of the Stately Home* (New Haven and London: Yale University Press, 1997).

Mandler, P. (ed.), *The Uses of Charity: the Poor on Relief in the Nineteenth-Century Metropolis* (Philadelphia: University of Pennsylvania Press, 1990).

Marcus, L. S., *The Politics of Mirth: Jonson, Herrick, Milton, Marvell and the Defense of Old Holiday Pastimes* (Chicago: University of Chicago Press, 1989).

Marling, K. A., *Merry Christmas! Celebrating America's Greatest Holiday* (Cambridge, Mass., and London: Harvard University Press, 2000).

Mauss, M., *The Gift: Forms and Functions of Exchange in Archaic Societies* (New York:

Norton, 1967).

Merryweather, J., *York Music: the Story of a City's Music from 1304–1896* (York: Sessions Book Trust, 1988).

Miall, A., and P. Miall, *The Victorian Christmas Book* (London: Dent, 1978).

Miller, D., 'A theory of Christmas', in D. Miller (ed.), *Unwrapping Christmas* (Oxford: Oxford University Press, 1993).

Miller, D. (ed.), *Unwrapping Christmas* (Oxford: Oxford University Press, 1993).

Miller, E. H., 'New Year's Day gift books in the sixteenth century', *Studies in Bibliography*, 15 (1962).

Moore, T., 'Starvation literature in Victorian Christmas fiction', *Victorian Literature and Culture*, 36:2 (2008).

Moss. M., and A. Turton, *A Legend of Retailing: House of Fraser* (London: Weidenfeld and Nicolson, 1989).

Nava, M., and A. O'Shea (eds), *Modern Times: Reflections on a Century of English Modernity* (London: Routledge, 1996).

Nissenbaum, S., *The Battle for Christmas* (New York: Vintage, 1996).

O'Shea, A., 'English subjects of modernity', in M. Nava and A. O'Shea (eds), *Modern Times: Reflections on a Century of English Modernity* (London: Routledge, 1996).

Oldstone-Moore, C., 'The beard movement in Victorian Britain', *Victorian Studies*, 48:1 (2005).

Owen, D., *English Philanthropy 1660–1960* (London: Oxford University Press, 1965).

Pemble, J., *The Mediterranean Passion: Victorians and the Edwardians in the South* (Oxford: Clarendon Press, 1987).

Pickering, M., 'White skin, black masks: "nigger" minstrelsy in Victorian England', in J. S. Bratton (ed.), *Music Hall: Performance and Style* (Milton Keynes: Open University Press, 1986).

Pimlott, J. A. R., *The Englishman's Christmas: a Social History* (Hassocks: Harvester, 1978).

Pimlott, J. A. R., *The Englishman's Holiday* (London: Faber and Faber, 1947).

Popple, S., and V. Toulmin (eds), *Visual Delights: Essays on the Popular and Projected Image in the Nineteenth Century* (Trowbridge: Flick Books, 2000).

Porter, R., 'The gift relation: philanthropy and provincial hospitals in eighteenth-century England', in L. Granshaw and R. Porter (eds), *The Hospital in History* (London: Routledge, 1989).

Prochaska, F. K., 'Philanthropy', in F. M. L. Thompson (ed.), *The Cambridge Social History of Britain 1750–1950. Vol. 3: Social Agencies and Institutions* (Cambridge: Cambridge University Press, 1990).

Prochaska, F. K., *Women and Philanthropy in Nineteenth-Century England* (Oxford: Clarendon Press, 1980).

Rappaport, E. D., *Shopping for Pleasure: Women in the Making of London's West End* (Princeton: Princeton University Press, 2000).

Restad, P. L., *Christmas in America: a History* (New York: Oxford University Press, 1995).

Richards, T., *The Commodity Culture of Victorian England: Advertising and Spectacle, 1851–1914* (Stanford: Stanford University Press, 1990).

Rieger, B., *Technology and the Culture of Modernity in Britain and Germany 1890–1945* (Cambridge: Cambridge University Press, 2005).

Rieger, B., and M. Daunton, 'Introduction', in M. Daunton and B. Rieger (eds), *Mean-*

ings of Modernity: Britain from the late-Victorian Era to World War II (Oxford and New York: Berg, 2001).

Roberts, D., 'The paterfamilias of the Victorian governing classes', in A. S. Wohl (ed.), *The Victorian Family: Structures and Stresses* (London: Croom Helm, 1978).

Robinson, H., *Britain's Post Office. A History of Development from the Beginnings to the Present Day* (London: Oxford University Press, 1953).

Ross, E., 'Hungry children: housewives and London charity, 1870–1918', in P. Mandler (ed.), *The Uses of Charity: the Poor on Relief in the Nineteenth-Century Metropolis* (Philadelphia: University of Pennsylvania Press, 1990).

Ross, E., *Love and Toil: Motherhood in Outcast London, 1870–1918* (New York: Oxford University Press, 1993).

Roud, S., *The English Year* (London: Penguin, 2006).

Rowell, G., 'Dickens and the construction of Christmas', *History Today*, 43 (Dec. 1993).

Russell, D., *Popular Music in England, 1840–1914*, 2nd edn (Manchester: Manchester University Press, 1997).

Schmidt, L. E., *Consumer Rites: the Buying and Selling of American Holidays* (Princeton: Princeton University Press, 1995).

Searle-Chatterjee, M., 'Christmas cards and the construction of social relations in Britain today', in D. Miller (ed.), *Unwrapping Christmas* (Oxford: Oxford University Press, 1993).

Seddon, L., *A Gallery of Greetings* (Manchester: Manchester Polytechnic Library, 1992).

Shiman, L. L., *Crusade against Drink in Victorian England* (New York: St Martin's Press, 1988).

Steedman, C., *Strange Dislocations: Childhood and the Idea of Human Interiority 1780–1930* (London: Virago, 1995).

Sughrue, C. M., 'Continuity, conflict and change: a contextual study of three South Yorkshire longsword dance teams' (unpublished PhD thesis, University of Sheffield, 1992).

Tamarkin Reiss, P., 'Victorian centrefold: another look at Millais's *Cherry Ripe*', *Victorian Studies*, 35:2 (1992).

Thompson, E. P., *Customs in Common* (London: Merlin Press, 1991).

Thompson, E. P., 'Time, work-discipline, and industrial capitalism', *Past and Present*, 38 (1967).

Thompson, F. M. L. (ed.), *The Cambridge Social History of Britain 1750–1950. Volume 3: Social Agencies and Institutions* (Cambridge: Cambridge University Press, 1990).

Thompson, P., *The Edwardians: the Remaking of British Society*, 2nd edn (London: Routledge, 1992).

Thompson, T., *Edwardian Childhoods* (London: Routledge, 1981).

Tosh, J., *A Man's Place: Masculinity and the Middle-Class Home in Victorian England* (New Haven: Yale University Press, 1999).

Tudor, B. A., 'Retail trade advertising in the *Leicester Journal* and the *Leicester Chronicle* 1855–71', *Journal of Advertising History*, 9 (1986).

Vickery, A., 'Golden age to separate spheres? A review of the categories and chronology of English women's history', *Historical Journal*, 36 (1993).

Vernon, A., *A Quaker Business Man. The Life of Joseph Rowntree 1836–1925* (York: William Sessions, 1987).

Waddington, K., '"Grasping gratitude": charity and hospital finance in late-Victorian London', in M. Daunton (ed.), *Charity, Self-Interest and Welfare in the English Past* (London: UCL Press, 1996).

Waits, W. B., *The Modern Christmas in America: a Cultural History of Gift Giving* (New York and London: New York University Press, 1993).

Walton, J. K., *The English Seaside Resort: a Social History 1750–1914* (Leicester: Leicester University Press, 1983).

Wearing, J. P., 'Edwardian London west end Christmas entertainments 1900–1914', in J. L. Fisher and S. Watt (eds), *When They Weren't Doing Shakespeare* (Athens: University of Georgia Press, 1989).

Weightman, G., and S. Humphries, *Christmas Past* (London: Sidgwick and Jackson, 1987).

Whitaker, W. B., *Victorian and Edwardian Shopworkers: the Struggle to Obtain Better Conditions and a Half-Holiday* (Newton Abbot: David and Charles, 1973).

Wohl, A. S. (ed.), *The Victorian Family: Structures and Stresses* (London: Croom Helm, 1978).

Wilson, A. E., *Christmas Pantomime: the Story of an English Institution* (London: George Allen and Unwin, 1934).

Winstanley, M. J., *The Shopkeeper's World 1830–1914* (Manchester: Manchester University Press, 1983).

Index